Coincidence or Destiny?

BOOKS BY PHIL COUSINEAU

STORIES
The Book of Roads

POETRY
Deadlines: A Rhapsody on a Theme of Famous Last Words

ANTHOLOGIES
Soul: An Archaeology: Readings from Socrates to Ray Charles
The Soul Aflame: A Modern Book of Hours
(photography by Eric Lawton)
Prayers at 3 A.M.: Poems, Chants, Songs, and Prayers
for the Middle of the Night

NON-FICTION
Once and Future Myths
The Art of Pilgrimage
A World Treasury of Riddles
UFOs: A Manual for the Millennium
Riders on the Storm: My Life with Jim Morrison and the Doors
(by John Densmore with Phil Cousineau)
The Hero's Journey: Joseph Campbell on his Life and Work
Design Outlaws: On the Frontier of the 21st Century
(with Christopher Zelov)

Coincidence or Destiny?

stories of synchronicity
that illuminate our lives

phil cousineau

FOREWORD BY Robert A. Johnson, author of He, She, and Inner Work

CONARI PRESS

Grateful acknowledgment for permission to reprint the following:
Excerpt from Fred Alan Wolf's *The Spiritual Universe: Quantum Physics Proves the Existence of the Soul.* New York: Simon & Schuster, 1996. Reprinted by permission of the author.
Excerpt from an interview with Huston Smith "The Way Things Are," by Timothy Beneke, *East Bay Weekly*, March 8, 1996. Reprinted by permission of Huston Smith.

Cover Design: Claudia Smelser
Cover Illustration: *Blue Universe* (detail), © Cassandra Chu
Book Design: Jennifer Brontsema
Author Photo: Rich Reynolds

ISBN 1-57324-824-X

This has been previously catalogued by the Library of Congress under this title:
Cousineau, Phil.
    Soul moments: marvelous stories of synchronicity—meaningful coincidences from a seemingly random world / Phil Cousineau.
        p.   cm.
    Includes bibliographical references.
    ISBN 1-57324-079-6 (pbk.)
    1. Coincidence—Psychic aspects—Case studies. I. Title.
BF1175.C68   1997
138.8—dc2197-1301

Printed in Canada.

02 03 04 05   TC   10 9 8 7 6 5 4 3 2 1

To my son, Jack:
it's more than coincidence,
a world beyond chance,
no quirk of fate,
but a marvelous
synchronicity
that you appeared
out of the blue
and changed
our destiny,
too.

First a shudder runs through you,
and then the old awe steals over you.

—Plato

Consider a world in which cause and effect are erratic.
Sometimes the first precedes the second,
sometimes the second the first.
Or perhaps cause lies forever in the past
while effect in the future,
but future and past
are entwined.

—Alan Lightman, *Einstein's Dream*

Every time I have become aware of a synchronicity
experience, I have had an accompanying feeling
that some grace came along with it.

—Jean Shinoda Bolen

Coincidence or Destiny?

III. THE PASSING STRANGE

IV. THE GRACE OF GREAT THINGS

The Soul of Synchronicity

by Robert A. Johnson

W hen the Swiss psychologist, Dr. Carl Jung, was asked the question, "Will we make it?" he always answered, "If enough individuals do their inner work."

To do one's inner work means to work on dreams, meditation, active imagination, drawing, music, poetry, or even gardening, fishing, or achieving a "runner's high." True inner work puts one into contact with the inner world and helps reveal the meaning of one's life.

For Dr. Jung, one of the most fascinating but perplexing ways an individual can find meaning is through an experience of synchronicity. To him the phenomenon of the "meaningful coincidence" was a missing piece to the puzzle of the psyche. By the end of his life he was convinced that Synchronicity was such a potentially powerful experience it should be taken as seriously as dreams, as messages from the unconscious world, and an example of "individuation," the unfolding of the unique life of each soul.

But as intriguing as Jung's own writing on the subject may be and as interesting as many of the recent books are, there are too few stories from this marvelous realm of synchronicity for us to truly enjoy, let alone understand the phenomenon.

That is, until now. Phil Cousineau's book, *Coincidence or Destiny?: Stories of Synchronicity that Illuminate our Lives,* accomplishes just that. Here are more than eighty morsels of marvelous coincidences, gathered from around the world. They range far, from birth and death stories to animal stories, trickster stories, tales of remarkable love and romance, and some that simply defy categorization. In this time that longs for intimacy, when people grieve for their loss of feeling and are strangers to their own souls, we need stories like these. These synchronicity experiences reveal the fugitive moments in which people realize their connection to the great web of life.

After reading them, however, I just have one question: "If synchronicity is true, is it not always true?" If there is this interconnecting web between all of life, is it not always there? And what does it say about human nature that we so seldom recognize it? One has to wonder if the inability to recognize synchronicity is one more example of the loss of inner life due to the deadening trade people have made in modern life for sheer material gain.

I have a simple story that helped me to understand the faith that is necessary if we are to understand the different ways that life unfolds. This is notoriously difficult to nail down, but I will try. A few years ago I was visiting a friend in San Francisco who lives near Grace Cathedral. He told me that we were having a guest for dinner, a young fellow. "I met him one evening," he told me. "He had been sitting on the stone steps of the cathedral across the street from Grace when I left for a recording session with my harpsichord, and, when I came home at 6:00 P.M., he was still there. I went over and asked if he was hungry, then invited him up for dinner."

"It turns out that the lad had hitched out from the Midwest and was of the firm opinion that if he sat there long enough somebody would come to help."

"I asked him what if I hadn't come around."

" 'Oh, but you did!' "

That young man's faith is something I'm not used to, a kind of faith in the synchronistic principle that is at work in the universe.

I suspect that it is the job of psychology and art to reveal this pattern and faith to people. But psychology has another task.

Since our capacity is severely limited to actually witnessing or experiencing the connections that are all around us every hour of every day, we must filter them out. I know I couldn't make it through the rest of the day if every moment had momentous significance. Who could stand that? Better to witness just a piece of the miracle, so one's ability to stand synchronicity is not overwhelmed.

The evidence is overwhelming that people go even further and deny any significance whatsoever in their lives, including the connections that make life meaningful. Think of the one who runs through life casually mocking and taking a stance *against* the reality of the numinous.

The churches come into play here. Traditionally they have two duties: to take you to heaven and to protect you from it. The Jewish skullcap is there to protect against too heavy a message from God.

There are many defenses against meaning and severe limitations to man's capacity to stand meaning. There is a danger of taking people into water too deep. Our capacity to endure as well as our capacity to have radiance of God is limited. Resistance is part of the defense humans hold and probably need between them and the numinous—the sheer radiance—in case God might come too fast.

This means that most people really don't want to change or be too deeply moved. Our ability to take the pure vision of something like the burning bush in the Old Testament is limited. So God said to Moses, "Yes I am near but you must hide your head or you will be destroyed. You may peek just as I disappear, you may see my back as I leave."

This majestic image reveals just how much radiance man can take.

However, while we must observe the natural resistance against the numinous powers of life, we must also observe how these experiences can open us to the meaning of an often profound depth. I am deeply moved to see that in the stories collected here in Phil Cousineau's book, we learn of the various ways that people have had their own "glimpses" of what he calls the "soul moments" in life. It gives me great pleasure to know that these experiences will be shared by others. There is joy and grace in the exchange of stories like these.

I am reminded of the Grail Legends where the Fisher King said to Parsifal, "Go down the road a little way, turn left, cross the drawbridge . . . and you will be a guest for the night." Parsifal follows the instructions but, tragically, fails to ask the famous question that would heal the ailing king and hence the Wasteland, *Whom does the Grail serve?* That is, in utterly failing to make the adventure conscious, Parsifal fails to end his own alienation. Twenty years later in his quest for the Grail, he is instructed by an old hermit, "Go down the road a little way, turn left, cross the drawbridge . . . and you will be a guest for the night." This time he retraces his path, asks the fateful question, and breaks the spell on the kingdom. He realizes the meaning of life is not only in the quest for one's own well-being but lies in the service of something greater. The realization that life serves something greater than one's self is the revelation of the Grail castle.

So, too, with the phenomenon of synchronicity. Again and again in these remarkable stories, we learn of newfound respect for connection to a life greater than one we have been living and that the mystery of our lives can be revealed with the asking of the fateful question, *What is the meaning here?*

Finally I am reminded of the time I was inspired to search in the dictionary for a definition of the word *happiness* which was defined as "an exultation of the spirit, gladness, delight, the beatitude of heaven or paradise." I feel *happiness* knowing that these things have *happened* to people, but also *joy* that their stories have been gathered here. And, as the dictionary distinguishes between happiness and joy, the stories here highlight the difference between mere coincidence and synchronicity, "a chance happening" and an "exultation of the spirit."

Reading them, I can appreciate the joy Dr. Jung must have felt when he heard his friend, the quantum physicist Wolfgang Pauli, first describe his revelation of a "dancing universe."

In a world longing for the joy of connection and ecstatic experience, we can be shaken out of our stupor by the sublime energy of stories as soulful as these.

*Ye Olde Curiousity Shop
of the Soul*

The world is *suddener* than we admit. We know it's true. The world *strangifies* every time we're startled awake from a disturbing dream, astounded by a vision, or are struck by a revelation. Each time the world surprises us with its twisting time-bends, a shiver runs through our soul. We blink and we're suddenly ten years older; we sleep in one morning and our children are ten years older. A parent dies without hearing from us what needed to be said. Late one night we're challenged and realize we have seconds to explain our entire lives. Early one spring morning the light in the park seems to dance, and there is the smell of an impending storm and—suddenly—we are eight years old again and ecstatically playing in the rain, and a wave of longing sweeps over us.

Then the moment is over. Or is it?

One morning, one smell; whole worlds collapse in on each other and time bends to meet the curve of our souls. *Coincides,* I mean to say. *Parallels* for a fleeting, poignant moment. Either we meet it halfway—or we don't.

"The world will not perish for want of wonders, but for want of wonder," said J. B. S. Haldane, the geneticist and mathematician, because "reality is stranger than we could ever imagine."

Of all the ways the world suddenly reveals itself, the strange coincidence is one of the most tantalizing. The prickling anticipation of a phone call seconds before the ringing, the premonition dream exactly nine months before the birth, the eerie realization of a loved one's death half a world away, the odd juxtaposition of numbers that brings a sweat to our brow, the toss of the coins that evokes the message that goes straight to our heart, or the chance encounter that was long expected.

Like dreams, coincidences come in many varieties and intensities. Due to the popularity of the work of psychologists like Carl Jung, author Arthur Koestler, and even the rock star, Sting, the idea of significant coincidence, *meaningful* coincidence, has become part of the cultural conversation. But coincidence has been around forever, at least since our ancestors first noticed the uncanny and inexplicable way the outer world sometimes paralleled their inner world—their thoughts, dreams, and visions of the future—and sensed that the mysterious coinciding *meant* something to them. Perhaps it was a dream of a mammoth herd that came thunderingly true a day later or a flock of black-winged pterodactyls hovering over the mouth of the cave that proved to be an omen of death.

Looking back over history for meaningful coincidences is a fascinating exercise, similar to peering back over one's own life and noticing how experiences cluster together and how our memories tend to adhere to those experiences precisely because they literally stand out. In his book, *On the Apparent Design in the Fate of the Individual,* the German philosopher Arthur Schopenhauer remarked that this kind of backward gaze can reveal a life that has unfolded like the chapters of a well-written novel. But then, what to make of it? "To ascribe an intention to chance is a thought which is either the height of absurdity or the depth of profundity—according to the way we understand it."

As Marie-Louise von Franz points out, the ancient Chinese actually compiled their histories this way, finding the clustered events of a particular time. So, too, Robert Grudin alerts us in his tonic of a book, *Time and the Art of Living*, that the place to look for insight about the uncanniness of time is in the world's great dramas, from the myths and legends to contemporary novels and movies.

"Great drama, like the energy implicit in every atom, is eternally around us and within us, but liberated only by coincidence, ceremony, creativity, periods reaching completion, pressures reaching the bursting point, and the simple but painful cultivation of awareness."

Going back several thousand years to the great Hindu *Ocean of Story,* there is a round of marvelous tales whose heroes dream of lovers they are determined to find in real life—and in plot twists and turns startlingly familiar to any modern movie-goer, their dreams eventually *coincide with reality.* In other words, their dreams *(coincidentally)* come true, perhaps the very origin of the phrase.

The Greek myths are also studded with coincidences. As a matter of fact, writes Murray Stein in *In Midlife,* "With considerable justice, it can be said that the Greeks named the experience of synchronicity 'Hermes'." His timely appearances during the Trojan War, to cite but one stage he cavorted on, were inevitably audacious visits to a hero in crisis by the soul-guide. As the god of the crossroads and messages and the inventor of language, he is the connecting power, the antidote to slumber, and the link between silence and communication. One of Hermes' favorite ways to reveal meaning is to cross borders and guide the soul through the underworld. Likewise, Jung recognized the mercurial and quicksilver nature of the meaningful coincidences he saw occurring again and again during his own soul-crises and those of his patients. He detected a pattern of sudden visits by the trickster of synchronicity during dramatic changes of life.

In the foreword to his book from 1952, *Synchronicity: An Acausal Connecting Principle,* Jung wrote, "As a psychiatrist and psychotherapist I have often come up against the phenomena in question and could convince myself how much these inner experiences mean to my patients. In most cases they were things people do not talk about for fear of exposing themselves to thoughtless ridicule. I was amazed to see how many people have had experiences of this kind and how carefully the secret is guarded. So, my interest has a human as well as a scientific foundation."

The Sagacity of Serendipity

From the earliest days of science, sudden, seemingly chance experiences, chance observations prominently and delightfully figure in the long and winding story of human perception. However, here they tend to be treated like the crazy uncle in the basement. Serendipity, first cousin to coincidence, and twin brother of synchronicity, you might say, threads together the very history of science. The word was coined in 1754 by Horace Walpole, who explained to his friend Sir Horace Mann that he had come across a lovely fairy tale, "The Three Princes of Serendip" (an ancient name for Ceylon and now Sri Lanka), in which they "were always making discoveries, by accidents and sagacity, of things which they were not in quest of . . ."

Nearly one hundred years later, Louis Pasteur connected the way in which accidents become discoveries. He declared, "In the field of observation, chance favors only the prepared mind."

Royston M. Roberts, in his wonderful overview of this territory, *Serendipity: Accidental Discoveries in Science,* makes another helpful distinction when he chronicles the *happy accidents* of history. Citing memorable stories such as Archimedes' sudden realization while taking a bath of how to measure a king's crown, Newton's transformative observation of the falling apple, Jenner's chance sighting of cowpox scars on the hands of a milkmaid, a spore plopping down into Fleming's petri dish, Kekule dreaming of a serpent eating its tail (the exact image of the carbon molecule he was searching for), Roberts asks, "What is the prepared mind, and how can it be acquired? I feel there is an inborn ability or talent for discovery in many of those who benefit from serendipity . . . [and] the dominant characteristic . . . and by many others who turned accidents into discoveries, constitutes mere curiousity. They were curious to understand the accident they had observed."

Shifting hallways in the pantheon of history we find that Russian novelist Boris Pasternak admitted in a letter to English literary critic Edmund Wilson that he used the "frank arbitrariness of coincidences" to show the "unrestrained freedom of life." He went on to say, "My sense of reality—the whole—has always been this: that there is a purpose, an end, a *telos,* a reached sending . . . . Whatever the cause, reality has been for me like a sudden, unexpected arrival that is intensely welcome."

In popular culture, no one more than the American adventurer and bon vivant, Robert Ripley, is associated with bewildering curiosities, including amazing coincidences. Introduced to his audiences as "that incomparable, inimitable, illimitable, inestimable introducer of immeasurable, incalculable, and incredible explanations," Ripley searched the world over for the peculiar and preposterous and made a fortune from popularizing them among his charming collections of tales in bizarre cartoons, books, and documentary films. All of which he left his readers, and visitor to his Odditoriums, of course, to "believe it or not."

In the electric shadow world of movies, where an *un*believable coincidence can provoke hisses from an audience (the chance parking space for the road racing hero in any San Francisco movie!), there is the English thrillmaster, Alfred Hitchcock, who prided himself in concocting his plots around innocent everyman heroes trapped in bizarre coincidences. If we roll away the reel world we find Cary Grant in *North by Northwest,* caught up in a thrilling run for his life because he *coincidentally* looks like the wrong man at the wrong moment. Just a case of mistaken identity or more? Hitchcock's famous closing shot of Grant and Eva Marie Saint safely ensconced on a train roaring through a tunnel suggests that despite himself, our heroes find their destiny. This is a celluloid version of the helping hand of synchronicity guiding a soul on its labyrinthine path.

And yet, coincidence, which is generally dismissed as mere chance, is usually just entertaining. Far more perplexing is that form of coincidence that haunted Jung in his own life and in his consulting room. Western psychologists didn't suddenly invent synchronicity, any more than physicists suddenly invented gravitation or botanists the echolocation powers of bats when these natural phenomena were suddenly revealed and named. But until Jung there was no word to describe the kind of coincidences that affect people's destiny, other than blind chance operating in the shadows of life's dramas or miraculous intervention from above. But as Koestler paraphrased Goethe,

When the mind is at sea

A new word provides a raft.

The raft that rescued Jung's confusion-tossed mind was his own newly minted word *synchronicity,* which he defined as "meaningful coincidence." Though he was not perfectly comfortable with the word, it at least gave him something to cling to when arguing for a principle not to replace but to complement ordinary cause and effect.

Much has been written on the subject since Jung's book was first published. Psychologists, physicists, and phenomenologists alike have been searching for the explanation of how synchronicity *works,* as if they were on the medieval quest for the Holy Grail. Theories abound, ranging from "the acausal connecting principle" to "the unifying principle behind meaningful coincidences, individual consciousness and the totality of space and time," to "the activation of archetypes" and "unconscious compensation" in the psyche.

As intriguing as the theories may be, this book turns the attention to what I believe is the heart of the matter, the stories themselves. If isolated, a synchronicity story can give the impression of being an anomaly, or a mere case study. But when read as part of a collection, something wonderful happens. They take on the aura of parables or appear like a cross between ancient Sufi teaching stories, Carl Sandburg's deliciously peculiar tales, *Foibles and Foobles* and Rudyard Kipling's "Just-So Stories."

Our fondest hope that there is still magic and mystery at work in the world can be reconfirmed by a story about a man who paints the face of the woman he will marry years before meeting her; or that the book we have been searching for for years mysteriously arrives the day we need it; or that the shuddering appearance of black birds over a house can presage a death in the family. But they also confirm an ancient belief that stories from the deep recesses of the soul will always defy our cleverest attempts at explanation.

From each of these stories there is something to learn and ruminate on. Some are marvels, some subtle and elusive. Others appear almost ordinary in their revelations of seemingly everyday coincidences. All prove to be profoundly symbolic in the life journeys of the contributors.

The soul of these stories is perhaps best described in a gnomic passage by the philosopher James P. Carse, in his remarkably soothing book of meditative essays on the mysticism of ordinary life, *Breakfast at the Victory*, "However, this hope, that we will one day see what is there precisely as it is there, is being challenged at the same time that it is growing. And the challenge is coming from those who have most vigorously encouraged the quest we get to the real the stranger it becomes, more and more unlike what we expected it to be. The most hardminded researchers into subatomic reality, for example, find themselves drawn into wild speculation about what is really there . . . But in fact they are describing things more dreamlike than real, more made of empty space than substance. Far from relieving us of all need for interpretation, the need for it has grown. In fact, each attempt to end an interpretation calls for a new and more imaginative interpretation. If philosophy begins in wonder it also ends in wonder."

What the contributors in this book have tapped into are moments of what I like to call "empirical mysticism," the experience of deep connection, if not outright *oneness,* with life. They refract and reflect the deeply real experiences of ordinary people through the ages.

What is revealed in the following pages approaches what Carse calls "the presence of winged life," a beautiful metaphor for the presence of soul suddenly gliding through one's life. "There was a presence to which I was present," he writes in a startling passage that helps make the distinction between the kind of people who obsess on how everything in every day connects to *them,* as if they were the hub of the world and all the spokes converged on *them,* and the humble, genuinely wonderstruck souls who are humbled by their observations, and especially the numinous *otherness* of the world.

For me—someone haunted by the somersaulting nature of time and the Möbius strip–like quality of space; someone who, as a writer, filmmaker, and wide-ranging traveler, lives alternately in the past, present, and future—synchronicity is less a phenomenon to be proved than a fascination to be lived. For as my old friend Joseph Campbell once said, "Life isn't a problem to be solved, but a mystery to be experienced." Naturally, he told me once, there are problems that cry for solutions, but life, *our* lives, need to be experienced and reflected upon, rather than *figured out*. The soulful moments must be seized or else we risk the possibility of finding ourselves in what T. S. Eliot referred to as "The Wasteland," suddenly realizing we've lived life—but missed the meaning.

For these reasons I've collected these marvelous stories from around the world. But rather than a theoretical blueprint for the Rube Goldberg machinery that may or may not prove the existence of the collective unconscious or be a metaphor for the curiouser and curiouser behavior at the quantum level, the heart of synchronicity is the literally dramatic story.

The Clues Divine

For me, synchronicity is an inexplicable but profoundly meaningful coincidence that stirs the soul and offers a guiding glimpse of one's destiny.

Consider, if you will, the words,

"The strangest thing happened to me recently. . ."

"Did you ever hear the amazing story about. . . ?"

"Once upon a time, in a land far, far away she dreamed. . ."

"In a time before time a stranger arrived at the door just as. . ."

Are you not leaning forward, feeling the gravitational pull of these ancient story openings? There is the promise that all stories carry like an electrical charge, but also the possibility, hinted at in the cadence and rhythm of the words, of something . . . marvelous about to happen, and with it the wild but wonderful connections of characters in the collision of time. The great stories of the world often suggest that there are myriad ways other than cause and effect to describe how things happen.

Once long ago, and a long time it was. If I were there then, I should not be there now. If I were there now and at that time, I should have a new story or an old story, or I should have no story at all. . . .

As Mara Freeman explains the hypnotic power of traditional Irish story openings like the one above in her essay for *Parabola* magazine, "The everyday mind is arrested and confused, as time loops back on itself, the world of cause and effect is suspended, and we enter those marvelous realms where what seems like a day's visit turns out to be a hundred years. The world is turned upside down, and the listener dizzily emerges in the Otherworld."

Or as Emily Dickinson wrote in her inimitable cadences,

So I must baffle at the Hint
And cipher at the Sign
And make much blunder, if at last
I take the clue divine—

If, as they say, there are only six kinds of stories that are repeated over and over, where does coincidence, chance, plot, or destiny fit in? What's the difference? Does it matter? What is divine about a story?

Asked by my cousin, Michael, recently, "Do you believe in coincidence—or is it all just chance?" I confess to being stymied for a second. Then I swear I heard Johnny Mathis' silky voice, and was inspired to reply, "Well, 'Chances Are' awfully good there's more than meets the eye. . . ."

Let us consider, then, three different kinds of coincidence stories: first, the infamous story of Hugh Williams, cited in Alan Vaughn's entertaining book, *Incredible Coincidences*:

"On December 5, 1664, the first date in the greatest series of coincidences in history occurred. On this date, a ship in the Menai Strait, off north Wales, sank with 81 passengers on board. There was one survivor—a man named Hugh Williams. On the same date in 1785, a ship sank with 60 passengers aboard. There was one survivor—a man named Hugh Williams. On the very same date in 1860, a ship sank with 25 passengers on board. There was one survivor—a man named Hugh Williams."

This classic coincidence story baffles, stymies, and snarls the usual powers of explanation. It is almost *too* incredible to be true. What does it *mean,* if anything, other than to reinforce such homilies as "Truth is stranger than fiction"?

Sheer trivia, many would say. Mere chance; a statistical aberration.

Speaking of trivia, how about the German housewife who discovered a ring she lost forty years before—inside a potato! Or the day a woman named Charlotte Muse and her coworkers were chasing a fly around their office and were futilely swatting at it with rolled-up magazines. *San Francisco Chronicle* columnist Leah Garchik reports that when the hapless fly landed on the pages of a heavy book some clever soul simply slammed it shut. Coincidentally enough, when the book, a dictionary, was opened people saw with astonishment that "the ill-fated insect had been smashed against the word 'housefly,' " which left Ms. Muse "with a lingering sense of mystery."

And speaking of chance, I'm reminded of the story from

Worcester, England, about the unfortunate motorcyclist Frederick Chance who crashed into a car driven by another benighted fellow named—Frederick Chance!

And speaking of tragic fate, what of Edgar Allan Poe's horripilating story about three shipwrecked sailors in an open boat who cannibalized their cabin boy named Richard Parker, eerily presaged an actual shipwreck a few years later when a cabin boy named Richard Parker was shipwrecked along with three other survivors—and suffered the same terrible destiny as his namesake by being cannibalized by his fellow mates?

In their book, *Phenomenon,* John Michell and Robert Rickard relate the peculiar story of the crossword puzzle published in London's *Daily Telegraph,* days before the Normandy landing of June 6, 1994—which included several of the top secret code names for the operations: Omaha, Utah, Mulberry, and Neptune, as well as the blanket code for the attack on D-day itself, Overlord. However, as they write, "Military Intelligence investigations could get no further than the bafflement and protested innocence of the compiler, a schoolmaster."

Another oft-cited example of logic-busting coincidence was noted most recently by Arthur Koestler who reported that Morgan Robertson, in his 1898 novel, *Futility,* foresaw the disastrous sinking of the Titanic. In the book, a ship called the *Titan* collides on its maiden voyage with an iceberg in a fateful place in the Atlantic near the spot the *Titanic* sunk fourteen years later. Pushing the coincidence one step further, Koestler reprinted a letter from a ship's captain describing a moment in 1939 when he was sailing through the same waters where the *Titanic* sunk. On a sudden hunch, he stopped the ship just in time to avoid a fatal collision with an iceberg. The name on the side of his ship? The *Titan.*

Tall tales like these tend to make razzle-dazzle party conversation, quick-flip reading for the commode, or relief from the coups-and-earthquakes news in the Sunday *Times*. Despite the pleasure a mind-bending story gives (seemingly in our time, especially the science-defying kind), mere coincidence stories tend to blur and bore if overdone, and inevitably they frustrate. For, as novelist Rebecca West has written, our time is marked by a "desperate search for a pattern." Chaos is a given; a pattern is longed for.

Not coincidentally, perhaps the most common object linked with coincidence is the clock, not only the symbol of time, but its mechanism for our observation, witnessing, and honoring of its passage, and, it seems, its inexplicable suspensions. In his book, *Man and His Symbols,* Jung writes, "It often seems that even inanimate objects cooperate with the unconscious in the arrangement of symbolic patterns. There are numerous well-authenticated stories of clocks stopping at the moment of their owner's death; one was the pendulum clock in the palace of Frederick the Great at San Souci, which stopped when the emperor died. Other common examples are those of a mirror that breaks, or a picture that falls, when a death occurs; or minor but unexplainable breakages in a house where someone is passing through an emotional crisis. Even if skeptics refuse to credit such reports, stories of this kind are always cropping up, and this alone should serve as ample proof of their psychological importance."

An unusual example of this kind of Kiplingesque "Just-So" story comes from Winnipeg, Canada. It seems this particular grandfather clock stopped when its seventy-two-year-old owner died. Nobody, however, could fix it; they couldn't even find a problem with it. According to family tradition, the clock was supposed to be passed down to the oldest son, but what with no sons or grandsons at the time of the—ahem—grandfather's death, his widow held on to it, though unable to get it running again. One day, she returned home and was astonished to find the clock tick-tocking loudly. Somehow it had wound itself back up and was keeping time for the first time in years. No more than a few moments later her telephone rang with the news that her first grandson had been born fifteen minutes beforehand. One might call this a "happy accident," in Royston Roberts felicitous phrase, an example of "serendipitous coincidence," one that mystifies more than clarifies and defies rather than mollifies with meaning.

Consider the following trilogy of unlikely appearances of an innocuous dessert in nineteenth-century France, as reported by the French pursuer of the phenomenal, Camille Flammarion, "A certain M. Deschamps, when a boy in Orleans, was once given a piece of plum-pudding by a M. de Fortgibu. Ten years later he discovered another plum-pudding in a Paris restaurant, and asked if he could have a piece. It turned out, however, that the plum-pudding was already ordered—by M. de Fortgibu. Many years afterwards M. Deschamps was invited to partake of a plum-pudding as a special rarity. While he was eating it he remarked that the only thing lacking was M. de Fortgibu. At that moment the door opened and an old, old man in the last stages of disorientation walked in: M. de Fortgibu, who had gotten ahold of the wrong address and burst in on the party by mistake."

File these under: Inexplicable Quirks of Nature. These stories delight, even stagger, but what is their relevance other than as clever material for bar bets or research into unconscious precognition?

However, as the archaeologist remarked, we can dig still deeper. Or as Jung himself is said to have admonished a depressed patient, "You haven't gone deep enough." So it is with our subject. There is another realm of coincidences that alternatingly haunts and inspires, catalyzes and galvanizes, electrifies and enlivens us.

Certain stories that form "a beveled edge," to borrow a phrase from my old days on construction sites, between the realm of predictable causality on one side and the unpredictable quantum world on the other. Deep coincidence. Odd juxtapositions that invite us to "Think sideways," as Edward de Bono describes them, which can awaken us out of the long slumber of strictly linear life.

"Tell all the Truth, but tell it slant," as Emily Dickinson suggested.

So counterpoised to the timely coincidence story is the timeless synchronicity one—soulful stories in which past, present, and future all converge like rivers into a delta and many of our most fundamental beliefs are challenged, if not shattered.

Of Jung's own cases none is more vivid then the following story, the "paradigm for synchronistic experiences," in the word of physicist Victor Mansfield. (Uncannily enough, just as I was jotting down these words I realized I was clutching a *pair of dimes* in my other hand to use in a pay phone. For me, it's another quirky example of the punning nature of synchronicity, plus an alert to the very language we use to describe it.)

"My example concerns a young woman patient who, in spite of efforts made on both sides, proved to be psychologically inaccessible. The difficulty lay in the fact that she always knew better about everything. Her excellent education had provided her with a weapon ideally suited to this purpose, namely a polished Cartesian rationalism with an impeccably 'geometrical' idea of reality. After several fruitless attempts to sweeten her rationalism by a somewhat more human understanding, I had to confine myself to the hope that something unexpected and irrational would turn up, something that would burst the intellectual retort into which she had sealed herself. Well, I was sitting opposite her one day, with my back to the window, listening to her flow of rhetoric. She had had an impressive dream the night before, in which someone had given her a golden scarab—a costly piece of jewelry. While she was still telling me about this dream, I heard something behind me gently tapping on the window. I turned around and saw that it was a fairly large flying insect that was knocking against the windowpane from outside in the obvious effort to get into the dark room. This seemed to me very strange. I opened the window immediately and caught the insect in the air as it flew in. It was a scarabaeid beetle, or common rose-chafer (*Cetonia aurata*), whose gold-green color most nearly resembles that of a golden scarab. I handed this beetle to my patient with the words, 'Here is your scarab.' This experience punctured the desired hole in her rationalism and broke the ice of her intellectual resistance. The treatment could now be continued with satisfactory results."

To further illustrate the triggering effect of synchronicity, the following story comes from Trish O'Rielly, a photographer and yoga instructor in Solana Beach, California, written shortly after receiving my letter inviting her to participate in this project. The letter, incidentally, included the previous story of Jung and the airborne scarab.

"I was enthralled by the ideas you shared in your recent e-mail. I pondered the poignant stories and reflected back through my life remembering my own moments of synergy and coincidence. I recalled chance meetings and instances of piercing clarity when the final piece of a lifelong puzzle fell into place. Where was I, who was there, and why such strange juxtapositions? The sheer surprise of certain events had been enough to turn my mind from its usual state and provided a doorway into a deep knowing, a bodily knowing of the interrelatedness of seemingly disparate events in my life. After my musings, I reentered my day

embracing the mystery of life's unfolding with an infused awareness of the grace and intelligence of life itself. Thanks for the
meditation.

"I was occupied for the next several hours with the chores of
daily maintenance and then a funny thing happened. I went to
check the mail, and, as I walked through the front yard, the plants
and air swarmed with the presence of hundreds of blue-green
scarabs, their iridescence brightly reflected in the sun of midday.
I thought, 'Am I dreaming?' But the beetles stayed for thirty-six
hours or so, and then they disappeared as quickly as they had
arrived.

"Your mail prompted an insightful day. Perhaps the flow of synchronicity is continuous and uninterrupted rather than special or
epiphanous. I usually just forget that I have the means to link to it."

As baffling as the scarab's sudden appearance in Jung's consulting room or in the photographer's backyard, is the episode
that helped trigger Arthur Koestler's dramatic discovery of psychic phenomena. In his book, *The Challenge of Chance,* Koestler
describes the horror of being imprisoned by Franco's regime in
Spain in 1937, where he was sentenced to be executed.

"In such situations one tends to look for metaphysical com-
forts and one day I suddenly remembered a certain episode in
Thomas Mann's novel *The Buddenbrooks.* One of his characters,
Consul Thomas Buddenbrook, though only in his forties, knows
that he is about to die. He was never given to religious speculation
but now falls under the spell of a 'little book'—which for years
had stood unready in his library—in which is explained that death
is not final, merely a transition to another, imperfect kind of existence, a reunion with cosmic oneness. . . . There clung to his
senses a profound intoxication, a strange, sweet, vague allurement
. . . he was no longer prevented from grasping eternity. . . ."

Miraculously, the Red Cross came to Koestler's rescue, and, after he was released from incarceration, he contacted the great German novelist Mann, to thank him for the consolation he had felt from that single passage—referring to the 'little book,' which had been Schopenhauer's essay on death. Mann replied that he hadn't read that particular piece for forty years, but that, coincidentally enough, only a few minutes before he was handed Koestler's letter by the postman, he had the sudden impulse to take the book from his library and reread it.

On the shoulders of stories like these we cross the Rubicon of Sheer Happenstance to the Shores of Meaning. In the context of the famous scarab story and the woman's deep soul crisis, every element explodes with meaning. It reverberates with the curiousness of all coincidences, but it also shimmers with what von Franz regards as the distinguishing trait, "a symbolically expressed message." As she interprets Jung's breakthrough insight, synchronicity refers specifically to a "meaningful coincidence of outer and inner events that are not themselves causally connected. The emphasis lies on the word meaningful." The insect that thumped on the window and flew into Jung's hand was no ordinary bug. The scarab has perennially symbolized transformation and metamorphosis, the very things that, as Jung interpreted it, the woman's unconscious was calling out for. In Jean Shinoda Bolen's elegant insight, "the outer event eerily paralleled her inner dilemma," as if the struggle in her soul had been projected like a powerful movie image into the outer world as Jung interviewed her.

Likewise, in Koestler's story, the element of the spell is evoked when the "Library Angel," as Koestler came to refer to the phenomenon of "the right book at the right time," is at work, and the muse is invoked, the personification of inspiration and the reverence for learning. As if on wings from heaven, the right words can appear and change our lives.

Uncovering deeper layers, like an archaeologist of the soul, can reveal in coincidences previously dismissed as arbitrary, new dimensions of meaning, connection, guidance, significance, individual destiny, words that lace through the stories in this collection.

For me, one other key element highlights these classic stories and other synchronicities that reveal the source of their alluring mystery: beauty. For all its usual brevity, an experience of synchronicity is marked by elegance, symmetry, vividness, suddenness, poetry, or a truth that speaks to the heart, often finally a sense of the unforgettable, as if Nat King Cole himself was whispering in our ear that this moment will not—cannot—be forgotten.

In such a way, synchronicity emerges as unthinkable as pure chance and points to a hidden order, a shadowy pattern, more a kind of coincidental serendipity. To paraphrase Herman Hesse, there are no accidents in the circle of synchronicity. At least not when one is on the path with heart, the path of destiny. But how do we find that path—out of all the paths into the dark forest of life?

An Indian elder's advice to scholar Jamake Highwater leans us in the right direction: "You must learn to look at the world twice. First you must bring your eyes together in front so you can see each droplet of rain on the grass, so you can see the smoke rising from an ant hill in the sunshine. Nothing should escape your notice. But you must learn to look again, with your eyes at the very edge of what is visible. Now you must see dimly, if you wish to see things that are dim—visions, mist, and cloud people, animals which hurry past you in the dark. You must learn to look at the world twice if you wish to see all that there is to see."

It is just this brand of giving the world "the once-over twice," as Detroit rocker Bob Seger, growls it out, that leads to the missing link in our search, meaning itself. Despite the postmodern vogue for demeaning meaning or Samuel Goldwyn's witty injunction to his screenwriters, "If you want to send a message, use Western Union," the hue and cry will always be there for a glimpse behind the curtain, behind the tapestry to see what threads make up our world and what the stories of our lives mean. As Mansfield writes in *Synchronicity, Science, and Soul-Making,* an episode of synchronicity ". . . always pivots around some critical meaning closely related with the person's individuation at that moment. A period of intense emotionality often precedes them. Without connecting these experiences, and the ones that follow, with the details of soul-making, the events would only be anomalous experiences—freaks of nature. Instead they are revelations of the self in both the inner and outer world, revelations of meaning seeking to transform the individual."

The Missing Link

There is a marvelous play just waiting to be written about the now caught-in-amber origin story of synchronicity. In a letter to Dr. Carl Seeling in 1953, Jung reveals the roots of his idea of synchronicity as being in a series of dinners with the redoubtable Albert Einstein in Zurich, Switzerland, between the years 1909 and 1913. The encounters of the young physics professor and the young maverick psychologist tantalize the imagination.

"Professor Einstein was my guest on several occasions at dinner," Jung wrote in a letter many years later. "These were the very early days when Einstein was developing his first theory of relativity, [and] it was he who first started me off thinking about a possible relativity of time as well as space, and their psychic conditionality."

For many years Jung couldn't get these beguiling exchanges with Einstein out of his mind, nor the intriguing implications they had for the numerous stories of baffling coincidences that his clients were revealing to him in his consultation room, his arcane studies, and most troubling of all, in his life.

However, it wasn't until 1930 that he used the term publicly, and only then in his memorial address for his friend, Richard Wilhelm, the elegant translator of the *I Ching,* also called the *Book of Changes.* Jung's attempt to explain the workings of the ancient Chinese wisdom book inspired him to try out his recently minted word, synchronicity, which he saw as a parallel to the perplexing way that the *I Ching* had undoubtedly worked for millennia.

Five years later, Jung delivered the "Tavistock Lecture" in London, where he pointed out the parallels between the Tao, the ancient Chinese belief in an underlying order to the universe, and for him, its Western equivalent. For the first time, he took a stab at defining the connections that were hounding his imagination, ". . . a peculiar principle active in the world so that things happen together somehow and behave as if they were the same, and yet for us they are not."

He formally presented his theory in a monograph at one of his own Eranos Conferences in 1951, then published several revisions over the next few years, not only out of intellectual fascination, but for the profoundly personal reason that "it is chiefly because my experiences of the phenomenon of synchronicity have multiplied over the decades." These incidents he memorably described as being "more than chance, less than causality," and as a "confluence of events in a numinous or awesome atmosphere." He had become convinced that synchronicities arose during points of crisis in people's lives, and moreover, contained insights, seeds of the future, and signs of destiny, if only people learned how to read them.

His encounters with Einstein may have helped give him the courage of his convictions that there might be another order of things, previously unknown forces in the soul comparable to those being discovered at the quantum level. But it was his association with Professor W. Pauli that truly set him on his way. Pauli's famous "exclusion principle of mathematical symmetry" proved the existence of nonlocal causality, in other words, that there is something else operating in the universe besides cause and effect. It was a major contribution to science, involving, in the words of F. David Peat, "the discovery of an abstract pattern that lies hidden beneath the surface of atomic matter and determines its behavior in a noncausal way."

For Jung, it was thrilling proof, in the form of scientific principle of noncausality to parallel his own unifying or connecting principle of synchronicity, that at heart, the world was one, a *unus mundi,* as the mystics had always said.

The confluence of these ideas about the hidden order of the inner and outer worlds, respectively, helped forge one of the first substantial bridges between physics and psychology, and, over the years, bridges between Eastern philosophy and Western science, even in our way of thinking about the left and right brain. At the quantum level of nature, life *dances* and is constantly unfolding, but according to a hidden and dynamic order. For those whose minds are sensitive to the subtle changes around them, as Peat suggests, synchronicity is a natural occurrence.

After long discussions together, Jung and Pauli's ideas converged in a book they co-authored in 1952, *The Interpretation and Nature of the Psyche,* which linked the world of objective reality with the human soul, while implying that each influenced the other. The book gave a theoretical structure for the magnetized moment, the times of sheer grace when an outward event coincides with inner changes and it feels as if our very destiny is affected.

In this sense, an experience of synchronicity is a soul moment, an electrifying experience, as sudden as a visitation by a god, a palpable inrush of grace and power, one of the defining moments in life, a sudden conviction that we might move beyond fate and realize a hint of our destiny.

The Meaning of Meaning

Somewhere, the brilliant Mexican writer Octavio Paz writes in an unabashedly Zen mood, that "The meaning of meaning is to *mean*."

The philosopher Ernest Becker, made infamous after his own death by Woody Allen conspicuously carrying his Pulitzer Prize winning book, *The Denial of Death,* around with him in *Annie Hall,* pointed to Huizinga and more recent writers like Josef Pieper and Harvey Cox, as exemplars of thinkers who had come to believe that "the only secure truth men have is that which they themselves create and dramatize; to live is to play at the meaning of life." The eminent religious historian, Huston Smith, in *Forgotten Truth,* states categorically, that "If it be asked, 'But what did the nonscientific approach to man and the world give us?' the answer is: 'Meaning, purpose, and a vision in which everything coheres.'"

If we are, indeed, meaning-seeking creatures, as the poets and philosophers have pointed out over the centuries, then a startling but deeply significant coincidence, which occurs somewhere along the border between myth, dream, and destiny, is one that calls for more exploration if we are concerned about the matter of meaning in our lives. In other words, meaning *means* because we suddenly created it from within or suddenly realized it from without.

When Hugh Moorhead queried the existentialist Hazel E. Barnes for his book, *The Meaning of Life*, she responded by answering, "To create meaning where there has been none . . ." The poet, Richard Eberhart replied, "To your question what is the meaning or purpose of life, read all the great poems of the world and you still won't find out. But read them anyway as if you could. Life keeps its secrets." The novelist Lois Gould answered, "The purpose of life is to leave one's mark upon the cave. The *meaning* of life is revealed at the point where all our marks converge." Elsewhere, Canadian ethnographer, Richard Kool has written, "Yet, the elders said, at times the world became too predictable and the challenge began to go out of life. Without challenge, life had no meaning. . . ."

In her masterful series of interviews, *Dialogues with Scientists and Sages,* philosopher Renée Weber writes of her encounter with physicist David Bohm and his startling proposal that meaning itself is a form of being. "In the very act of interpreting the universe," she writes, "we are creating the universe. Through our meanings we change nature's being. Man's meaning-making capacity turns him into nature's partner, a participant in shaping her evolution. The word does not merely reflect the world, it also creates the world . . . In one of our sessions, he suggests that what the cosmos is doing as we dialogue is to change its idea of itself. Our doubts and questions, our small truths and large ones are all forms of its drive toward clarity and truth. Through us, the universe questions itself and tries out various answers on itself in an effort—parallel to our own—to decipher its own being.

"This, as I reflect on it, is awesome. It assigns a role to man that was once reserved for the gods."

It is just this call to meaning that James Hillman calls into question in his seminal essay, "Peaks and Vales," "The question of what is trivial and what is meaningful depends on the archetype that gives meaning, and this, says Jung, is the self." Elsewhere, in his "Senex and Puer" paper, Hillman describes those times in one's life that exhibit a "meaningful discontinuity or the order of chance governed by fate," as if with a deep bass note playing in the background. He adds, "So the sense is given wholly by the experience itself as a *gift of soul* [my italics]. And one feels through such experiences that there is meaning, that one is in meaning, that one is personally meant."

I can't imagine a more beautiful evocation of that soulfully subtle thought than the story that concludes Keith Thompson's interview with the brilliant scholar of comparative religion, Frederic Spiegelberg. In their discussion, Spiegelberg reveals an unlikely but deeply moving source for the most powerful expression of the spiritual search he ever heard, a brief but unforgettable moment when he was a boy standing at a window with his mother.

"There she stood by the window, looking out upon the street underneath, horse carriages going by, sparrows and other birds feeding on our balcony. After a silence, she spoke quietly, 'This old mother, this stupid old mother, sometimes must ask, *Was soll das alles?* "What is the meaning of it all this?"' There she stood, astounded, bewildered, by the miraculousness, the immenseness, the unexplainableness of it all, standing there asking that. And knowing at the same time that it is a 'stupid' question, for clearly she was pointing to something which cannot be answered but must be asked and lived time and time again."

This is a particularly poignant concatenation of insights for our whole question of synchronicity: What emerges in the stories of *Coincidence or Destiny?* is a series of parables, some simple, some so extraordinary they challenge our belief system, in which men and women from childhood to elderhood, in countries around the world, find and confirm a moment that *means* a great deal to them and has grown to become a significant moment in their own soul's journey through life.

Remembrances of Synchronicities Past

When looking in the rearview mirror of my own life, I see the reflections of still-strange milestones on the long and winding road.

One episode in my life that remains unexplainable occurred in the late 1970s. At the end of a particularly grueling house-painting week in the Haight-Ashbury district of San Francisco, I ventured over to my favorite used bookstore in the city, Green Apple Books on Clement Street. After wandering around for an hour, I was drawn by that magical force known to fellow booklovers to the book that would change my life. In this case, it was a copy of Richard Henry Dana's masterpiece, *Two Years Before the Mast.* I recall being intrigued by the jacket copy that referred to the author's death-defying journey around Cape Horn to California and his observations of the Bay Area shortly before San Francisco was founded. As a newcomer to the city and one still interested in putting its colorful story together, it sounded like the right book at the right time.

That night I was so captivated by the book that I read until dawn, marking the page numbers at the back of the book of the three episodes I found the most riveting. The next day I regaled my painting partners about the book while we dangled from the fourth floor scaffolding, focusing on those episodes. I described to them as vividly as possible the breathtaking scene of the California Indians tossing the cow hides off the tall cliffs near Point Concepcion to the sailors they were trading with on the beach below; the cruel flogging punishments onboard that stunned readers and later helped inspire the first laws to protect sailors at sea; and how the ship's crew camped on an island in what is now the heart of San Francisco Bay and stared in wonder at the vista of hills surrounding the lone Presidio Fort, imagining a grand city someday springing up there.

When I returned to my small apartment in Berkeley that night there was a package from my father on the doorstep. Inside was a paperback copy of *Two Years Before the Mast;* same edition, same condition. Tucked within was a yellow index card filled with the red ink of a marking pen recommending that I read the book immediately, because it would give me the background to my new life in the Bay Area. My father pointed out how Dana was a friend and influence on Herman Melville, and then he listed his favorite scenes in the book—*the same three scenes* that I had noted and retold to my friends on the paint-splattered scaffolding that day.

I was struck with nothing less than a sense of wonder. Moreover, the peculiar convergence made me feel *connected* to my father in a way I hadn't been for years, or at least *aware of* the connection that had been there all along. The incident defied explanation, but more importantly helped me focus on my relationship with my father in a way that is at the heart of the mystery of synchronicity. A mirror had suddenly been placed in front of me, and everything in my life seemed altered. My two years on the scaffolding, which I had resented as a waste of time, now seemed like two years before the mast, a period of difficult but invaluable learning.

When I contacted my father about the coincidence he was

dubious. Then as I elaborated—and shared my sheer delight—he was soon amused and even proud of our bond through the book. Most amazingly he continued sending me "the right books at the right time" for the rest of his life. Through this one moment, this simultaneous discovery and gift, which had slashed into my ordinary and predictable day-to-day life, I sensed the indescribable beauty of the *symmetry* of life. Only then did I begin for the first time in years to reconsider my belief in how different he and I were, and to think instead about how similar our interests and fascinations had always been.

In the summer of 1986, I was staying in a small Paris apartment with a friend I had met at Shakespeare and Company Bookstore. I was attempting to organize an art and literary tour for the following summer, but my plans were in shambles. It was as if the fates had conspired against me. Three of my announced guest lecturers had suddenly backed out. My scheduled hotel claimed to be booked up. One of the oldest restaurants in the city where we had reserved a banquet room was attempting to gouge me.

On my last scheduled morning in town, poetically rainy and gray, I paced the room wondering if I should cancel the tour, cut my losses, and get out while I could. Then, on a hunch, as I've often done throughout my life for inspiration, I randomly picked up a book off my friend's bookshelf. It just happened to be Shakespeare's magnificent *Richard III*. Absentmindedly, I riffled through the pages until I stopped as if on command to a page whose first line read:

"Stay you, bear the course, and set it down. . . ."

Immediately, I read this as a sign, not in a generic, impersonal sense like a newspaper horoscope, but as a finger-from-the-clouds kind of sign to *me*. There was nothing cosmic about the moment, but a cool confidence began to brim at that very moment. Whatever had been so painfully disconnected in me about Paris suddenly felt reconnected. I read the moment as more than coincidence. I knew on a gut level that I must not procrastinate any longer, and instead must commit to the daring but doable tour. It even dawned on me that I could stay on after the tour and live there for several months, something I'd wanted to do since I was a boy.

Virtually within hours the phone was ringing with calls from three lecturers who had heard I needed replacements, a hotel that had just had a cancellation and now could take my group, and an affordable three-star bistro on the Île St-Louis agreed to host our banquet. For the coup de grace, later that day I finally got a commitment from the legendary George Whitman, owner of Shakespeare and Company, to use his landmark bookstore (what he loves to call "The Rag and Bone Shop of the Heart"), as a daily meeting place.

As with most synchronicities, the moment I found the Shakespeare quote was marked with blazing clarity and a sense of intense purpose, as if I'd suddenly recalled some ancestral ability to read omens.

Years later, during the research for this book, I came across a reference to David Bohm's book *Unfolding Meaning* in Joseph Jaworski's book *Synchronicity: The Inner Path of Leadership.* Unfolding the meaning of that provocative episode in Paris is exactly what I've been doing for years, which is often the case with tantalizing coincidences. Jaworski points out that Bohm developed a theory of dialogue for weekend seminars that encouraged free-flowing discussion, an idea partly inspired by his discovery that the Greek root of the word "dialogue" was "meaning flowing through." For Bohm, dialogue was analogous to superconductivity, where "electrons cooled to a very low temperature act more like a coherent whole than separate parts. They flow around obstacles without colliding with one another, creating no resistance and very high energy. At higher temperatures, however, they begin to act like separate parts, scattering into a random movement and losing momentum."

Looking back to my startling experience of synchronicity in Paris, Bohm's comparison of dialogue or communication to superconductivity seemed to fit. In Paris I had become discouraged, angry, restless. But the moment I "let go" of my expectations, when I went with the "flow," the "sign" appeared in the pages of a book, and three quick, guiding references to Shakespeare. An undeniable, but previously hidden pattern appeared: when my life is "cool" there is "flow." On the other hand, when I "overheat" or get "hot-headed," my life, like Bohm's electrons, scatters into random movements.

(I was warned that this would happen: that synchronicities would multiply for me if I worked on a book like this. The moment I typed in the lines above my doorbell rang. Trusting my intuition that I should take a short break, I answered the door. It was UPS with a package from my sister, Nicole, back in Michigan. I opened it immediately and was stunned to see she had beautifully reframed an enormous photograph of my father that had hung in the basement our entire childhood. It showed Sgt. Stanley H. Cousineau in Fort Jackson, South Carolina, giving a lecture at a blackboard. He is pointing at chalk white words that read: *Electron Theory*.)

Each time I think of this remarkable overlapping of the word *electron* and the ineffable sense of affirmation and guidance I felt at that moment from my father I hear the words of Huston Smith. Over one of our ritual lunches he regaled me about the year he spent teaching in Asia during which the books of Fritjof Schuon, the greatest oriental philosopher of the time, kept magically appearing at the very moment he needed guidance. "What are the odds, Phil," Huston asked me with sublime reverence for these mysteries, "what are the odds?"

One more shade of synchronicity story will serve to set up the rest of the stories in this collection. In the summer of 1996, I was lecturing with the psychologists Robert Johnson and Robert Moore at a "Journeys into Wholeness" conference in North Carolina. One afternoon I retold the remarkable and still pertinent episode about Mentor, one of my favorite characters from Greek mythology. As Homer rhapsodizes, when Odysseus sailed for Troy he left behind his uncle, Mentor, to care for his baby boy, Telemachus. Homer vividly describes how wise it was for a warrior to have the presence of mind to leave behind a trusted teacher with his son so the boy would have strong and soulful guidance until he returned from the wars. Ever since, Mentor's name has signified the wisdom of elders. For it was he and the goddess Athena who guided young Telemachus until the return of his father twenty years later. Even Telemachus' name signals something profoundly symbolic about the role of "mentoring," for its Greek roots, *teleo-machia,* means "the end of fighting." One of the universal functions of a mentor is to take the war out of young men.

A few hours later, I picked up phone messages from my home in San Francisco. The third one that day was startling and disturbing: "Hello . . . This is Allan down in Los Angeles . . . If you're the same Phil Cousineau that I know, then I haven't seen you in twenty years . . . So that should give you a clue . . ."

For a few slicing seconds I thought the call was a hoax from my twenty-two year-old nephew, Adam Balcerek. I hit the replay button, heard the same strange voice taunting my memory, then saved the message. Immediately, I began a long series of phone calls to try and track down Adam in Arizona, where he had just recently moved after living with my mother for a few years in Northern California.

All night and throughout the following day I heard the taunting voice, "If this is the same Phil Cousineau . . . We know each other . . . ."

My original suspicions proved to be true. It was my nephew's father, Allan Balcerek. Adam hadn't seen him since he was two years old. I hadn't seen him either for many years, but had been looking for him ever since Adam turned eighteen and asked me in an emboldened voice, "Will you help me find my father, Uncle Phil?"

It was as if he had heard the voice of the goddess herself in the *Odyssey* who had prompted Telemachus at the same age with the immortal words, "Go seek thy father."

Uncannily enough, like the embattled, war-weary Odysseus, after exactly twenty years Allan had reappeared, first to me, the uncle who had long acted all along as mentor to my nephew, then to his own son. Adam's father had come home, as it were, after a hard-scrabble life in Los Angeles, sad and remorseful, but determined, to see his boy again, and to take on his responsibility of being a father.

The next day when I finally reached Adam his first words were, "Wow . . ." Then after a long throat-clogged pause, "I feel like I've been reborn, like I have a reason to live now," a poignant line that was echoed almost word for word by his father when I arranged a reunion two days later.

After learning of their reconciliation by telephone, I thought again and again of Neruda's lines from *Odes to Opposites,*

Luck was with me.
I walked arm in arm
with Joy.

As with dreams, the clue to the meaning of synchronicity can often be found hidden deep within the words used to describe it. In this case, the place where Adam had just moved is called Phoenix, after the blazing bird of rebirth.

One last story, offered up in the interest of balancing the solemn with the hilarious and the cosmic with the comic, comes from the further side of synchronicity. It looped in on me from the back of beyond when I was living in the Richmond district of San Francisco. One morning I woke up at dawn after a lousy night of writing and only a couple hours of sleep. I was grumpy, grouchy, and physically sore, as if, I remember mumbling to myself as I got dressed, I'd been in a boxing match with a rugged opponent in my dreams. I charged out of my apartment building like an angry bull and stomped across the street feeling pummeled by life itself. I was contemplating tossing in the towel on my entire writing career, when I was suddenly accosted by a wild-eyed homeless man in his late twenties.

"You think you've got problems!" he bellowed at me, "You think *you* had a rough night—I fought Mohammed Ali ten rounds last night!" He raised his fists into a clenched boxing pose, challenging me to step around him on the sidewalk.

His words and his ferocious expression stopped me cold in my tracks. It was as if he was reading my mind—or at least my face. I felt torn between being haunted and taunted, then thought, This is too strange. Is this just the Universe goofing with me—or is there something else happening here?

Fortunately, this one time the meaning was immediately clear. I felt contrite because I had to admit that my early morning brooding must have *read* like my dream, practically begging the world to feel sorry for me getting KO'd the night before by my own melodrama. I must have looked as bruised and beaten as a pusillanimous boxer, but it was self-induced from weeks of all-night writing.

I stared at the poor guy and then burst out laughing—not at him, but at the cosmic joke. I imagined a cartoon balloon filled with absurdist dialogue from a Gary Larson panel over my head. For an animated moment, I felt like one of his cartoon deer with the target painted on its back while the other deer in the woods snicker behind the trees. But, beyond the ludicrousness of the moment, there was the undeniable presence of the *thin blue line* between the dream world and the world of the mad ones, and the peculiar feeling of being unmasked by a stranger—or was it by strangeness itself?

Regardless, he turned, infuriated with my stupor, and staggered away, shadowboxing with the morning fog.

The Ancient Web of the World

"Everything causes everything else," writes physicist F. David Peat. "Only connect," novelist E. M. Forster recommended. "Everything is connected to everything else," remarked David Bohm to Joe Jaworsky. "We are not sure how this connectedness works, but there is a certainty, there is a 'separateness without separateness' . . . Yourself is the whole of mankind. That's the idea of the implicate order—that everything is unfolded in everything. The entire past is unfolded in each one of us in a very subtle way."

For Bohm, the only picture imaginable of this initially abstract notion of an implicate order is that of "a vast, scintillating hologram," as Allan Combs and Mark Holland in *Synchronicity: Science,*

Myth, and the Trickster, interpret him, because it's a modern image for each part containing the whole.

Chief Seattle said, "Whatever man does to the web he does to himself." For poet William Blake it was possible to "see the world in a grain of sand." To the ancient Chinese, "If you cut a blade of grass, you shake the universe."

For a perfectly average pitcher in the 1950s, Don Larsen, the only words he could muster moments after hurling the only perfect game in World Series history were, "Goofy things happen."

But then, what else *could* he say?

"We have to think with *feelings* in our muscles," is what Einstein recommended. It may also help to think alongside fellow human beings who can do so, or complement our own way of thinking. One of my own favorite examples of exhilarating connective thinking is the series of lectures mythologist Joseph Campbell gave with engineer Buckminster Fuller on a cruise ship at sea in the 1970s. According to Jean Erdman-Campbell, who told me in private conversation that Joe's metaphor for his talks was the Hindu net of gems, which he wrote reflected "the universe as a great spread-out net with at every joint a gem, and each gem not only reflecting all the others but itself reflected in all." Bucky's parallel was his model of the geodesic dome, still the lightest and strongest design of its kind ever conceived. In Jean's memory their lectures connected like their images, glinting and gleaming like Indra's jeweled gems. She has told me that it was exhilarating to hear them find a point of convergence in their separate but similar ideas about "the totality of the phenomena of the world."

Despite centuries of fighting what Marie-Louise von Franz calls the "monster of determinism," the soul still cries out for connection such as the ones Campbell and Fuller discussed out at sea.

Conceiving the world as consisting of patterns and connections of individual events would not have appeared strange to inhabitants of the Middle Ages, as von Franz has pointed out, nor to any of the traditional peoples of the world. It is only since the Newtonian revolution in physics that the West has viewed the world as: predictable, orderly, linear, and the result of cause and effect.

According to Combs and Holland, "The new mechanistic worldview powerfully cancelled out the earlier, more comforting view that saw meaningful connections between apparently discrepant events . . . the view of the world provided by religion allowed for the meaningful connection we today call synchronicity. Thus science discouraged us from looking into ourselves for the meaning of things."

In high contrast, writes Carolyn North in her little handbook, *Synchronicity,* "According to Taoist, Buddhist and Confucian thought, the whole Cosmos is perpetually in motion, every particle shifting in relation to every other particle, everything synchronized in time and space." Furthermore, she adds, "To the ancient Chinese, it was simply a fact that correspondences existed between our individual lives and the grand sweep of the universe at any given moment in time."

As evidenced by the recent fascination with ideas from the new physics, such as complexity and chaos theories, Westerners are beginning to recognize that on the microphysical level, the principle of causality is incomplete. In her book, *On Divination and Synchronicity*, von Franz writes, "We can no longer think of causality as absolute law, but only as a tendency or prevailing probability." Instead, she goes on, causality is simply one way of thinking that helps describe general trends or possibilities. "Synchronistic thinking, on the other hand, one could call field thinking, the center of which is time." Von Franz points out that in China thinking of the world in terms of fields leads not to Western questions such as "Why has this or that occurred?" but "What tends to happen together in time?" or "What complex of events happen together at a given moment?"

The soundest parallel Jung found to synchronicity was in the ancient Chinese book of wisdom, the *I Ching.* The hexagrams and the elemental concepts they symbolize, such as birth, death, fire, and water, Jung thought were remarkably similar to archetypes of the collective unconscious. He likened the acausal but significant relationship between the dream scarab of his patient and the real scarab he caught in his hand to the inexplicable relationship between the hexagrams and the real life action of tossing yarrow sticks or coins. He was convinced that the meaningful connection is the sudden discovery of profound meaning and timely guidance through a crisis of the soul.

The Heart of the Matter

And then, as Horace said, "Change the name and the story is about you."

Again and again in the following stories, we sense that truism about what is most personal is most universal. There is a palpable link between synchronicity and destiny. It is no mere coincidence that the word *weird* is often used to describe the experience of synchronicity since it comes from *wyrd,* the Anglo-Saxon word for fate. As used by writers from the anonymous author of *Beowulf* ("wyrd was very near") to Shakespeare ("the wyrd sisters"), the word has long described the strange pull of one's destiny.

These episodes appear to me to be examples of what happens when "souls communicate with each other," as one contributor writes. It is this experience, the fermenting in the soul, what

William James called the "blooming buzzing" of connection to the unity of life that lies at the heart of synchronicity. For those who experience these sudden moments of connection with the rest of creation, life becomes saturated with meaning, awe, and wonder. These tales remind us that the true task is the reenchantment of the world. It is joy that is needed to touch the soul, to realize one's true gift.

What links these stories together is that they offer deeply personal revelations of patterns, correspondences, parallels, and more: the experience of the great web of the world.

I have chosen these particular stories because a phrase, a tone, or feeling rang out to me, or I sensed the numinous charge of genuine awe and wonder that must have seized the writer when the synchronicity occurred. It is hoped that in reading them readers may find clues to the depths of meaning in their mysterious encounters with synchronicity.

Listen, then, for the simple truths in these stories. In them we can hear the quickening words of souls who have encountered threads from the great web that connects us all, and reminds us that, as Antoine de Saint-Exupéry wrote, "It is only with the heart that one can see rightly; what is essential is invisible to the eye."

Still the riddling question remains: how do we know which of our coincidences to take seriously, and which to let pass by as happenstance? To those still wrestling I offer this redolent Sufi story about "Deep and Shallow Questions," as told by Idries Shah:

"Someone went to the public session of a wise man, with two bunches of flowers. He said: 'One of these bunches is of real flowers; the other, made with the greatest cunning in China, is artificial. If you are as perceptive as you are supposed to be, I would like you to tell me which is which. But you must not hold them very close, you must not smell or touch them.'

"The sage said: 'A wise question is met with a wise answer, a shallow one with a shallow reply. This, however, is a horticultural one—bring a hive of bees!'

"The bees, of course, chose the real flowers."

The bee is the soul seeking out the real flowers, the real honey, choosing what is most fragrant and beautiful, and most real among the stories of the world.

I. The Waking Dream

There is a dream dreaming us.

—A Kalahari Bushman

The synchronicity stories in Part I seem to come to us from what the Australian aborigines, for forty thousand years, have called the Dreamtime. Some of them literally emerge from private dreams and move outward, in the way Jung described in his ambrosial book, *Dreams,*

"Anyone sufficiently interested in the dream problem cannot have failed to observe that dreams also have a continuity *forwards*—such an expression be permitted—since dreams occasionally exert a remarkable influence on the conscious mental life even of persons who cannot be considered superstitious or particularly abnormal."

Rather than put wires to the craniums of our contributors, like the lab technicians who hooked patients to an electroencephalograph they called "The Poetry Machine" in the belief it would render objective readouts of the brain waves of dream activity, we will trust that the stories can teach us something about the far reaches of human consciousness, the rewards of deep attention, and the marvelous ways people discover meaning for themselves. Strange to say, they may give us a glimpse beyond our conventional notions of time and causality, and the underlying dance of the life force, and to story, which is, in the chiming words of James Hillman, "something lived in and lived through, a way in which the soul finds itself in life."

Ironically, what matters here is no matter at all, as Flannery O'Connor suggests in the uncannily titled *Mystery and Manners.* For "[n]o matter what form the dragon may take, it is the mysterious passage past him, or into his jaws, that stories of any depth will be concerned to tell."

Anyone who has sat up through a long winter night with an Irish *seanachie,* or sat in the circle of Bedouins in the Marrakesh market, or listened to an African griot in a mudhut village, or sipped lemonade on the porch of a grandparent during a long lazy summer night hearing tales of ancestors, knows the mood. It is where myth, dream, and fantasy converge.

Here too is where the border between paranormal experience and synchronicity begins to blur, as Jung admitted in his introduction to the *I Ching,* as translated by Richard Wilhelm and Cary F. Baynes, "Telepathy, clairvoyance and precognition are all synchronicities—meaningful coincidences between persons and events in which an emotional or symbolic connection cannot be explained by cause and effect."

In ancient Kashmir, India, there was a tradition of the shared dream that foresaw an incident about to happen in real life. From the magnificent round of eleventh-century stories called the *Kakthasaritsagara,* the *Ocean of Story,* comes this story of love:

"A painter copied an image of a girl from a travel book. King Vikramaditya saw the picture and fell in love with the girl. That night, he dreamed that he was making love to the girl, but suddenly the watchman woke him up. The king banished the watchman in a rage, and was convinced that the girl existed, though he despaired of finding her. He told his friend about the dream: "I crossed the sea and entered a beautiful city, where I met a princess named Malayavati, the girl I had seen in the picture. We fell in love at first sight, were married, and entered the bridal chamber; and as I made love to her, at the culminating moment that cursed watchman woke me up. Now that I have seen

Malayavati in a picture and in a dream, I cannot live without her."

"The king's friend, realizing that this was a true dream, told the king to draw a map of the city on a piece of cloth. He showed it to everyone, until one day a poet came from afar and told this tale: "In the city of Malaya, the king's daughter, Malayavati, dreamed that she married a certain man and entered the bridal chamber with him. But just as she was making love with him in bed, she was awakened at dawn by her chambermaid. She banished the maid, in a fury, and vowed that she would die if she did not find that man in six months, of which five have now passed." When the poet had told this tale, with all of its striking similarity and agreement, the king rejoiced in his certainty, and set out for the city.

"He found it just as the princess was about to kill herself. When she saw him, she said, "This was my dream-bridegroom," and when Vikramaditya saw his beloved with his own eyes, just as she had been in the picture and in his dream, he regarded it as a marvelous favor from the gods, and he took her back with him to his city."

As if reflected in the Indra's Net of Gems itself, the theme returns again centuries later, in this brief retelling by Wendy Doniger of the Rudyard Kipling story, "The Brushwood Boy," from 1898, a story, as she writes, "that raises the most striking questions about the interaction of myth and reality in the twilight zone of dreams."

"A young boy dreamed again and again of a girl with whom he rode on horseback along a beach until a policeman called Day awakened him. He grew up and joined the cavalry in India, where he drew a map of the place in his dream. When he returned to his parents' home in England, he heard a girl singing a song about the sea of dreams, the city of sleep, and the policeman Day; he recognized her as the girl in his dreams. When he told her of his dream, she told him of the boy she had always dreamed of, in the same dream."

Terrified, the girl asks the young officer, "What does it mean?" to which he simply kisses her, then replies, "Perhaps when we die we may find out more, but it means this now."

Another variation on the theme comes from G.H. Lewis, the companion of the novelist George Eliot, who told the following story about Charles Dickens, quoted in *The Canadian Illustrated News, 1870–1880:* "Dickens dreamt that he was in a room where everyone was dressed in scarlet. He stumbled against a lady standing with her back towards him. As he apologized she turned her head and said quite unprovoked "My name is Napier."

"He knew no one of the name Napier and the face was unknown. Two days later before a reading a lady friend came into the waiting-room accompanied by an unknown lady in a scarlet opera-cloak, "who" said his friend "is very determined of being introduced." "Not Miss Napier?" he jokingly inquired. "Yes Miss Napier." Although the face of his dream-body was not the face of Miss Napier, the coincidence of the scarlet cloak and the name was striking."

A contemporary parallel to the dream-come-true genre is the baseball cult film, *Field of Dreams.* Our hero, Ray Kinsella, played by Kevin Costner, is "stuck" as the story opens as all heroes are when we meet them. Soon we realize he is estranged from himself, his wife, his daughter, his work, and the memory of his dead father. Suddenly, one day, out in his corn field, he hears a mysterious voice whispering, "If you build *it* he will come. . . ." Shocked and disturbed, but also challenged, Kinsella does indeed build it, and "he" ["disgraced" baseball star, Shoeless Joe Jackson] miraculously appears to play ball on Ray's beautiful baseball field. Ray's dream comes true, although not the one he or the audience expects.

That the story will take place in the dreamtime of synchronicity is signaled early in the book while Ray is researching Shoeless Joe, "As I read, I discovered some uncanny coincidences. Or are there ever coincidences?"

In light of this timeless question, the stories in this section are offered with brief comments on the common themes that emerge as the book, like synchronicity itself, unfolds. By flagging a few key words and themes the thread of meaning that ties these stories together, while evoking Marie-Louise von Franz's reflection on the goal of life, "The realization of 'meaning' is therefore not a simple acquisition of information or knowledge, but rather a living experience that touches the heart just as much as the mind."

In "The Marvelous Moment," by cultural historian Keith Thompson, the author, like the hero in many an epic journey, is stuck as the story begins. He is in crisis about the dreaded transition between his twenties and thirties. Then in the telltale coincidence, a set of curiously significant numbers on his alarm clock startles him so much that time seems to stop, and he begins paying attention, finally admitting that, "I could only marvel at the moment." Elsewhere Thompson has written about "the astonishment of being," and commented on the curious "repression of the sublime" that modern culture has perpetrated. For him, the significance of a synchronicity is not *why* it happens, but *that* it happens. The phenomenology of such a moment asks only to be told, not proved.

In his whimsical tale, musicologist Atesh Sonnenborn hears a voice in a moment of career crisis, which, to his everlasting relief he listens to. What struck him was the "sheer discontinuity of the heavenly voice," signaling a break with ordinary time. Then, lo and behold, "doors open where there were no doors before," as Joseph Campbell once described this idea of following your call in life.

In "Dreamtime," Australian filmmaker Sophia Kobacker begins her vivid story with the revealing phrase, "missing link," which evokes the classic opening of an adventure journey that leads her toward her meeting with aborigine artists. Her juxtaposition of their "dreamtime" with the museum's "closing time" is a poetic touch. The story is a beautiful example of Jung's distinction of teleology in incidents of true synchronicity: the way an individual is drawn toward her goal or destiny, and being merely pushed along by fate. As someone involved with many indigenous cultures, Kobacker adds elsewhere that incidents of synchronicity are common when working with native people.

"For no apparent reason . . ." writes Katherine Van Horne of the key moment in her peculiar road movie of a story, "Square Wheels." In so doing, she spontaneously echoes the most common way that synchronicity is distinguished from commonplace or meaningless coincidences. "There was," she writes, "a definite connection to our timing and the dream . . . ."

In "Fire and Water," Lesha Finiw describes her ominous dream like a German expressionistic scriptwriter, with phrases such as "a house at crazed angles" and "too terrified to dream," or an alchemist as she describes the power of her transmuting dreams. Her story unfolds with choppy transitions, exactly like a leaping dream, and seems to be ruled by what psychologist Robert Aziz calls "images not one's own." Yet, she finds them to be "a wake-up call" while reflecting with a heart-felt expression about "the marvel of web connecting me to others." This almost exactly evokes Von Franz's definition, "For Jung, individuation and realization of the meaning of life are identical—since individuation means to find *one's* meaning, which is nothing other than *one's* connection with the universal Meaning."

For Trish Saunders, her experience was a "turning point," after which she began to listen more to her active dream life, whereas for author and teacher Valerie Andrews, the dilemma is how to interpret her prolific dream life and incorporate it into waking life. "Keep listening," she finally admonishes herself and her students. To Denise Burke, powerful dreams are "a deep saving connection," a poignant phrase to describe the power of all these stories. To Lisa Rafel, writer and actress, a mysterious voice presages a long, strange journey to the site of the ancient Eleusinian Mysteries in Greece, which results in an unexpected epiphany.

Finally, in his introductory letter to me regarding his touching reminiscence of his bodhissatva philosopher father, Alan Watts, Mark Watts writes, "For some time I have felt that when we are on track synchronicity is the confirmation of our connection." His story makes a case for mere coincidence being an unreflected-upon synchronicity, while conversely, synchronicity may be a deeply reflected-upon coincidence.

In each of these finely wrought stories an inner crisis parallels an outer event in a way that is inexplicable, uncanny, significant, and memorable to the writer. What's been called the "fine hand of synchronicity," appears to be at work here.

As Jung, von Franz, Bolen, and others have defined the phenomenon as acausal, the contributors in this book remark again and again how explanation is far less important to them than the experience itself. Or as the Hindu lover said to his beloved at the beginning of this roundelay, "It means this *now.*"

In the preface to his book, *Caravan of Dreams,* Islamic scholar Idries Shah retells one of his favorite stories from *A Thousand and*

One Nights, a remarkable example of how synchronicity is woven into the very fabric of many of our ambrosial myths, legends, and fables. *Not* coincidentally, this comes from a book I fondly remember my father reading out loud to my mother, sister, younger brother, and me, half a world and seven centuries away from the caravansaries of the ancient deserts that inspired these immortal teaching tales.

"In one of the best tales of the *Arabian Nights,* Maruf the Cobbler found himself daydreaming his own fabulous caravan of riches. Destitute and almost friendless in an alien land, Maruf at first mentally conceived—and then described—an unbelievably valuable cargo on its way to him.

"Instead of leading to exposure and disgrace, this idea was the foundation of his eventual success. The imagined caravan took shape, became real for a time—and arrived.

"May your caravan of dreams, too, find its way to you."

THE MARVELOUS MOMENT

I was about to turn thirty—just another birthday, or so I imagined. But as the biographical milepost drew nearer, I found myself surprisingly uneasy. It wasn't the predictable American concern about aging too fast; to the contrary. My best friends and closest colleagues have generally been my senior, thus it has been easy to equate the gaining of years with the development of insight, wisdom, character, and substance. I even celebrated my first gray hair as precursor to some John Forsythe-like *gravitas* that would, I supposed, come to me simply by enduring. Still, if the impending end of my second decade was really a welcome rite of passage, why then were my palms in such a ferocious sweat?

The problem, it seemed, was generational. Every child of the 1960s had heard the legendary refrain of counterculture performance artists Jerry Rubin and Abbie Hoffman: Never trust anyone over thirty. Naturally, of course, I didn't really believe that. I knew the third decade cutoff actually signified new era values of the '60s that couldn't be reduced to something as literal as a birthday count. I knew many people who had made it past thirty with their integrity and idealism intact.

Yes, but something about the thirty-as-endgame mythology had taken root in my psyche in ways I didn't exactly understand, not unlike the symbolic power of the millennial juggernaut constantly stirring the collective mind, sparing not even those who most loudly insist, "It's only a date on a calendar."

On February 25, 1984, I set off on a walk at dawn alone to the top of nearby Mt. Tamalpais, to greet the final day of my twenty-ninth year. Later, I was toasted by friends and coworkers who gathered to welcome me to the ranks of the generationally unfit. Returning late at night to the small hillside cabin I called home in those days, I lit a small candle and watched shadows dance on the ceiling. A breeze rattled a window, giving me a start. The owl that sometimes perched in the sprawling oak above my house called out to the night: *wwhhoo-wwhhoo*. Soon I extinguished the candle. Then came sleep: dreamless, bottomless, giving no hint that it could ever end.

But end it did, so abruptly in fact that for a time I had no idea where or who I was. At length I recognized the bedroom ceiling. Not exactly a voice, rather a strange and unfamiliar compulsion "told me" to turn to my immediate right.

There on the nightstand the red-lit digital dial of the clock-radio read as follows: 2 26 54. In one sense, this was nothing special: two hours, twenty-six minutes, and fifty-four seconds in the morning; another passing instant in a vast cosmos that intended me neither well nor ill, personally. And yet, and *yet,* I could only marvel at the incandescent display. For I was born on 2/26/54. I had wakened and looked over precisely "in time" to see that combination of numbers.

Ancient Greeks conceived of the ordinary passage of time— incessant, impersonal, non-negotiable—as belonging to the god Kronos, from whose adventures the term *chronology* is drawn. But the Greeks realized that not all time is *ordinary*. They reserved the term *Kairos* for *special* time: moments when something extraordinary punctuates mundane existence, reminding them that the origin of being is ever-present and shimmering. Similarly, Celtic mythology speaks of "thin places" in the universe, places where the visible and the invisible come in closest contact. Or as William Blake advised, "If the doors to perception were cleansed, every thing would appear to man as it is, infinite."

On the other hand: In the embryonic hours of my thirtieth birthday, it was indeed half past two in the morning, and nothing more, according to Kronos, not a god to be easily detoured. His relentless minute-hand marched forward . . . soon twenty-eight after the hour, then twenty-nine, soon *thirty*. As the digital display of the clock restored the dominion of the *mundane,* it occurred to me that perhaps nothing significant had happened after all. Probably I had read too much into sheer happenstance. Kronos? Miss a beat? Not likely.

I smile at that thought now, just as I smiled at it then. Kronos will never say so, but there was more to 2 26 54 than chronology. "Time must have a stop," insisted Shakespeare's Hotspur. The night belonged to Kairos, and so it will forever.

—*Keith Thompson*

DREAMTIME CALLING

I had been working at my home in Sydney on some short stories about a young woman's journey, and one morning, came to the realization that there was a missing story in the collection. It was obvious that my character still needed to travel to the central Australian desert, so as to apply what she learned there to events that came later in life.

Some months earlier, I had met a group of Australian women elders out in the desert. I had been invited to walk their country with them and learn their language and ways. It was important to wait for the right time. They had said, "One day we will telephone you and say, 'Come.'"

I had not yet heard from them and had expected they were all off together in the bush, but, on the morning I realized there was a missing link in my story sequence, I called the only Napangadi woman in the group who had a telephone line.

Pannaji sounded so matter-of-fact when she answered the phone in Alice Springs. She had been expecting my call. Earlier that morning, one of her sisters had walked into town from the desert and come to Pannaji's house asking about me. The Aboriginal women had collectively decided that the time had come for me to join them.

The two women had turned Pannaji's small house upside down looking for my phone number, but couldn't find it. The sister from the desert had shrugged her shoulders and said, "Don't worry, she'll call."

They had simply decided to wait, the way Aboriginal people do. And having waited on the Spirit before knowing when to move and in which direction, they were confident the time had come for me to travel with them and that I would call.

So certain was my desert sister that I would phone that day and arrive soon after, she had left Pannaji's house to walk to the women's art center to finish off a dot painting she had begun for me—a painting I had not yet asked for.

When I telephoned that morning, Pannaji had been sitting by the phone waiting for me to name the day I would arrive. Without thinking, I told her I'd be there with a four-wheel-drive within a week!

Since all the Aboriginal women were talented artists, I then asked Pannaji if one of them might paint a canvas for me.

Pannaji said, "Yes, it'll be finished by this afternoon!"

It was only then that she told me the sister had walked in from the desert less than an hour before, and that they were all now waiting for me.

The amazing coincidences of that day did not end there.

Pannaji told me that one of her kin sisters, whom I hadn't yet met, had gone to Sydney with paintings for a big art exhibition. She said I should go to the Art Gallery of New South Wales where several of her relatives were about to create a big sand painting. These sand paintings in desert ochres depict powerful dreaming stories, and they are a direct link with the Ancestor Beings.

When I arrived at the gallery that afternoon, I was told by the staff that the Aboriginal exhibition would not be opening for another three days and that the area was closed to the public. Pannaji had been very specific about when the ritual sand painting would be created. She had said "They'll be doin' it in the late afternoon."

It was closing time when I walked past the security guard into the Aboriginal wing of the big art gallery. There, I was greeted by the Aboriginal artists like an old friend. They shooed away the flustered security people saying, "We know her. She was invited." Yet I had never met any of them before.

I still don't know how it happened, but as I sat with the Aboriginal artists, watching as the huge sacred story took shape in red sand on the floor of the deserted gallery in central Sydney, while a fierce electrical storm raged all around us triggering the gallery alarms to echo through its empty halls, I knew I was meant to be there!

—*Sophia Kobacher*

SQUARE WHEELS

In the early fall of 1989, I had a dream. In the dream, the car I was driving at the time had developed suddenly, for no apparent reason, four square tires. In the next segment of the dream I was asked by a friend to drive the car up a specially designed ramp. The setting was a grassy area bordered by trees on which the ramp just appeared for square tire checking, I guess.

In day reality the following morning, I drove over to the Marin Headlands outside of San Francisco where my son, Zach, was spending a couple of nights with his fifth grade's nature field trip. I'd been asked to spend the day with them hiking. As I looked down the faces of the cliffs on that cloudless, still, late morning, the tide was out a remarkably long way. The bay rested in a calm pond, which I registered and mentioned.

At the end of the educational and joyful day, I was asked to drive home three strangers—two precious fifth-grade girls, who had stated they felt anxious or frightened about spending the night, and one mother I'd not met before either, who needed a ride back to the East Bay.

As we approached the relatively low span heading north on Highway 101 just past the exit to Stinson Beach and Tennessee Valley, I was thinking of two friends in the Tennessee Valley area who lived near a grassy section of road similar to that of the dream from the night before. Just as the van I was driving drove onto the low span that lifts over the turn to Tennessee Valley with the bay on the right, the sensation I felt was that the van had *four square tires!*

I laughed to the three new acquaintances in the car and asked if they were experiencing something odd about the ride. Each answered that she was and that it felt like all our tires were moving "catiwampus" at once. I mentioned that I thought I'd lost it altogether, as if I'd dreamed this very situation the night before. At the same time, the car radio reception went fuzzy, and the thought occurred to me that something was worth pulling over to check out when the car suddenly recommenced driving completely smoothly again. Several other cars had pulled to the side of the road for some reason. Yet with all systems except the radio working in top form, I proceeded along and the four of us visited with the radio off recollecting the beauty of the day.

Once we had crossed the Richmond–San Rafael Bridge and were heading along 580 East toward Highway 80, I noticed the traffic was moving sporadically. Then as we entered 80 just above Gilman Street in Berkeley, a car suddenly careened from the freeway up over the ice plant, taking a long irrigation pipe with it. I said nothing except to the woman passenger, "I think I'll take the University exit."

When we did, there were clusters of people outside buildings and windows were broken. I leaned out my window and asked a man at the light, "Is something going on we maybe should know about?"

"The Big One!" he cried back.

By not stopping the car in Marin to check the tires and simply shaking my head at the fact that we each were experiencing my dream of the night before, we had managed to make it onto the Richmond–San Rafael Bridge just before the Highway Patrol closed it due to the 1989 Loma Prieta earthquake.

—*Katherine Van Horne*

FIRE AND WATER

I was vacationing in Washington, D.C., at the time of the Oakland Hills fires in California in 1990. Unfortunately, newspapers on the East Coast were not very specific about where the fires were located. The general human interest in any disaster story is always magnified when you have something personal at stake. I feared for some friends who were living in the area, but it wasn't easy to track them down, what with the evacuation. Eventually I was relieved to find that they and their home escaped the worst.

When I returned to San Francisco, there was no getting away from the media coverage of the disaster. The smoke was still heavy in the air. Thousands of people were homeless. The fire was the only thing anyone could talk about. In earthquake country, people learn from every nuance of disaster. We see that it can happen, anytime to anyone. Everybody knows someone who's been affected. We grieve for the losses. We are grateful for the people and places that live to see another day. We watch for survival tips and pray that when our time comes we will rise to inspired acts of heroism.

One night after I had gone back to work, I dreamt an elaborate dream saturated with water. Huge waves rose and flared over the tops of buildings, crashing over the roof peaks. I guess I'm too terrified to even dream of fire. It looks to me like my dreaming mind has translated all the video images of fire to images of water, maybe because I like to swim and have a better chance in water.

In my dream: I have been transported to my brother Ron's house in Scituate, Massachusetts. It is on Oceanside Drive, right on the Atlantic Ocean. Ron and my sister-in-law, Marisa, live on the inland side of the road. The only thing between them and the ocean is the True family's house across the street. There is an empty lot full of large rocks and boulders just to the right of their place, so there is a clear view out to sea. The ground floor is almost all windows, designed to show off this view.

I am sitting in the recliner downstairs, watching a ferocious storm. Huge waves crash over the top of the True's house. Though I am impressed by the sight of the towering waves, I feel completely safe. I know that I am not in any danger, that Ron's house is not in danger, and that I am simply there to observe. I witness in detached wonder as neighboring houses begin to float down the street, as if they are floats on parade. Several houses drift by. I am fascinated to see them slowly twirling and spinning as they go down the road.

On the following evening, I am sitting in my own recliner, feet up on the hassock, watching the evening news with one eye, while reading the mail. I only half-hear what the announcers are saying, something about President Bush. There's hurricane damage at Kennebunkport, Maine.

Quick mental geography. Maine? It's higher up the coast from Ron and Marisa. No bother to me and mine. Quick glimpse of damage estimate. Doesn't look that bad to me . . . . More talk that I don't pay attention to until the sign-off: "This is so-and-so (didn't catch the name) for (don't remember which station) reporting live from Scituate, Massachusetts."

Suddenly, my eyes are up and alert, straining to catch a fleeting glimpse of the town as the camera cuts away. I think I recognize the place but it's too fast. Were they reporting down by Scituate Harbor or trying to find more scenes from the storm?

I lurch for the phone. Not surprisingly there is no answer at Scituate, so I try to get through to my sister MaryAnn in Boston. She answers: Ron and Marisa are OK, the main house is OK, but the deck's damaged and the stairs were ripped off by the storm.

So it turns out that my dream *was* transmuting fire to water. It was actually eerily accurate in its own way. The True's house held firm, withstanding the pounding of the towering waves. But many neighbors' houses were lifted off their foundations and spun around. Much of the landscape of Oceanside Drive was rear-ranged. The house immediately behind my brother's was split in two. The one next door (across from the empty lot), was pushed back off its foundation and tilted at a crazy angle. Its back door was crushed into the ground, while the front door was lifted way up to face the sky. Ron's neighbors, Fritz and his elderly mother-in-law, were trapped inside, but Ron was eventually able to get them out.

I never quite know what to make of such dreams. I don't know if they're actually prescient, or more often, like news bul-letins to let me know that something serious is happening that affects the people I love. Sometimes I wish I could put these visions to better use—but then I retract that wish. It would be too great a responsibility. What if I didn't get through in time? Even if the dreams are predictive, I'm not good enough at divining their meaning. I usually connect them to the real event only after I hear from the other people involved.

But these dreams do have a very important effect. I am always looking for the meaning. When I have a dream this vivid, I know I need to start asking questions, looking for correlations, checking in and checking up on the possible source—that is, I am remind-ed to keep in close touch with my friends and family.

Not a bad reminder, in any case, but it's a wake-up call, giv-ing me a strong sense of urgency.

—*Lesha Finiw*

DREAMING OF STONES

In July of 1996 I journeyed to Nova Scotia, Canada. While there, I was drawn to collect the beautiful, mysterious stones along the beaches and coves of the Atlantic Ocean. A week after my return home, I had plans to meet a friend at the Ann Arbor Art Fair. My friend was going through a difficult time, so I had a present for her to help lift her spirits. The present was beautifully wrapped and I wanted to place one of the Nova Scotia stones in the center of the package. But no matter what I tried, the stone wouldn't stay put. So I decided to put the stone in my pocket and place it on the package just before I presented it to her.

Since we weren't going to meet until mid-morning, I had a chance to walk around the art fair alone for a while. I happened upon the booth of an artist, Gregory Strachov from Venezuela, who painted beautiful, mysterious, large stones. His paintings were watercolors that looked like photographs. They were haunting. I was pulled into the booth to look closely at these stones.

The first question I asked the artist was, "Do you dream these?"

He said yes.

I felt an overwhelmingly deep affinity for his work. I wanted so much to buy one of the paintings, but financially I couldn't. I told him how deeply his work touched me. Then I left.

As I walked away, I absentmindedly put my hand in my pocket. I felt the stone. Instantly I knew! The stone didn't belong to my friend, which is why it wouldn't stay on the package. It belonged instead to this marvelous painter of stones.

So I quickly returned to his booth and told the artist and his wife about my original intention for the stone, but how the stone [seemed to] know differently.

My story gave them goosebumps. The artist told me that wherever he was in all the world my stone would accompany him. He and his wife asked me to please sign their book with my name, so they would know who I was. When I signed my first name, *Mary,* they audibly sighed and told me that in Spanish the name *Maria* means *Mary* and both their grandmothers' names had been Mary. They went on to say that the first date they had was at a *Cafe Maria,* and that the artist's first studio was on *Maria Street.*

A circle of deep affinity and resonance was present. I walked away from that booth knowing that lives can deeply touch with the briefest of magic.

—*Mary Rezmerski*

GEORGE

When I was in the eighth grade, I began to make a commitment to write down my dreams upon waking. I had this idea that writing them down would help to make me more psychic—ESP, ya know?

Anyway, by the time I was in the tenth or eleventh grade, I got quite good at recalling my lucid images in the form of words on paper. One day, I stayed home from school because I was sick with a cold. I slept late and remembered my dream, which was a long one. In my dream I had been to my prom date's house, which I remembered vividly. In real life I had never been to his house. We had a plan to go to his prom together, but we weren't that close. So it was unusual for me to dream of him.

Anyway, that day he called me on the phone. Since we rarely called each other, I told him what a coincidence I thought it was that he happened to call on the day that I had dreamt about him.

When I told him about the dream and how vivid his room was, he said, "What did it look like?"

I said, "Well, there were twin beds."

He said, "I used to have twin beds, but not anymore. What else?"

I told him that there were round rugs on the floor. He said he had round rugs in his room and asked, "What color were they?"

I said, "They were all different colors."

He said, "That's what my rugs look like, alright."

I thought, "Wow, how cool."

Later, when my mom came home I told her about the phone call and the coincidence and recalled the rest of the dream to her, then said, "But there was this other part of the dream where you and I were in our old house, in the upstairs bathroom. It had a secret room attached that I never knew about. There were pictures in there of all our relatives and one large family photo that looked a lot like 'The Last Supper,' except that George Washington was in place of Jesus."

In my dream I couldn't believe that we were related to George Washington and asked my mom why she never told me we were. She said, "I don't know. I just never told you."

As I was casually telling my mom this especially vivid part of my dream, her jaw slowly dropped. She said, "I think you should go into the kitchen and read the letter that's on the counter. I just received it today."

I did as she suggested and discovered that it was a letter from a man who was researching his family history and was stuck on someone who was related to my Aunt Ida Clark. He wondered if we knew anything about her family history or this distant relative of hers that he was stuck on.

The relative's name was "Mr. George Washington Clark."

Coincidence? I can't say. But it was a turning point for me in that it validated my early morning writing exercises. I also began to listen more to my dreams, in a way I hadn't known before.

—*Trish Saunders*

THE DREAMING

I had studied piano and composition and, for awhile in the late 1970s, I dreamed music, which I would then wake up and write down.

One night I dreamed that Lizst had met Chopin, in Paris and together they had composed a certain piano piece. It was a kind of funeral march. When I woke up, I sat down at the piano and played the first few bars.

By 1981, I was working in London at a job that had nothing to do with music. I was promoting the first women's international marathon and held a dinner with a public relations firm we'd just hired. To my surprise, I found myself seated next to Rosemary Brown, the English psychic and pianist, who had just recorded a selection of Chopin's compositions she had channeled. Her son was a friend of the young woman who was writing our press releases, and they'd come to the same restaurant. Rosemary and I spent the night talking about the idiosyncratic phases of Chopin and Liszt, and I told her all about the funerailles I had received in my dream.

"Keep listening, my dear," she said, "that's exactly how I get mine!"

—*Valerie Andrews*

THE WOMAN FROM MY DREAMS

In 1994, I began dreaming of an Indian woman. She always gave me sound advice and told me to come and see her. Later that summer, I attended a dream seminar with Dr. Stephen Aizenstat. I was walking with a friend when a picture fell out of a book. It was the woman from my dreams. He told me she was Mother Meera, the avatar from India.

Later I dreamt: I am walking arm-in-arm with Mother Meera and Mother Teresa. They are showing me how to make holes in the soil with my finger. I tear open a packet of seeds: They are my tears. I slowly begin to plant them.

Later that week, I go to see my mentor. As soon as she sees my face, she exclaims, "So you have connected to Mother Meera?"

"Yes," I tell her. "How did you know?"

"I can see her in your eyes, as I have just come from seeing her."

—*Susan Foster*

THE WARNING

"That underlying connection (with others) is the Tao, and a synchronistic event is a specific manifestation of it."
—Jean Shinoda Bolen, *The Tao of Psychology*

Several years ago, I organized a Northwestern University reunion of my sorority sisters. We were all to stay at a sister's home in Santa Rosa, California. A group of about twenty of us were able to come, some from as far away as New York. I had planned rather outrageous, California-style events for my old gang, ranging from mud baths and glider rides in Calistoga to horse-drawn carriage rides through the vineyards of Napa. I was immensely excited about the reunion and was especially looking forward to the arrival of my best buddy from Ohio.

The afternoon prior to her arrival, I received a long distance call from her. She said, "My suitcase is packed and my ticket is in my hand, but I just don't think I can come."

It seems her son had called and begged her not to go. He had had a very powerful dream in which she was in a fatal accident at the reunion. My friend said that based on that alone she wouldn't have changed her plans. But her son had confessed to her that he had also had a similar dream three years before that his father would die very suddenly. Five days after that dream his father died while taking a shower. He was forty-eight years old.

The son felt somehow responsible for his dad's death, and due to his guilt had never shared this information with his mom. But now he was desperate to convince her to stay home.

The first day of our reunion was incredible. A little devil inside of me gave me great joy as I watched these tense, middle-aged Midwestern women trying to immerse themselves in the stinky, hot, slimy Calistoga mud baths, and as they took off, white-of-knuckle and clenched-of-tooth, on their glider rides through Napa Valley. Everyone was a great sport and had a lot of fun.

"Now how are you going to top *this?*" they asked at the end of the first day.

The plan for the second day was a horse-drawn, open-wagon ride through the vineyard countryside. That morning, nine of us climbed up on the first carriage as the driver was in the process of hoisting his large body into the driver's seat. Suddenly, the two horses mistook a loud sound for a signal to go. They lurched forward, throwing the driver on the ground. With no one to keep them in check, we were soon going at a full gallop!

Picture this big, fat man yelling, "Whoa!" while puffing and running like hell in chase after a carriage with nine hysterical women, which is only funny in hindsight (no pun intended). The horses were galloping at what seemed like the speed of light. I reached up to the driver's seat and pulled back on a large wooden lever, which seemed like it should be the brake. Naturally, it didn't work, but I held onto it for dear life. Others threatened to jump, but I begged them to hold tight.

As we were racing out of control, my mind kept screaming, "This is Barbara's fatal accident; this is what her son saved her from." All of a sudden, we realized the freeway was straight ahead of us and the damn horses were heading straight for it. At that point, my friend Lynn decided to jump rather than face the dangerous prospect of crossing the freeway in a runaway carriage.

But as the horses approached the freeway, they took a sudden ninety-degree turn on two wheels onto a frontage road. It seemed as if we were doomed to roll over at that point, but we didn't. The problem was we were then tearing down a road lined with telephone poles, and our horses were attached together by a large wooden yoke. At full speed, they headed directly for one of the poles—which went right in between the rampaging horses, smashing the yoke and freeing them. Everyone but me was violently flung out of the carriage, which wrapped around the pole right through to the middle. Women lay strewn on the ground like rag dolls. No one sustained serious injuries, but when the police and ambulances arrived an officer asked me the names of the others. They were all good friends, but I was so shaken up I couldn't remember one name.

I kept wondering, "What would have happened to Barbara if she had gone with us?"

I think that a deep connection between mother and son saved her life.

—*Denise Murphy Burke*

TWINS

When my sister Lisa and I were growing up in a little Missouri town called Webster Groves, many people believed we were twins. We were actually two years apart, but since I was slightly big for my age, and she slightly small, and since we were very close as far as sisters go (not to mention the fact that our mother dressed us alike!), I could easily see how folks might have come to such a conclusion. Lisa and I thought it was fun to pretend that we were twins, since our father and his brothers were twins.

We spoke alike, gestured alike, and laughed alike. Sometimes when we would speak to each other on the phone, I could hear her voice in my ear, even when I would be the one speaking—as if our voices were one and the same! Our friends were often amused at how we addressed each other as "sister," and how we ended our sentences in unison. When we conversed with each other, we would say the same thing at the same time so often that one of us would eventually sigh, "I don't know why we talk to each other, I already know everything you're going to say!"

As we grew older, Lisa eventually moved eastward to a little town in West Virginia, and I moved westward to a little town in California. More than once we would call home to Missouri within five minutes of each other; and even more often, while our mother or brother would be talking on the phone to one of us, the other would click-in on call-waiting at the same time.

Once, when I was visiting mom's house in Missouri, helping my brother type a paper for school, Liz arrived that day, having driven eight hours from West Virginia. She looked at my type-writer, confused, and said, "Oh—did I leave my typewriter here last time?" Then suddenly she gasped, "No way!" she blurted out. "I can't believe it! That's the *exact* same typewriter I bought in West Virginia!" Sure enough, in different states, of all the brands and models of typewriters available, we had purchased the same one, a Smith-Corona; even the model was the same, an SD-650.

Perhaps many of our childhood similarities might be trivially explained away with nature/nurture theories. After all, we were similar due to heredity and an atmosphere of identical upbringing. And maybe what we considered eerily synchronistic might have sometimes have very well been only a coincidence.

But coincidences can't explain everything that's happened.

A few years ago, I was working on a ship on the West Coast, near San Francisco. Although I normally do not let sadness get the best of me, I had one of those days when nothing went right. I was working ridiculously long hours; I missed my family; I was men-tally exhausted; and I had unfortunately had my heart broken by a gent I quite admired at the time.

Depressed and drained, I curled up on my bunk around 11:00 P.M. and submitted to a fine dose of self-pity and a well-deserved cry. My feelings felt exceptionally deep, as if I was in a state of meditation miles inside my head.

In port the next day I called Lisa, as there is no finer consola-tion in the world than a sweet sister. When she picked up the phone she said, "How weird . . . I had the feeling you were going to call. I woke up last night about two o'clock in the morning and sat straight up in bed and said, "Something's wrong with Paula!"

It was quite a comfort to hear her words. They honestly didn't seem strange at that moment, as we have often remarked about our innate ability to sense a strong emotion in the other. But after we hung up the phone, it hit me that she was 3,000 miles away. How could she have felt my pain? What was this energy that could travel such a distance? I wondered then why she woke up precisely three hours after I was in bed.

Then, as if a splash of water had hit my face, I realized that I had not considered that I was on Pacific time, and she was on Eastern, which meant that she did not wake up three hours later. Instead, she woke up at exactly the same time that I was in the depths of my sadness.

—*Paula Jean Pfitzer*

NIGHT OF TERROR

My throat ached with an excruciating pounding. It was my heart! I felt as if I had swallowed it and was gasping for breath as I tried to suppress the thundering. It was so loud that I was sure I would be detected in my third hiding place in the shed. Who was this madman stalking me with a gun? What did he want with me?

Finally, catching my breath, I braved a peek around the corner of my shelter and decided to run for cover in the main house again. I dashed through the clearing toward the house, slipped in through a side door, and gingerly slid the lock shut so I wouldn't be heard by my predator (if he was still within ear shot).

I fell back against the wall and slid down into a heap, still gasping for breath. Just as my heart began to slow down a bit, I heard a wild screeching of tires in the driveway. With anguish, I rolled onto my knees and, with all the strength I could muster, pushed myself up to eye level with the bottom of the window. Through a tear in the curtain, I could see the maniac in the driver's seat heading straight for the house at full speed! His eyes were like great dark holes with flames flashing out of them. The hatred was spewing out of his every pore, tightening the reddened skin around the bones of his face, as he shouted and raved while steering the car directly toward the front door.

Jolting with terror, I leapt to my feet and ran out the back door toward the orchard. I thought that if he was going to crash into the house, then certainly I would have a chance to run for it. I knew I was running for my life and tried to ignore the aching pain clawing at my throat and limbs. In a flash I heard the car behind me. I turned the corner of the house and the wheels screeched after me. My God, this was it—I was going to die!

I bolted upright in bed stricken with terror. My heart was thundering in my chest and throat. It took me several minutes to realize that I was home and was experiencing a nightmare of gargantuan proportions. The fear lingered. I was so shaken by the experience that I made myself get up and walk around to stay awake. I turned on music and sang out loud to dispel the mood so there would be no chance of reentering what was a very real, frightening place. I knew this was no ordinary dream. It was 2:00 A.M., so I had some tea and, after an hour or so, somehow managed to get back to sleep.

Two days later, I was speaking with my mother who lived several states away. She related a horrifying story to me about how she and my sister had been chased into hiding by my sister's crazy husband who had threatened to shoot them. They frantically tried to find a place to hide. They hid in the shed, then in one of the cars, where they slept all night in the pouring rain. They were truly terrified for their lives.

It happened at 2:00 A.M on the very night of my own nightmare.

—Joanne Warfield

THE HEAVENLY VOICE

Quick cash for rent and groceries were called for. I figured the best way to get some would be to sell my vintage, fifties' Volvo 544, one of four classy cars handpainted by Christos Katechis in a cardinal elements series of earth, air, water, and fire. Mine was *fire*, a pale yellow mobile mural, tongues of orange and red flame covering it from hood to trunk. It was beautiful.

I parked my car on busy Union Street that afternoon, with red and white "For Sale" signs on either side of the car inscribed "Inquire Within" and settled down with a newspaper. It was cloudy, drizzling fitfully. Suddenly the clouds parted in the west, just enough so that a single beam of sunlight could leap to light my car, my face.

Then I heard a great, reverberant voice command, "Get over to the union hall!"

Quite cinematic, mind you.

I looked around at the folks on the street, but there wasn't a glance in my direction. I was the only one who had heard the voice or seen the light.

Now the percentage of actively gigging union musicians in San Francisco back then was small compared to Los Angeles or

New York, and though I had checked in at the union hall when I got to town months earlier, there had been no hope of work through them, and I hadn't even thought of Local 6 since the year before. My inner makeup being what it is, though, I hightailed it over to the Tenderloin district, found a (impossible) space directly across Jones Street from the entrance of the hall, ran up the stairs into the office, and business rep Tommy Alexander called out from his office, "Don't you play piano?"

"Yup," I agreed. He was at that moment on the phone with a request for a piano player from the now-defunct Mocambo Club on Polk Street, for that very evening. Three hours later, I was warming up the crowd for comedian Henny Youngman's set, which paid more in one night than I'd seen in a long, long time.

The sheer discontinuity of the heavenly voice and getting the gig are what make me continue to marvel about life.

—*Atesh Sonneborn*

THE VOICES OF ELEUSIS

In 1988, I changed my life. I had been walking up a hillside in an eastern section of Nepal called Namsaling. It was a strange feeling that stopped me in a tall grove of bamboo. The air was warm and fragrant, but I was stopped by the sound of the air passing over and between the leaves of the trees. I stood there and realized that my life was without internal music. I wanted the beauty of this moment to be a part of me, and so I decided to leave my job and to become a person who lived from a poet's heart.

I had been writing profusely for six months before this journey, and when I returned I began performing my poetry anywhere

I could. I realized that there were parts of myself that I had no idea about, and I felt that the best way to learn about them was to listen to what I was saying. My writing took me deeply into the nature of myself as a woman. I watched the audiences responding to my work and was encouraged to go even more deeply. I expanded into the nature of relationships.

One evening, I was performing at a small club on La Brea Boulevard in Los Angeles, when a man whom I had talked with before and who knew my work approached me and handed me a flyer telling me about a trip to Greece. The flyer said that a well-known poet and therapist, a dance specialist, a theater director, and a dream interpreter were all going to re-create the Eleusinian Mysteries with a small group of participants. I didn't know anything about the Mysteries but the flyer said that the people who had performed them up to 2,500 years ago had heard the voices of God. This fascinated me.

Up to this time, I had been reluctant to tell people the full truth regarding what happened to me in Nepal for fear that they would disbelieve me. I had heard a voice there. It had been specific and insistent. The voice made it clear that I must survive there and that life is a test of courage and strength. Although I mentioned this in the poetry book I wrote about the journey, I did not know how to talk about it. I had not visited New Age bookstores or shops. I had no New Age friends when this happened.

I can't describe how I knew I had to go on the trip to Greece when I saw the flyer. I just knew it. I didn't have the money for the trip, but I sent in my deposit anyway. Then the Iran/Iraq war broke out, and there was talk that the trip would be canceled. But I kept looking at the flyer. I had learned to pray in Nepal, and I prayed now. A month later I got a job that paid for the trip. Another month passed. We watched the events of the war carefully. As the date approached, the leaders of the tour checked with the State Department and it was agreed. We would go.

The first night we arrived in Crete, we gathered in the conference room of the hotel. We formed a large circle and the leader asked us to share with each other why we had come. When my turn came I was excited, but I casually said that I had come because I was intrigued by the Voices-of-God statement on the flyer.

The leader looked at me curiously. "There's nothing like that on the flyer," she said.

I was shocked. That flyer had been on my desk for months.

She then reached into her notebook, found a copy of the flyer and showed it to me. It wasn't there. There was nothing like it on the flyer. But that was why I had come.

—Lisa Rafel

DREAMING OF SUPERMAN

In September 1991, I had the following dream:

My husband and I are hosting a political fundraiser at our home. In the dream, my husband is Christopher Reeve (Superman). Our house is beautiful and ornate like an Italian museum. There are pieces of art everywhere, Michelangelos, Van Goghs, and Matisses. Everything is framed in gold, as are the fixtures in the house. I feel uncomfortable and out of place. I wish I could leave, but I do not know how. I feel like I do not belong in this world of my husband's. He leaves to go ride his horse. I put on a happy face and begin serving champagne to the guests.

I hear a commotion outside and see a group of men carrying

my husband. They put him in a wheelchair. He has been paralyzed from the neck down. I think, now I will never be able to leave him. I think now that he is paralyzed, however, perhaps we will get along better.

I send everyone home and take him upstairs to give him a bath. I undress him and put him in the tub. He is heavy and hard for me to manage. I turn to get some towels and as I turn back, he has slid down in the tub. I frantically try to lift him out before he drowns, but I cannot. He dies. I begin to cry. I feel around in the tub, holding him. Suddenly, our son Wesley pops out of the tub and says, "Hi, Mom. Don't worry, everything will be all right. I reach down into the tub and Wes (Christopher Reeve) is gone.

I realize that I should have pulled the stopper to let the water run out, and I wonder at my stupidity. I wake up.

The next night I awake to the sound of running water. I go upstairs to find my then husband drowning in the bathtub. I try to pull him out, but remembering my dream I pull the stopper out of the tub, saving his life. He did, however, leave.

The other obvious coincidence of course is Christopher Reeve's fall from the horse. This dream occurred several years prior to his accident. My associations at the time were that my husband bore a strong resemblance to him and to a crippled Superman animus (mine).

—*Susan Foster*

FROM TIME TO TIME

My father, the late Alan Watts, used to say that human beings are constantly trying to straighten out the wiggly world of nature. We try to explain life in rational terms, but this is our attempt to confine a multi-tracked universe to a single line. When he was writing about the Tao in the early '70s, I drove up from Big Sur one day to help him prepare visual language charts for his new book, *The Tao: The Watercourse Way.* I was to meet him at his studio aboard an old ferryboat moored across the bay from San Francisco, and since there was scarcely an hour before our planned meeting I sped along in an effort to arrive on time.

I reached the boat at the appointed hour and found my father sitting absorbed in his work with a freshly inked brush in his hand. He was contemplating the calligraphic figures drying on the roll of paper in front of him. Quietly I joined him at the table, and after a long moment he glanced up and said, "This is a tricky one— I don't think most Westerners will get it. However, it is closely related to the original sense of our word for nature." The Chinese character in question was *tzu-jan,* meaning at once self-so and nature, or that which-is-so-itself, and, in the process, true to its own nature. He returned to his brushwork.

From the hours spent driving up the coast, I felt a slight muscular tension extending from my forehead and behind my eyes to my neck and shoulders. I stood up to stretch, feeling suddenly that I was somehow there ahead of myself. Breathing deeply, I stretched my arms back, and then downward. After a long moment, lost in the sensation of energy filling out behind me, I heard my father chuckle, and say, "Spread your wings back . . . that's it . . . now touch the water." I knew he drew this image from the birds we saw sunning their wings along the shoreline every day. As I continued to relax and stretch out, I suddenly felt the sensation of backward spreading feathers touching liquid and drawing up, as if a quill were drawing wet ink. We were on the same page, as it were, and spent the rest of the afternoon following the evolution of Chinese characters and preparing the charts for his book.

The next time I started to rush to get somewhere, I remembered that the last time I had hurried only to arrive on time, but somewhat ahead of myself. In the following months, I began to develop a new sense of being "on time," or perhaps more accurately, "in time." It was characterized by a clear head and a very tangible sensation of being neither ahead of nor behind myself, but comfortably centered between the heart, belly, and hips. I had begun to notice that many of the things I did regularly tended to pull the physical sensation of being upward from this center and project it out ahead of the upper body, but that by taking a moment to sink back into the center, balance could easily be restored.

For me this energy exercise offered a physical parallel to the essential Buddhist idea of a middle way. From its center, body energy flows evenly but is never stagnant, and it ripples along in a dynamic balance between balance and imbalance. It also seemed that to be "out of time" was, as far as I could tell, a uniquely human condition. I began to go out and paddle around in an old canoe and to practice a sort of water meditation out on the water. Egrets and geese set the tone punctuated by occasional visits from the local otters.

Against this background, my thoughts stood out as somewhat artificial constructs, and I noticed that at times someone I knew would pop repeatedly into my head, but in connection with a usually trivial thought or memory. I began to realize, however, that these spontaneous arisings often held a significance other than the one my conscious attention had connected with it. I was thinking about the right thing, but I was thinking the wrong thing about it!

The recognition that something else was going on opened another door, and seeming intuitions about the thoughts began to surface. Then, as I drifted along, I became aware of a field of thought *outside* my head, an almost visible layer of collective mind hanging in the atmosphere over the water. Paddling again, I began to see how this level of thought worked in parallel to my own thought process. It was an informing agent, with the potential to put me in touch with events I would not usually perceive.

As I became comfortable with this prospect, I decided to try an experiment. Instead of bringing that source into my mind, what if I were to go out into it? So I began to tune back into the sensation of the field, giving myself over to its intelligence. Then, an extraordinary change of perception overcame me, and my surroundings disappeared in a vision of the same setting, but as it must have appeared a hundred years earlier. The buildings were gone from the distant shoreline, and in their place were trees and marshes. The freeway overpass at the end of the bay was gone, and instead a moose waded out along the water's edge. And above it a mountain grew up out of hills, still in their pristine state. Recognizing the mountain, the spell began to break and, as my eyes fixed on a little spot halfway up its slopes, the vision crumbled, the distant roar of traffic resumed, and I said to myself I should go for a walk up to that spot on the mountain sometime.

The following year my father passed away, and I found I needed to be in the area more often to continue some of the projects we had begun. I had been sending records of his talks to public radio stations across the country, and one day I went into the local post office with a stack of record boxes in my arms. In line, I found myself behind a philosophy instructor I knew from one of the local colleges, and we began to talk. When he found out I was planning on moving back into the area, he said, "You know, I have a little room next to my house I was thinking of renting. It is pretty small, but it might be just right for you." The location turned out to be the exact spot I had focused on during the vision. I lived there for more than twelve years, until I married and we grew out of the cabin; after a few years away, we will soon move back into the house next door. And still, from time to time, I take a moment to see what else is going along with thoughts that come to mind.

—*Mark Watts*

II. Sudden Appearances, Uncanny Encounters

Synchronicity can pave the way for people coming together. By unraveling the circumstances through which two people meet to enter a significant relationship, the delicate, unseen hand of fate, destiny, synchronicity, or underlying Tao—by whatever name the matchmaker is called—can be discerned.

—Jean Shinoda Bolen

In his book, *The Challenge of Chance,* Arthur Koestler called the spirit that appeared to him when he was stuck with his research his "Library Angel." This is the magic realm of the muses that mythologist William Irwin Thompson alludes to when he wistfully remarks, "A university can provide you with a library, but what makes the book you are not looking for fall off the shelf and into your hands is not understood by any university."

In *Synchronicity: Science, Myth, and the Trickster,* Allan Combs and Mark Holland cite an example of the Angel at work in a story that Dame Rebecca West sent to Koestler from her research of the Nuremberg war crimes: "I looked up at the trials in the library and was horrified to find they are published in a form almost useless to the researcher. They are abstracts and are catalogued under arbitrary headings. After hours of search I went along the line of shelves to an assistant librarian and said: 'I can't find it; there's no clue; it may be in any of these volumes.' I put my hand on one volume, took it out, and carelessly looked at it, and it was not only the right volume, but I had opened it to the right page."

Another tonically baffling anecdote about book synchronicity comes from Francis X. King's *Encyclopedia of Mind, Magic, and Mystery.* There he describes a story from 1971, in which the novelist George Feifer's personally annotated copy of his own novel, *The Girl from Petrovka,* was stolen from his car in London. After the film rights had been sold, Feifer went to visit the casted star, Anthony Hopkins, in Vienna.

Hopkins revealed to him a strange coincidence that he had just undergone. As soon as he inked the contract to appear in the movie version of the novel, he tried in vain to find a copy of the book. However, on his way home, his attention was drawn to an open package on a bench in London's Leicester Square Underground Tube Station. Because of recent terrorist bombings, he was wary of the parcel but for some reason (a common motivation in these stories) he risked looking inside. There he found a copy of Feifer's novel, which he had been searching for all day.

Hopkins handed over the book to the bemused Feifer, and it turned out to be the author's own annotated copy, lost, presumably forever, two years before.

Retelling this story, my mind moves sidelong, and I think back to an afternoon in 1993 in a small seaside village on the west coast of Turkey. I was leading a mythology tour and that particular morning I had stood on the "windy walls" of Troy and had coaxed my group to read outloud from several translations of the immortal *Odyssey* so they might get some idea of the different voices that have interpreted Homer through the generations. Afterward, we had threaded our way through the tumbledown ruins on the hill of Hisarlik that the enigmatic archaeologist Heinrich Schliemann discovered more than eighty years before. Pausing at the site where he and his wife reputedly found the gold "Treasure of Priam," I described the controversial discovery that both shocked and dazzled the world. At that point, one of the members of the tour, Sue Beaton, just happened to ask me where the treasure was now. Glad to field such a pertinent question, I reported that Schliemann had secreted the hoard out of Turkey and taken it to Berlin, where it was subsequently plundered again at the end of World War II by the retreating Russian army.

Suddenly, I remembered a fugitive line I'd read weeks before in *World Press Review* about a rumor that the treasure had recently been sighted in a Moscow museum warehouse along with dozens of invaluable Impressionist paintings. Supposedly they had been found during a painstaking inventory of the loot that had been locked away since the end of the war. With a sly grin, I shared the rumor, partly out of my irrepressible reflex of embellishing stories, but also because we were there, at Troy, after reading Paris and Helen, Achilles and Hector, all my life, beginning at my father's knee as a boy, just like Schliemann had with his father. I wanted it to be true.

Hours later, in the seaside *lokansi,* we were having a fantabulous lunch of fresh fish, salad, and ouzo when my Ahmet, my Turkish co-leader, triumphantly appeared waving the national newspaper in the air and shouting, "Phil, Phil, look, look!" I spread open the paper and immediately recognized the old photographs of the archaeologist and his Greek wife adorned in the gold jewelry from the "Treasure of Priam," and could even get the gist of the headline in Turkish: "Schliemann's Treasure Discovered in Moscow!"

"How did you know?" a fellow romantic bellowed from down the table. "Hey, you must have read that somewhere yesterday," charged Steve, the group skeptic. "Wow, outrageous!" came another voice.

I didn't; I couldn't have; but of course it was, as synchronicity always is.

Cross-cutting to the stories in Part II of our collection, we find a welter of images that convey the phantom appearances and uncanny encounters that populate so many synchronicity experiences. Once again, the stories need less analysis than they do attention to the details that accumulate and accrue to form a vivid picture of what can happen when one is suddenly overcome in the middle of nowhere, and as Jamake Highwater puts it, "sees something out of the corner of my eye." Baffled, he learns to be "profoundly aware of the miracle of life."

In Kate Bullard Adams' remarkable narrative, the mythological metaphor of being "stuck" at the beginning of an epic journey is evisceratingly realized. The North Carolina novelist uses the vivid metaphors of Frankenstein, zombies, and paradoxical visions to convey the eerieness of her experience. Her fears of "screwing up" are startlingly expressed, as is her wise conclusion that she had "to make a mistake so as to see."

So too in physicist Fred Alan Wolf's story, excerpted from his book, *The Spiritual Universe*. Like an Alex in Wonderland, Wolf unabashedly reveals how "a strange thing happened," which catalyzed a reverie in him, and to his astonishment he felt connections but also was also humbled to find he knew "nothing." The disturbing appearances of three crippled men, one right after the other, forced him to finally realize that they were not an aberration, but a metaphor for his own soul crisis. For this he describes his own prescription, in his own indubitable phrasing, this "one-legged life form has to change."

Likewise the other stories in this section evoke the ghostly feeling that the phenomenon of synchronicity so often evokes. The photographer Eric Lawton captures the essence of memorable encounters on the back roads of the world with his picaresque description of feeling connected to someone in a way that defies rational explantion.

"If you don't go down willingly into the underworld, the gods yank you down," the Roman writer Salutius once said. Two thousand years, or so, a mighty hand might have punched a hole in the earth and reached up and grabbed us if we weren't doing our proper soul-work. Today we travel by car cross-country, like astrologer and travel director Jeannette Hermann did twenty years ago, until a blown tire signals she'd better stop and look around and see what's cookin' and what's not. Just when she thought things were back to normal, a magical fish appeared, revealing that *change was in the air*. In amusingly similar fashion, during one peculiar stretch of his life not one but *seven* fish mysteriously appeared to Jung himself, which he read as a sign. . . .

"Coincidence, we don't think so," remarks Dennis Slattery about his own "change" and concatenation of synchronicities, though he could have been commenting on the stories that buttress his here.

A few more phrases will set the stage for the rest of this section's stories:

"This soul-task of mine," as film producer Christy Baldwin expressed the way she embraced her goddess project after an auspicious sign. Playwright Judith Lutz says of her encounter with doves, "The insight was immediate for me . . . reminding me of the deeper trust in life." And film producer Gary Rhine remarked, "Ironically, my destiny was to merge."

Of her sighting of a fox, Mary Rezmerski concludes, "Seeing the fox affirmed the spirit in everything; I know I am connected to a power stronger." For performer Megan Wells, the sighting of a rabbit brought about a "paralyzing fear," and to bluesman Rand DeMattei the close encounter with a crow brought a rush of joy. Each of the soul moments in these stories evoked gratitude and signaled great change.

Significantly, these stories also underline what our last contributor here, editor Shirley Christine, concludes about her common coincidences, "the meaning is in the connection."

EMPTY SPACE

The pass over the Zigana Mountains in southeastern Turkey is a rift between two landscapes.

The rugged road breaks away from the lush, damp greenery of the coastline and climbs steeply upward through dusty forests that grow out of walls of gray rock. Suddenly the land changes again to the arid Asiatic plain covered with tough, thorny scrubs and clouds of yellow dust.

Driving is extremely difficult. My friend Zaferyap squeezed into her corner of the taxi and clenched her fists in fear, closing her eyes and making a soft, doleful sound. She was so nervous we had to stop occasionally for rest. But even when we momentarily climbed from the rented taxi, my friend was pallid and speechless. Fear had taken complete control of her.

While I was taking photographs of the curious houses of the district, with their stacks of corn husks piled high around a central stake, Zaferyap made an effort to talk to our driver and explain her concern for our safety. "Too fast...too fast," she admonished. But the man had turned surly and was clearly annoyed to be criticized by a female.

"What can we do?" Zaferyap sighed in resignation. "We are miles from a town where we can rent another car and get rid of this nasty fellow. And he knows it."

When we got back into the car, the driver immediately roared up the road, hardly giving us time to close the doors. The mountains dropped behind us. Abruptly we found ourselves approaching the sheerest roadside cliffs that I have ever seen. Not even the spectacular cliffs of the Spanish Costa Brava compare to the horrendous drops along the roadsides of southeastern Turkey.

The highway was not really wide enough for two lanes of traffic, but regardless of the danger, our driver thundered along, the music from his cassette player howling. I kept recalling the twisted wrecks we had seen strewn like crushed beer cans along the roads of eastern Turkey. I felt certain that at any moment a truck would vault around a curve and smash into us, sending our taxi into empty space.

At times the world disappeared entirely from our windows as we rose to a summit where we could see nothing but suffocatingly vacant space. But now the fear that nagged at me turned into anger. I became resolute that the driver would obey Zaferyap and slow down. I ordered him to do so, but he ignored me. Momentarily we dropped into a tiny valley, and I was overjoyed to see trees and grass and solid land again. But the valley was hardly more than a dip in the unending ascent of the road, and we began at once to rise out of the glen at a terrible speed.

When I was about to vent my anger on the driver, I was suddenly overcome by what I saw before me. It was a wooden hut just beside the road. It stood there in the middle of nowhere, and in front of the hut was a very old man with a white beard and a peasant's cap. I tried to comprehend why he was waiting there in this desolate region and why, just as we approached, he rose slowly from his position on the ground and waved us on with a little white flag. Later, when I tried to recall that moment, I couldn't understand its meaning or even be certain that it actually happened. I shall never forget the expression on the man's wrinkled, brown face as he gestured to us, as if beckoning us onward toward that terrifying ascent.

Then, as suddenly as he appeared, he was gone.

It was only a moment later, as we took a wide, hairpin turn, that there was a terrific burst of energy and sound. I briefly saw *something* out of the corner of my eye.

I was baffled by what I saw, until I realized that the object was the front wheel . . . the entire front wheel of our vehicle, flying off, bounding up an embankment, ripping through the trees, and then tumbling back down toward us, crashing with a sickening thud into the door beside me, and finally flying high into the empty air before it vanished from sight, falling, falling down into the valley hundreds of feet below us.

There was a horrendous screech as I felt the car going out of control. The howling metal was twisting under me. The axle plowed along the narrow road, sending up huge sparks and smoke and making a dreadful noise, like a beast being torn apart. For a moment we swerved furiously to the right, and then we began to spin gradually around as we headed straight for the edge. There was no chance to leap out and save ourselves, though the automobile seemed to be moving in slow motion. Strangely calm, I simply sat and watched the small trees at the edge of the cliff moving in on us as the world began to disappear on both sides of the car, and all that was left was an enormously empty sky.

Then we stopped.

Zaferyap had fainted. The driver was hysterical as he scrambled out, with no concern for his passengers.

Zaferyap's face was filled with a strange mixture of rage and fear. Her voice shook with aggression and desperation, one feeling overtaking the other.

Then she glanced at me for the first time since the accident. Her eyes are were filled with confusion. She looked as if she was about to scream. But abruptly and unexpectedly she began to laugh.

I had no idea why she was laughing, but the laughter was so filled with relief that I too began to laugh. This furious merriment was strangely infectious, and gradually it filled the entire car. One by one the passengers began to smile and snicker. Soon the sound of laughter overtook us.

Then, as our car rumbled down the perilous mountain, people at the side of the road stared at us. Through our open windows poured a wide resounding wake of laughter, spreading out behind us as we clanked and clattered down the mountain.

"Look at us! We're alive!" we shouted.

That was what our laughter celebrated. Suddenly, each of us became profoundly aware of the miracle of our lives. And everyone in the car roared with uncontrolled mirth as tears streamed down their faces and life overflowed into the dusk that was falling over the wide landscape.

—*Jamake Highwater*

A STICK STUCK IN THE HEAD

When I think of really big synchronicities in my life, the one that overshadows all others occurred in July 1994, when I attended the Sewanee Writer's Conference for the first time. The incident was really more on the order of a waking dream, a vision, if you will, but I think it falls into the synchronicity category, too.

Going to the writer's conference for the first time was a big deal for me. I'd heard that it was pretty tough and competitive, and I'd never been into that kind of thing before. Also, it meant being away from home for almost two weeks, which meant making elaborate arrangements to keep my household of (at that time) husband and two children going. I spent several frantic days cooking, cleaning, doing laundry, calling babysitters, and trying to get everything ready. I finally took off on a Tuesday morning and successfully navigated the nine-hour drive to Sewanee, Tennessee, only to find out I had arrived on the wrong day. Registration wasn't until Wednesday, and the information packet had made it quite clear that no provisions would be made for early arrivals.

I was mortified and felt sure this was a sign that I never should have come. As I stood in the campus student union, utterly miserable and wondering if there was any way to salvage this misbegotten muddle, two teenage boys dashed in who were participants in a high school music camp that was being held at the university. (It is pertinent to the unfolding of this story to know that I was a pianist and played the piano extensively in high school.)

The two boys approached the information desk and told the attendant that a girl was coming in who needed emergency medical attention. "She's fallen down," they said, "and gotten a stick stuck in her head. It goes in one side and comes out the other."

I immediately envisioned Frankenstein walking in the door so I started paying attention to the unfolding scene. Sure enough, in a few minutes, a teenage girl along with two more boys walked in. I stared at her, but from where I was standing there were no signs of a "stick stuck in her head," as they had described it. Or it just wasn't visible from where I was standing. In fact, she looked fine. I can't remember now whether or not I actually heard anybody say this or if I made it up, but my impression was that she had fallen, and a splinter of wood had passed through her skin, maybe through her cheek, so that it went in one place and came out another. At any rate, my understanding of the situation was that she did, indeed, have a stick stuck in her head, but it wasn't visible. She looked perfectly fine.

The girl sat down in a chair and in a few minutes, emergency medical personnel arrived. They asked her a lot of questions as they began to put a wide plastic collar around her neck and assemble a stretcher. Then I started hearing the name *Kate* being repeated, and realized that, like me, this girl was named Kate. I thought that mildly interesting, since I could easily count on one hand the number of Kates I'd known in my life.

By this time I was listening very closely. When they asked her for her last name, I heard her say "Bullard." I then heard her spell out "B-u-l-l-a-r-d."

My whole body blinked. Bullard is my maiden name. I have never, ever, in my entire life known anyone else named Kate Bullard. When I heard her name, I felt somewhat dissociated, like I was watching a movie in a dream, a sensation. I had a definite sense of recognition, although there were some distinctly creepy overtones. How would you feel if you saw yourself carried out on a stretcher with a big, plastic collar around your neck and put in an ambulance?

I've been working with this pretty astonishing episode ever since. For me, there were enormous implications to every aspect of this vision, and I'll probably spend the rest of my life sorting them all out. Certainly the most immediate and absolute insight that came with it all was the sure knowledge that, for whatever reason, I was meant to arrive at the conference a day early by mistake so I could witness this event in the context of having made a mistake in order to see it. Part of my reason for going to Sewanee was to try to find an agent or publisher for my first novel, which is somewhat autobiographical and deals with the period of my life when I *was* Kate Bullard. During the course of writing the novel, I had started using my full name of Kate Bullard Adams again, although for most of my married life I'd dropped the Bullard name.

Finally, thinking of the Sewanee Kate Bullard who was attending the music camp there, I haven't played the piano to speak of for years because of a hand injury, but shortly after returning from the conference that summer I started taking voice lessons and reincorporated music into my life in a more immediate way.

—*Kate Bullard Adams*

THE SOUL-TRICKSTER

The spring of 1977 in San Francisco was a crisis period in my existence. I was on the edge of some major life changes and was quite stressed out as a result. . .

I was batting with two strikes against me and was especially anxious about the future, when I found that the Tibetan Karmapa, the spiritual teacher of the Dalai Lama, was coming to San Francisco to lead a ceremony for world peace. I'd received an invitation to attend and decided to see what it was all about.

The ceremony was held in a large auditorium on Nob Hill. Many thousands were in attendance, and I had a seat in the high mezzanine area, so my view, although unobstructed, was from some distance. As the audience came in and quieted down, the ceremony began. At first, the director of the institute who had made it possible for the Karmapa to visit came on the stage and told us this was, indeed, a very rare event—that the Karmapa rarely ever left his sanctuary high in the Himalayas to do this kind of thing. But these were rare times, and many felt the need to bring the East to the West in the form of spiritual teaching.

As the director was leaving the stage, a strange thing happened. The Tibetan spiritual teacher Trongpa Rinpoche, who then led the Buddhist Nairopa Institute in Boulder, Colorado, suddenly limped into view from a position just offstage and behind the curtain. He said to the audience, very loudly and in a somewhat drunken slur, "Don't be fooled." He then limped off the stage and vanished from sight.

I asked my friend, "What was that all about?" She told me Trongpa had been drinking alcohol nearly all day, having suffered an automobile accident in Colorado that shattered his right leg. I thought I had noticed that along with his crutch he was carrying a bottle of booze with him when he came on stage. Of course I knew the rinpoche would have had some connection with his spiritual leader, the Karmapa, but, nevertheless, I was surprised to see him on stage, seemingly joking, and in the condition he was.

But then the great long horns sounded and the ceremony began. It was as if I was watching a living *Tonkha*—a spiritual painting—come alive as the ceremony continued. The Karmapa donned his black hat and blessed the whole assembly. Many were surprisingly moved by the long ceremony. I was a bit bored. I wanted more action. As the ceremony reached a particularly high point of silence—perhaps better said, soundlessness (which for me was the height of boredom)—suddenly the drunken rinpoche once again, with crutch under his arm, limped on stage and said, "Keep your shirt on."

I turned to my friend who, entranced with the ceremony, was not bored. I was about to ask her if she had seen Trongpa, when I thought better and decided not to interrupt her reverie. I couldn't believe he would have done it again—disrupted a sacred ceremony. I was feeling a bit anxious during the ceremony and laughed at the message. To me, keeping one's shirt on meant slowing down and being patient—a lesson I had not learned.

After the ceremony, as we were all leaving the auditorium, I asked my friend, "Did you see the rinpoche?" She said, "Of course I did, don't you remember? I told you so at the beginning of the ceremony." I said, "No, I don't mean then, I mean later when he came on the stage and said, "Keep your shirt on." My friend, rather astonished, looked at me and said she hadn't seen him come on a second time and she certainly didn't hear him say, "Keep your shirt on."

I was a little mystified at this, but I attributed it to her being in a somewhat mystical state herself during that part of the ceremony.

Later that week, while I was home in my flat in San Francisco, I received a phone call from a man I didn't know. He said he was calling me from San Jose, sixty or so miles south of the city. He had heard that I was interested in the Qabala, and, as he had some interest in the subject, he hoped to discuss the connection between the Qabala and quantum physics.

I was interested, but not knowing this person, I was a little apprehensive during the call. Nevertheless, I invited him to come to my apartment in San Francisco. He told me it might take him a little while because he didn't have a car and wasn't sure about the public transportation between the two cities.

I agreed to wait for him. After about three hours I was concerned because he hadn't shown up. I took a peek out of my upstairs window and noticed a man coming up the street. He was visibly limping, had a crutch under one arm, and was having difficulty climbing the upward-sloping street. I noticed he had a very bad limp. He rang my bell, and I let him in.

In about five minutes he was already out the door, acting very disgusted with our meeting. He said, "I went to a lot of trouble to get here, and I find you know nothing." He was also a little intoxicated and that, coupled with the strangeness of his call and his bad leg, had me quite mystified. Had I received a visit from some clone of the rinpoche? Whatever it was, I had to admit, in spite of the obvious discomfort of my visitor, it was strange and a little humorous.

I didn't think about it very much after that. Several months passed and my low self-esteem crisis had not eased nor had my impatience or anxiety. I was feeling quite despondent and still hadn't any idea about just what I would do to make my way in the world. Then, one day while I sat on a park bench looking down at the ground feeling even more depressed and anxious, a small wild bird with a broken leg hopped up to my shoe and pecked at it.

I had to laugh. The trickster had finally made it clear to me. As a one-legged life-form it had to go slowly. First appearing as a drunken spiritual teacher reminding me to be patient during the long ceremony, then appearing as a drunken hobbling man, slowly climbing a hill, coming sixty miles to simply present to me a reminder that going slowly did not mean not achieving one's goal, and finally, a one-legged bird patiently pecking at my shoe—the trickster had finally gotten through to me. It was too expensive for me to maintain my depression. By being patient the depression would lift. The chaos of my life would be brought to some order by my simply learning to wait. Whatever I was going to do, I needed patience. To this day, when it comes to patience, although I still have difficulty with it, I usually slow down when I remember the patience needed to hobble along on one leg.

—*Fred Alan Wolf*

KALIMPHONG TO PARO

After a personal loss in 1985, I found an affinity with the Kagyu tradition of Tibetan Buddhism. In working my way through the outer layers toward its ancient wisdom, I encountered K., a translator and gifted teacher who embodied the alchemical mixture of Western "open mind" and Eastern "empty mind."

When I told K. of my plans to travel alone to the Himalayan villages of Darjeeling, Sikkim, Nepal, and Bhutan, he introduced me to S., a Bhutanese on an extended stay in Los Angeles. S. was a Buddhist rinpoche who had left his monastery and position for a secular life. He said he would give me a letter to deliver in Bhutan, to a friend he hadn't seen in years. His friends would be able to provide certain insights into this otherworld. S. knew of no way to contact his friend, but I thought I might be able to find him. He gave me a sealed envelope addressed in a script I did not recognize. I resolved to make this delivery a special mission in my journey.

After some weeks in the mountains of Darjeeling and Sikkim, I slept a weary night in the village of Kalimphong. It had been arranged that the following day I was to arrive in Siliguri before noon, to meet a driver who would take me into Bhutan. If I missed this driver, I could not enter. Leaving Kalimphong at first light, my Tibetan driver, Nima, had just crossed the Teeste Bridge when our way was blocked by a jeep freshly flattened beneath a mountain of stones.

I lifted my astonished eyes to trace the road that disappeared into an immense mound that had been the mountainside above until just then. My eyes ranged back along a frozen file of jeeps and trucks, confronting the migrant mountain in stillness and silence.

Nima bolted for our jeep and yelled for me to jump in. He crushed the throttle to the floor, hurtling us into the vacant oncoming lane for a careening mile to the head of the stunned, indignant line. He eloquently defended our maneuver during the hours it took to dynamite and, stone by stone, heave the countless shards into the raging river below.

In time, the stones were cleared enough for two boys to sprint madly toward us across the rock field, dodging random boulder cascades all the while. At last we thought it stable enough to attempt a crossing from our side. Two men inched across the narrow path so as not to slide down the loose slope into the voracious waters below. When they disappeared around the bend, Nima let out a shout and our jeep shot out in a wake of rattling debris. My eyes were riveted to the sight of the precarious outcroppings above.

To my astonishment, he slid to a halt midway across the road. I squinted through the dusty windshield through which I faced thirty oncoming Army trucks occupying the full width of the pathway ahead. In an instant, the diminutive Nima was out the door and locked in fervent discourse with the commanding officer.

I will never know what he said, but the entire column backed up to let us pass.

We arrived in Siliguri by mid-afternoon. The Bhutanese driver was not there. Unable to wait any longer, he had left word for any following driver to take me if there was room. One arrived two hours later. He had also been delayed by bad roads.

I heaved my bag into the car and wearily fell into the seat beside the driver. His name was Thinley Dorji. He spoke some English. We climbed the serpentine roads through mountains inspired by clouds and pierced by beams of light that erupted into color wherever they fell, and we descended into fertile valleys and landscapes of wordless intensity and dimension.

We spoke of the ancient landlocked ways; of a place protected until recent times by earth's highest mountains; of the world of Bhutan unfolding to the world beyond; of the education of their best and brightest in Europe (*all* of whom returned); of the rotation of the members of government to a different branch every few years to avoid entrenchment; of Guru Padmasambhava who brought Buddhism to Bhutan in the seventh century by flying from Tibet on the back of a winged tiger; of gridlock in Manhattan; of the interweaving of an ancient culture with a vision of the future; of a life of purpose and compassion; of Bhutan's young king.

He spoke of his life as a traveler and as an artist. I spoke of my life as a lawyer, as a pilgrim, as a Western man trying to reconcile the intuitions of the East that had led me to this place. We shared a gaze into the passing faces of the stone-breakers at the side of the crumbling roads, laboring to fill the gaping holes, their empty eyes foretelling their imminent, tubercular fate. Throughout the journey he had a glow of familiarity that defied any rational connection, but I could never have encountered him in the past.

On our arrival into Paro Valley seven hours later, I saw the ancient textures of a timeless, suspended light as it flowed over the thatched roofs and abstract fields, dissolving into dusk. We had finally reached my destination. I stretched and lifted my bag from the car. I turned to thank him and remembered the letter I had carried the past three weeks. Pulling it from my pocket, I held it out to him and asked, "Do you know how I could find this man?"

He examined the envelope and turned it over in his hand.

"That won't be hard," he replied. "It's me."

—*Eric Lawton*

GHOST STATION

The other day I asked a man at Universal Studios' Victoria Station Restaurant about their station sign: East Grinstead. "Yes, ma'am, it came from the real East Grinstead Station," he said proudly. I felt a little like Alice in Wonderland when she saw the grin without the cat, because when I lived with my family in England on the edge of Winnie-the-Pooh's Hundred Acre Wood, East Grinstead Station had been our stop.

It took us an hour by train from London to E. G. Station, as we called it. My husband, Alex, liked it especially, because Agatha Christie used it as her location for *Ghost Train,* a mystery in which he had played the juvenile lead one summer on Chebeague Island, Maine. He remembered the stage train blinking and hooting into the station when least expected, making fearfully eerie sounds. The real E. G. Station was a low, red brick building, the roof dark wood with large overhangs providing shelter from rains, mists, and fogs. Inside, high-backed benches and walls, carved of the same dark wood, were varnished to mirror glass. We usually ran through the station to climb aboard just as our train was chugging out, so we seldom talked to the stately stationmaster who dispensed tickets with perpetual courtesy.

It was here I became irrevocably convinced as to the reality of synchronicity.

We lived twenty-five minutes from E. G. station, in Forest Row. Our house, built of Sussex flint, overlooked rose beds and apple trees, and was a perfect Agatha Christie country setting. Even the Vicar looked suspicious in such a peaceful place. We were within walking distance of a legendary yew tree, said to have been planted a thousand years earlier with foredoomed foresight by Viking warriors to provide bows and arrows for their descendants. Substituting as best they could, my kids, Jefferson and Winslow, spent hours clambering about its shaggy branches, wary of the ghosts of long gone attackers.

At the other end of the track from E. G. was London and Victoria Station. We usually stopped at the Victoria Hotel before our return journey, waiting in its historic lounge in deep sofa chairs, blindingly white well-starched napkins on our laps as we were served hot tea from silver teapots, brought in on silver trays by waiters in tails. Tea came with English scones, rich Devon cream, and silver jars of bitter marmalade. Tweedy country travelers ordered, drank, and left, etching the afternoon with their varied characters. This was the only place Alex ever came early to catch a train.

Alex liked to be late catching trains or even planes for that matter. I know this because we traveled extensively. He enjoyed running from parking lots down mile-long airport corridors with heavy suitcases, struggling to find misplaced tickets and passports. "Why not let him miss just once and see what happens," Winslow wondered one damp day as our red boots squished with satisfying "glurks" through the muddy grasses of Eeyore's Corner.

So halfway to the airport on our next three-hour drive to catch an intercontinental flight, I said, "You've got passports and tickets safe?"

"Me?" asked Alex.

Three hours later, we were back at this same green spot on the same journey, and I was finally silent.

"Don't worry," Alex reassured me. "The flight originated in India. Realistically, it's bound to be late."

I don't know about reality, but synchronicity being what it is, it was.

Even so, realistically, I opined, that might have just been

Alex's good luck, not synchronicity at all. The next time we had to catch a train, however, there was no doubt. Meantime, we enjoyed the peace of our Sussex garden girdled by hedges of fragrant honeysuckle and rambling roses. Sometimes a hedgehog hid conspicuously in its lower reaches. On the tip-top flowers, tiny spiders spun tiny webs, which, sprinkled with dewdrops and backlit by the morning sun, were transparent galaxies of otherworldly activity. Sometimes a blackbird landed on the green grass, listening for an early worm. Nightingales and English robins poured themselves out in profuse strains of unpremeditated song from the branches of our stately oak. The hedge was thickened by red-berried holly bushes, entangling blackberry brambles and the sharp-thorned hawthorne, white as snow in spring.

The sharp thorn in my side, however, was Agatha Christie's *Ghost Train*. Alex was competing for the role of engine rather than the juvenile lead, arriving at the station off schedule, unexpectedly, and with fearful surprise. "Let him take more responsibility," Jefferson offered in the silvery summer twilight, walking with Winslow and me over a phosphorescent carpet of leaves under a centuries-old beech tree, our feet kicking up cascades of pewter light.

I took courage from Jeff's supportive hard-heartedness, but weakened on the fateful day, wondering aloud why we were having breakfast at eight o'clock. "I thought eight-fifteen was time to leave the house, not the station," Alex explained cheerfully. We discussed this misunderstanding during the next twenty-five minutes through the dawn rain to E. G. It was really too late to worry, though. Alex surely had already missed the train, therefore his appointment, therefore his book contract. Changes would surely follow. This time reality was firmly in place and on my side.

I turned off E. G.'s quaint old Main Street with its Tudor

buildings and sharp-eyed merchants, drove quickly past the red, double-decker bus, and rounded the corner to the station as Alex shouted enthusiastically: "There it is, I knew it, the train's still here. Aren't you happy?"

I saw it. The train here. Just the station gone.

I walked over to the stationmaster, now standing out in the rain. "Ah, yes, dear lady," he leaned down to explain. "Last week the station was shipped brick by brick to Canada. It's to become a restaurant, I understand. I'm told the sign went to your country."

Alex hugged me goodbye with good-humored optimism. "Wish me luck," he grinned, hopping onto the already moving train. I blinked: He needed more? But you can always learn something important: "That's synchronicity," I nodded decidedly, as I drove home to our corner on the edge of Pooh's Forest. Under a canopy of snow-white, particularly sharp-thorned hawthorne.

—*Jane Winslow Eliot*

OH FACE, WHERE IS THY STING?

In the mid 1980s, I was still waiting to hear the call—which direction to shoot life's arrow. I had picked Los Angeles as the place to try and draw the bow. At this time, the rock star Sting had just become a solo artist, dissolving his hugely successful band, The Police. The fact is Sting and I could be brothers. Strangers would come up to me and say "Has anyone ever told you that you look like. . . ?" "Yes!" I'd cut them off. After a hundred times the novelty wears off. It made me queasy to be reminded how much I looked like Sting. We shared similar physiognomy, but behind his face, I saw everything I lacked—success, talent, and piles of money. My face was an imitation, his the genuine article.

I was eking out a living bartending. My entrepreneurial friends said I should at least try and cash in. One day, feeling my empty pockets, I visited "Ron Smith's Celebrity Look-Alikes," the agency for impersonators. I filled out an application ("What celebrity do you look like? Sound like? Sing like?") and turned it in. Just then the receptionist's phone rang. A music video needed a "Sting." The receptionist punched up her records. With my addition, she had two Stings. The director would be in tomorrow to see us. I returned the next day and waited with a cheery guy who looked like Sting—if Sting was 6'6" and had Mediterranean parents. We both went in, met the director, and I got the job. The video was to star the real Sting. It was his first as a solo artist and required scenes with a "good" Sting and a "bad" Sting. They couldn't afford to shoot Sting for both parts so a look-alike was needed. I did the video ("We'll Be Together Tonight"). Sting was friendly (he squeezed my nose when we first met), and I collected a small check.

A few months earlier, I had begun dating a woman named Debbie. She was a singer and songwriter, one of the hopeful thousands waiting for a break in Los Angeles. She vigorously sent demo tapes all over town touting her talents. When we first met she paid her rent by teaching piano and playing Top 40 songs in the cocktail lounges of downtown hotels. Shortly after my job in the video, Debbie got a call that one of her demo tapes had come into the hands of a new band that was forming. They needed someone who could sing and write songs, having recently lost their talented lead singer/songwriter. Debbie auditioned and got the job. The band featured the abandoned other two thirds of The Police—Andy Summer and Stewart Copeland. Overnight my girlfriend quit her jobs and stepped into the shoes last filled by

Sting. They named the new band Animal Logic. First my face, now my girlfriend.

Debbie's musical dream had come true. I went to a rehearsal and met Andy and Stewart. If it was awkward that their new lead singer's boyfriend eerily resembled their last, they were too much the millionaire rock stars to look bothered. The new demands on Debbie were formidable and our relationship withered quickly. For me, it was all for the best. It had become spooky to be shadowed in life by a famous man. Leaving her and the glare of Sting's world, I returned to look and own the face I was given. Now, years later, only rarely is the similarity mentioned. Having settled more firmly into who I am, I am not made insecure by the comparison. And, from the beginning, I always liked Sting. But now I've come to know my worth, too, and which way to look when I face the world.

—*Haydn Reiss*

RAINBOWS, TIRES, AND FISH

Wandering after college and trying to live in various states including Massachusetts, New Hampshire, and Minnesota, I was in a confused state. I had left my first advertising (college major) job on a metaphysical newspaper to go to a Rainbow Family Festival in Rocky Mountain State Park outside of Denver. I drove from St. Paul with a guy who was a self-professed witch (of which there were plenty in the St. Paul–Minneapolis area), who kept raving something about the Mississippi River being the kundalini of the United States with Minnesota as the crown chakra.

We got to the festival but soon realized it wasn't happening. As a child of the '60s, this 1972 version was a little underwhelming. So we decided to go to the Tetons and camp. Feeling my life was fairly rudderless, I thought I'd undertake a five-day fast in the mountains and await a revelation from God as to what was next in my life.

When we got outside of Jackson Hole, we parked the car and loaded what we thought we'd need to pack into the mountains for five days. To this day I still don't know why I insisted on bringing my five-pound geography textbook.

We trudged up to a small lake and pitched the tent, made the first of our numerous cups of tea with honey sitting around a campfire, and listened for the voice of God.

Five days later, cold, dirty, hungry, and by now practically deaf from straining so hard to hear God, we came down the mountain looking for some hot soup. Completely disgruntled and unhappy, I decided it was time to get back to my home state of Ohio. We poured over the map and chose the scenic route through Yellowstone and over the Cook City Pass into southern Montana. Yellowstone was gorgeous. Then we started driving higher and higher. The car was an old model, but so far so good. It was June but snow still clung to the high passes, and we saw some people skiing down glaciers. Just as we got to the top of the 10,000 foot pass, the front right tire blew. Slowly, we skidded and bumped to a stop at the side of the road.

Now this friend of mine may have been a very wise witch, but he sure as hell didn't know how to change a tire. I started wondering why he wasn't able to predict how we would travel together. We fussed over that tire jack for a good half hour, but then he couldn't get the bolts off to change the wheel. Since he wouldn't do it, I jumped on the tire iron to get more leverage, but nothing. We were stymied. It was a Saturday night. Weren't no one around to help us.

Well, the day dwindled as did my patience. Finally someone came by and helped us. It was a simple matter, he said as he just turned the wrench the opposite direction. Done in fifteen minutes. Sigh. Grumble. Tired. We headed down the other side of the mountain.

In those days, I didn't seem to worry much about traveling with emergency funds. But by the time we hit the next town, Red Lodge, Montana, elevation 5555, population 2222, being both broke and into numerology, I said, this is it for me. I'm checking into the first hotel I see and find dinner, then tomorrow I'll look for a temporary job to get me back to Ohio. So I spent my last twenty-five dollars on a room at the Bear Creek Lodge and a really awful pasta dinner. The next morning I went looking for a job.

Since the main street of the town was only four blocks long with storefronts on both sides, it wasn't too hard to scope out the possibilities. There on the corner was KRBN radio station, Red Lodge. Pulling out my advertising major persona, I went in. Hi, so and so, I am so and so, and I need a temporary job in your town. I can do this, this, that; my degree is such and such, *blah blah blah,* and besides that I am an astrologer.

"Oh an astrologer you say," he said, sitting up in his chair. "I've been thinking of starting an astrology show. If you stay twelve days and do a five-minute show each day after the noon news, I'll pay you xx. But you have to stay twelve days."

I said I'd think about it, because I had nowhere to stay and that would barely cover my room at the Bear Creek Lodge. So I left his corner building and tried walking to the lodge on one of the back streets. I passed two guys unloading all the fish they had obviously just caught. I stopped and looked and said something like, "Great fish, where'd you catch 'em?"

"Bear Creek," they said. "Hey, we got so many, why don't you take one?" Thinking of the hot plate in my room, I said thanks.

Then I was walking down the street carrying a recently alive fish, and up came a woman and her two kids. "Where'd you get the fish?" she said. I told her about the guys and the hot plate and the Bear Creek Lodge and the radio station. And she said, "I got a spare room at my house you can stay in for twelve days. Come tonight, and we'll cook the fish."

And so it happened, I became a local personality with an astrology booth at the town's annual international festival (representing the universe of course), did mini-readings for people during cocktail hour at the Carbon County Coal Company, and finally one person agreed to actually pay for a chart. We swapped dreams and goals one afternoon after his reading, and he told me about this ranch in Helena, Montana, that a psychic had told him about. It seemed to have everything I was looking for—spiritual orientation with a teacher, yoga, vegetarian, a commune-type situation. He was going to check it out, and we'd get together when he got back.

A week later, he took me to his wonderful mountain cabin, played lovely guitar music, and told me all about the Feathered Pipe Ranch in Helena. There was William just back from India who gave talks on Sundays; a woman named India, who had inherited these 100 acres and gorgeous log lodges from Jerry Duncan whom she met at Sai Baba's ashram in Bangalore; and the videotaped yoga classes; and on and on and on. They said he could come for the rest of the summer, no charge—and when he told them about me, they said I could come too.

Thus began my ten-year relationship with India and the Feathered Pipe Ranch and organizing astrology and other seminars, in addition to travel programs and meeting many wonderful teachers, travelers, and friends. I helped them start *Yoga Journal* and the Holistic Life University, and, eventually, I moved to

California and opened my own travel agency specializing in educational travel programs. One thing led to another, even to Paris. But that's another story.

—Jeannette Hermann

CHANGE

While camping one weekend at Lost Maples campground in Texas in 1995, we went out on a walk along one of the trails one morning. Under a tree, we saw a woman's change purse, a cloth one covered with a flower print. We picked it up and saw it was stuffed with $100, $50, and $20 bills. We put it in our pack and carried it to the car, where we quickly counted it. There was $1,300.40 in all. Down at the bottom of the purse was a woman's driver's license.

Should we just keep it all? we wondered for a fleeting moment. We decided to try to track her down at the park.

When we found the park rangers, we told them we had found a purse and left our name at the station, but we kept the purse.

Later, we were tracked down by a woman in a beat-up car with two young sons in the back. The money was all that was left of a child support payment check that her ex-husband had finally paid. It was the first support check he had ever sent her. She was going to use the money in the purse to buy clothes for her kids.

Relieved and delighted, we gave her back the purse. She thanked us and went off with promises of reward money forthcoming.

Okay, so we felt good about helping someone out.

Three weeks later, during a violent storm at our home in San

Antonio, a tree ripped from its roots in the backyard of our neighbor's house, crashing down against our wooden fence, and came to rest on the roof of our Subaru station wagon, creasing the roof, but not greatly.

We filed a claim with the insurance company, but had no intention of fixing the car, thinking that we would use the money for other necessities. After deductibles from the insurance policy, we were given a check for $1,300, exactly. Just forty cents less than the amount of money we had found at the campground and turned over to the woman who lost it.

Coincidence? We don't think so.

—*Dennis Slattery*

THE NOTE

Regarding myself and my mundane world, I had an experience when I was thirteen years old that unnerved me and left me wondering. There was a guy in my class, Steve, a big guy tending to overweight and not into physical exertions. We had the kind of running competition kids get into, not just schoolwork, but also arm wrestling bouts, which were harmless for the most part, but with a definite edge and unsaid boundaries.

One weekend I decided to go hiking with friends in the Pennines some twenty miles from Sheffield England in a particular ravine called Winnats Pass under the shadow of Mam Tor, the largest peak in the district. At one point, I decided to scrabble up a rock face, not so high—forty to fifty feet or so—but, before I set off, I did one of those things kids do. I wrote my home address and date on a scrap of paper and took it with me (note in a bottle kind of thing). Near the summit, I found a split rock jutting out, folded the paper tightly, and pushed it deep into the cleft. I don't know why, kind of like burying pennies.

A week later, I was in school and Steve approached me with his arm outstretched and fist clenched . . . was it the usual joke? Something slimy, something crude? Was it something bordering on physical confrontation, or did he genuinely have something for me?

"Open your hand," he said. A moment passed, and as one or two others had gathered round the old competition surfaced and I had to take the dare. Opening his fist, he dropped my note into the palm of my hand. This guy didn't walk anywhere he didn't have to, and rock scrabbling was for mugs . . . yet he had gone out to the same place just a week later, climbed the same rock face, and located my note.

—*Trevor Green*

THE VISIONS OF A FORMER MONK

I had ridden my Honda Gold Wing from my home in Sunnyvale, California, to Sonoma county—a journey of about two hours—on a bright, clear, and wonderful Saturday afternoon. The Westerbeke Ranch held me until the early evening, but suddenly it was time to go. I headed off with no jacket, just a flannel shirt and a Windjammer fairing to cut the flow of seventy mile per hour winds on the open motorcycle.

I had safely made it though Sonoma and Marin counties, and felt only a shiver. But when the shiver became a chill, which then became a gut-wrenching spasm of cold, I knew that it was time to find a motel room and immerse myself in a very hot bath—even though I was only fifteen miles from my warm and toasty home—or I'd drop the bike and die.

When I was groggily thinking these thoughts and becoming fearful that a hotel room was rapidly becoming out of reach, another rider came onto the freeway and joined me in my ride. He positioned himself in the same lane next to me, which heightened my awareness of danger but focused my concentration. We rode along together, almost as a single unit, tracking each other carefully and enjoying an unspoken companionship.

After what seemed like an eternity, I saw an overhead sign reading: Sunnyvale 1 Mile.

I looked back at my mysterious companion, and he gave me a thumbs up and gently exited the freeway. When he left me I realized I wasn't cold anymore; I had forgotten my hypothermia.

One exit later, I was home, smiling to myself and wondering where my guardian angel had come from and where he had gone.

When the moment of truth came, that moment of knowing how certain death might be if I dropped the bike, I didn't cry for help. I didn't cry for a vision or strength. If I analyze what might have happened in that single breath of time, the only thing I can say is that I released the fear to the universe. I put it out there in the time between thoughts of it. I let it go.

And that's when the angel appeared.

—*Steve George*

THE QUIET EYE

While living in Hong Kong in 1963, I met a painter, Sheila Isham, who was there as the wife of a consulate officer. The normal situation as a consulting family is to spend two years abroad and the next two years in D.C. As an artist, Sheila used these foreign experiences to expand her artistic self. This was later seen in her work, either directly or indirectly.

In Hong Kong, Sheila was studying calligraphy, as well as changing the forms of some of her canvases to resemble Chinese coins. Sheila's work was incredible. Her work resonated for me in a way that I had not experienced before, and we talked about this at times. I loved her work, and when we were transferred to Canada in 1965 I wanted to buy something from her.

Sheila brought a large (four by five foot) painting for me to live with for a few days while my husband was in Taiwan. One evening, when the children were away and the servants had retired for the night, I sat with a glass of wine and contemplated the painting. It was a deep blue, heavily textured with a palette knife, and in the center was a large symbol that looked like a Q. As I looked, I started to cry and couldn't stop. The word *profound* kept occurring to me as the best description of my reaction, although my inner chatter said, "Are you nuts? This is an abstract painting. How can you feel so intensely about it?"

I've known a number of artists over time, and since I thought Sheila would be especially interested in hearing of my experience, I called her. After I described the deep sense of the profound that I had felt in her painting, she said, "It's funny you should say that because the name of the painting is 'Profound Water,' and the symbol that looks like a Q is Chinese for profound."

—Beverly McDevitt

The Presence

The Greek goddess Athena came into my life when I was an impressionable adolescent with self-doubts. In sophomore English, myths about her inspired me with courage to rely on my intelligence, to focus on my goals, and to establish myself in a competitive world. In time, as I assumed the roles of wife, mother, and teacher, her image became less directive.

In 1978, a lifetime beyond high school, I committed myself to a project far afield from anything I had ever done. I was intellectually prepared, but technically untested. I was going to Greece to film a documentary, *The Presence of the Goddess: A Vision Whose Time Has Returned,* a title that had occurred to me as spontaneously as Athena's full-grown birth from the head of Zeus.

Again, I was faced, as in my youth, with the need to overcome self-doubts, and to focus on my adventure with confidence of success.

As I was boarding the Olympic Airlines 747, my attention was jolted by the name emblazoned on the nose: ATHENE.

Seeing that, I suddenly felt assured that she was beckoning me and would be ever-near in this soul-task of mine.

—*Christy Baldwin*

THE DOVE STORY

I have always loved watching birds, so I was thrilled when a family of doves made their nest in the tree just outside my balcony. I would find my way out there every possible moment, sipping tea, writing in my journal, fascinated as I watched them build their home. One day, just as suddenly as they had arrived, they were gone.

Soon after that, in meditation class where we allow images to come as gifts for each other, a woman turned to me and spoke of an image she had for me. She saw me with two doves carrying ribbons. My heart stirred; there was something peaceful in the way she described this. I thanked her but didn't mention the doves on the branch outside my patio. The following week, she turned to me again. Again, she described images of doves. Her description gave me a warm, pleasant feeling, and the image was one I was reminded of when I put together a photo collage for a workshop I was attending. I found an image of a dove and included it prominently. At the time, I was recovering from an illness, and I'd been shaking with fear from tests I'd had to undergo. I eventually ended up with a holistic doctor whom I felt safe with and who was able to help me heal. But the memories of the recent tests and an insensitive medical specialist still haunted me.

Soon after that, my boyfriend and I were returning from dinner out and heading back to the car when we noticed a dove standing in the grass at the street corner, perfectly still! As we got closer, we were surprised to find the dove didn't move. We came closer, then even closer. Still the dove didn't budge. Finally, just inches away, the bird simply stared at us. His feathers looked a bit ruffled, but we couldn't see any apparent injuries. In soft voices we concluded that he must be injured or in shock. We cooed at him for a moment, then David moved his forefinger to the dove's feet. Not skipping a beat, the dove moved onto David's hand. We decided to take him back to the apartment and put him in an open box on the patio, to get him away from any cats on the prowl for a nice dinner. If by morning he wasn't better, we would take him to the vet. When we got to David's truck, David handed me the bird. He stood easily on my finger as well, though his whole body was shaking with fear. I could relate! I cooed and spoke softly with him on the way back, hoping he'd know he was safe.

When we got home, we took him to the patio, and David went to the market to get birdseed and a box. He soon returned, and we created a little space in an open box with branches and birdseed, then left him there overnight. In the morning he was gone! I felt a wonderful sense of my own healing, having held this frightened bird who somehow was able to trust us, and then knowing he must have recovered enough to fly away.

Two weeks later, I looked out to the patio and noticed a dove standing there. I was in awe. No bird had ever come onto the patio before—the closest they'd ever come was a nearby branch. I moved slowly closer. He stood there, watching me. Then suddenly, he marched right past me and into the apartment! I was astonished! He walked through the living room, as if surveying it, then through the dining room and into the kitchen, along the perimeter of the kitchen, then back into the dining room, when he suddenly looked lost and started going in circles. David approached him slowly and extended his forefinger, and the dove immediately came forward and perched on it. He walked outside to the balcony. The dove pitched forward and flew away. We stood there silently, in wonder. Was this the same bird we'd rescued? Could it be?

Regardless, the insight was immediate for me. That a wild

bird could be so trusting in the face of fear reminded me that I needed to cultivate a deeper trust in life. I think of the doves often, and how they enriched my life in a very deep, unexpected way.

—*Judith Lutz*

A SIGN FROM GOD?

In 1970, I was nineteen years old and attending my first year of college. I had been studying the religions of the world, while at the same time participating in Students For a Democratic Society (SDS) and protesting against the war in Vietnam. My SDS activities had resulted in my feeling angry at my country, frustrated with my parents, and generally depressed about my life. I had an ongoing debate inside my head regarding politics and religion. Which was the best way to influence positive change in the world?

So, in the traditional manner, I climbed the highest mountain, pondering the question. I acknowledged that I wanted to believe that there was a God, but I wanted some proof before I was willing to commit. So I prayed spontaneously, probably for the first time in my life. I said, "Creator, if you're there, I want to believe in you and live my life in a way that will contribute to your will. But I need a sign. If you will give me a sign of your existence, then I'll dedicate myself and my passion to you for the rest of my life."

Suddenly, directly in front of me in mid-air, were two pairs of hummingbirds, two of them spinning around each other just to the left of my eyeline and two just to the right.

I wondered if this was the sign. Although I had never seen birds mate before, I realized that that's what they were doing. Not one pair, but *two* pairs mating directly in front of me.

Was this a coincidence, or was it a sign from God? I thought to myself, "What do you want? What did you expect?"

I decided to accept this as a sign. I committed myself to the spiritual path, and I've never looked back. (Ironically, my destiny was to merge the two paths of politics and spirituality!)

—*Gary Rhine*

THE GUIDE

On January 1, 1996, I listed my goals and dreams for the new year. One of my spiritual goals was to discover my animal guide. I've read and researched many accounts in American Indian literature about animal guides and truly believed in the deep connection between animals and people. A month later, in a meditation, I received a vision of a fox. It surprised me. I always imagined that my animal guide would be a dolphin or a hummingbird, because I have a strong affinity for these two animals.

In July of the same year, I traveled to Nova Scotia, Canada, with my husband. We were on our way to Cape Breton Highlands National Park, the northernmost part of Nova Scotia. One night we stayed at a pleasant inn. The next morning we left the small town without gassing up. Realizing this, we consulted a map and backtracked; finally someone told us that we could find a gas station in the town of Indian Brook.

When we reached Indian Brook, we drove along the two-lane wilderness road, not finding the gas station. My husband, Mike, decided yet again to turn back a couple of miles where there were three men talking near a parked pick-up truck and ask them where the station was. Mike usually never asks for directions, but this time he did. Years ago, I would have grown impatient with all the backtracking and wasting of time, but in the last few years I've learned to be patient, believing that things happen for a reason. I had the feeling something out of the ordinary was happening.

The men confirmed that we were on the right path and that we would find the gas station up ahead several miles. Relieved, we drove for a few miles, when suddenly Mike said, "Mary, there's an animal ahead just coming out of the woods."

He stopped the car. We watched as a red fox entered the road from Mike's side, crossed in front of us, then stopped at my side of the car. The fox turned and looked at me. To have a wild animal look into your eyes is an exciting experience but, to have it be the animal I felt to be my guide, gave me goose bumps. My dog at home communicates with me through his eyes. This fox looked at me like he knew me. I felt stunned by the recognition. It was that sense of recognition that made me believe this fox was my animal guide.

At this point, since Mike knows I am an avid photographer, he yelled: "Get your camera . . . take a picture." Instinctively, I said, "No. This can't be photographed."

Gracefully, the fox turned and recrossed the road, stopping near Mike's side of the car, to look back at us, then disappeared into the wilderness.

I had chills as I softly told Mike about my meditation and my wish for an animal guide. It was much harder trying to explain why I felt that the experience could not be photographed. When I saw the fox, I was transported to another realm, very trancelike, and if I would have searched for my camera, the spell would have been broken. I felt that if I aimed my camera at the fox, it would have disappeared. Respect, awe, and silence were what the moment needed.

I have always believed in the magical, spiritual side of life. Seeing this fox affirmed that the spirit I believe in exists in everything. I know I am connected to a power much stronger than myself.

Prayers and dreams are answered all the time.

—*Mary Rezmerski*

THE RABBIT STORY

My husband, Gary, and I returned from our honeymoon to our cramped apartment in the Bucktown neighborhood of Chicago and immediately began to look for a house. Our down payment was a gift from Gary's parents, but the payments would be our monthly mystery, because I had left my corporate gig to become a storyteller only one month before.

At that time, Gary was deeply immersed in the Men's Movement. After a weekend workshop, Gary returned home carrying a silver button cover imprinted with the image of a rabbit. I laughed when he showed it to me, because I had just spent the weekend studying Native American animal stories, including the old myth of Rabbit.

According to the ancients, Rabbit's medicine radiates from his ears. Rabbit hears everything, and also too much. So rabbit people are deeply sensitive listeners, who can project and be paranoid when out of balance. Imagine a rabbit paralyzed on the road staring at the headlights! Gary often felt this way about our impending purchase of a home, so *Rabbit* became our code word for paralyzing fear.

We found the house. We bought it. We moved within a

month. It was the fastest closing in our realtor's twenty-five-year history. On the day we moved into the house, I was standing at our kitchen window, sweaty, tired, drinking water from the only plastic cup we'd unpacked. I looked out into the yard, and there was a rabbit lounging in our backyard. This rabbit was catching the rays of the sun—belly exposed and legs stretched out long from his body. I called for Gary to come see. We stood in our new kitchen, holding each other, looking out at that rabbit.

Clearly, Rabbit was not afraid of anything!

It was fall, so I knew I needed to get a bulb garden going in order to have flowers for our first spring. I made a circular garden (a starter, mind you, quite small and manageable). I planted tulips, daffodils, and irises. As I covered each bulb, I prayed for fertility—come spring—that the bulbs and my belly would bloom with new life!

Winter came. Rabbit was sighted less frequently. I'd leave him carrots and salad scraps. From our kitchen window, I watched the snow slowly blanket my new little garden. I thought of Demeter and Persephone and the Greek myth of winter and motherhood. I was inspired to write a one-woman play, which I performed in January, thinking of my little garden and my big hopes.

In February, Mother Nature gave us a perfect snow, clean and white and packable. Gary and I went out into the backyard to make a snowman. But you know, it wasn't a snow*man* we built. We built a snow*goddess!* She was beautiful—all hips and breasts. We made her in honor of Demeter, Mother Nature herself.

When she was complete, we playfully made ritual love to her. From a friend, I had received two seeds of corn as a wedding present, which represented hopes for two children. We took one of the corn kernels, and using a stick, Gary impregnated Demeter with the corn and asked her to bless us with a child in the spring.

It was so loving and innocent and playful.

The spring thaw came, and I found the corn seed in our yard. It was cracked exactly in half. By late March, the bulbs were coming up. Every day I checked for blooms, coaxing the green buds up and up—but no flowers.

By Easter, Rabbit was returning more regularly and I'd joke with him about my fear that neither my buds nor my belly would ever bloom. Rabbit would crinkle his nose at me.

On April 20th, my home pregnancy test had a very faint positive sign. Gary didn't trust it, so on April 25th we went for a blood test. As we pulled out of the driveway, I noticed paper that had collected in the bushes and made a mental note to clear it when we got back. When we returned home, Gary went inside and I went to the bushes. As I kneeled over to collect the paper, I saw it wasn't paper at all. The white was the white breast of our rabbit. He lay still. I kneeled further. He was dead.

I picked him up and saw that he had two puncture wounds in his neck. He wasn't bloody, so I thought a cat must have killed him for sport. I stood to bring him into the house, feeling the need to make a ceremony of some sort for him. As I was walking toward the house, Gary came out. He saw I was carrying something and asked me what it was.

I said, "The rabbit died."

We stood paralyzed, looking at each other and the rabbit, taking in the irony of the phrase "the rabbit died," because, in my mother's day, doctors tested for pregnancy with rabbits: If the rabbit died, you were pregnant.

Later that afternoon, I made a ceremony for our little friend and buried him in the bulb garden. The next morning, the nurse called to tell us that my blood test was positive. Yes, indeed, I was pregnant.

"I know," I said to myself as I hung up the phone. "I know, because our rabbit died." I looked out to the rabbit's grave in our little garden. One sweet yellow tulip stood proudly open in our backyard.

—*Megan Wells*

RENEWAL

I'm a psychotherapist, and for several years worked with a client whose greatest sorrow was that she'd fallen out of touch with the near-ecstatic spiritual feelings that had often graced her as a child. We tried several avenues to help reawaken the sacred—prayer, meditation, ritual, automatic writing, and dream work. All these inspired her briefly and then fell flat.

One Wednesday, I was feeling downhearted when she arrived for her appointment, because the day before I'd been diagnosed as having a tenacious intestinal parasite. Somehow my cat and I had become infected, possibly through contaminated water. I would survive, but was heartsick to see my cat severely struck down, fighting for his life. The client arrived at her appointed time and announced she'd been feeling punk.

She said, "I found out yesterday that my bird and I are both infected with intestinal parasites."

I was flabbergasted. How many therapist-client duos and their beloved pets were all diagnosed with parasites on the same Tuesday in June? We lived more than thirty miles apart in separate towns with separate water systems. I kept my amazement to myself and spent the session attending to the client's anguish over her suffering bird. As she described the many veterinary treatments attempted in vain, one thought became prominent in my mind. I pictured her praying for the bird. Praying. Whether it lived or died, healed or languished, she would have to make a plea to the spirit world.

At last I asked, "Have you prayed about it?"

She burst into tears and wept for the rest of the session. That day marked the return of her spiritual practice. Desperation had pushed her to the brink and had reawakened in her a passion for daily prayer.

As for myself, I'd previously thought my spiritual life, consisting of fairly regular prayer, divination, and ritual, to be perfectly adequate. Yet I'd routinely forget to pray for simple things such as my cat. Inspired by the client's example, I began praying for him daily. Both pets hovered close to death for a while, but eventually they bounced back and recovered fully, to the surprise of their vets. The client and I recovered, too. But the most miraculous recovery (for which I thank the parasites) was the renewal of our shared passion for daily prayer. This humble practice has enabled me to tap into a vast well of gratitude for the simple things, and within that gratitude flow luminous strands of ecstasy.

—*Erica Helm Meade*

THE PERFORMANCE

This coming October, it will be four years since my husband, Phil, died. He had blond hair and blue eyes. We would have been married forty-four years . . . had he lived. When I first met him I was a freshman at NYU. I thought his hair looked red, and I had an immediate crush on the "cute red-head" in my class. Within weeks we were smitten, and within two years we were married and had started our life together in Los Angeles. That's the background to my short story.

Last week I was up in San Francisco to baby-sit my grandchildren, and on my final day my daughter and I roamed the area stores in Mill Valley waiting for school to get out, beginning my trip to the airport and home. We entered one store and were greeted by a friendly cat whose name we were told was Kennedy. He looked up at me with giant blue eyes. His full coat was blondish, and his ears and tail were reddish. He followed our every step and kept eyeing both of us, inviting us to pet him as we walked through the aisles. The store clerk informed us he was a frequent visitor, very friendly, but much more so today. She said he was "really performing!"

This was a garden store, and there was an almost empty wooden barrel offering some merchandise. I stopped to look inside, when Kennedy leapt up onto some boxes and walked the narrow rim of the barrel, gingerly, one paw in front of the other, carefully balancing himself to where I stood. We were eye to eye, his motor running. He put one paw on my shoulder. I'm a dog person with no cat experience, but I could easily see this was no usual cat! He clearly wanted me to pick him up, so I did. In all my sixty-four years, Kennedy was the first cat I ever picked up. He put his front paws around my neck and we hugged. His motor continued running. It was a blissful experience. Both my daughter and I felt my husband's presence.

As a matter of fact, her first comment when we entered the store and saw Kennedy staring up at me, meaningfully, was "It's Dad, Mom. He's come to join us shopping."

—*Rosalind Sorkin*

IN THE EYE

I was finally getting some time with not my oldest, but my closest, friend. We were walking a Topanga State Park trail in Southern California. The main topics were shadows, our natures, and the nature of it all.

I spoke of the journey inward and my attempts to cash in pain, anger, and the dilemmas of power and love for the price of admission to the shadow realm of my own psyche. We talked of reaching for a spirit of fullness through therapy and art, and the pursuit of meaningful moments.

He was troubled. Health issues arose. Family and economic pressures were high. Work was burdensome. There was little art and no magic; no grace in his recent history or foreseeable future. He spoke of how he had once seen the image of a gnome captured in the dead wood of a fallen tree, suspended above a creek.

His description evoked the powerful memory of a time, four years earlier, when I stood alone next to a river in Montana. I was a sieve to joy. My marriage was challenged. Work was difficult. There was no art or magic or wholeness. I prayed for a connection with a spirit that might restore to me some sense of flow, instead of a difficult, grinding passage.

I told this story to my hiking partner. I described how near I was to that Montana river and the small steep mount, a knob of earth some 500 feet tall, forested and covered in summer grasses and wild flowers. Past the last fence, I plunged into undergrowth at the base of the mount. Keeping to the vertical, my heart soon pounded, and my burning legs carried me up the light and shadow-stippled slope.

I stopped at the sight of a dried tree stump. Without thought or reason, I seized it, pulled it straight up from the ground, and flipped it over. Its stump fell straight back into the hole. The snarl of its dead root system faced up into the sunlight. I saw the Rorschach blotlike face of a bird of prey with prominent eyebrows and a hooked beak.

I turned and continued the climb. The top of the hill provided a green and azure view of the softly curved river valley. I built up the remains of a fire ring with stones. With pine needles and deadwood, I lit a smoky fire and stood in the sun watching the ashes glow and dark billows rise.

My eyes tracked up higher into the sky, to the ringing voice of a large bird of prey. As I stared at it, a second osprey rose up from the left into my peripheral vision. It floated effortlessly on an invisible column of air ascending toward its mate. It tilted its wings, then soared down to hover not fifteen feet above me and the fire. Only individual feathers subtly moved along the edges of its brown and white wings. It cocked its head back and forth and looked me in the eye.

Minutes after finishing my tale, my friend and I rounded a bend in the Topanga trail to a view of the precipitous Eagle Rock—its contours and ledges form an eagle's beak, hollows its eyes, the upthrust rock gives it altitude and attitude. The land was layered, laced with stones long since turned by water. Eagle Rock was sedentary, carved from time and ocean bottom and sky. Swallows nested in its face and populated the air between it and the valley below. Near the crest of the rock cliff stood the black shape of a large raven.

We scaled the rock, sat at the crest, and laughed at finding the raven shape to be an illusion of shadow in a concavity of rock. But then, a raven flew into our view and down to a facing ledge. As we stared at it, a second rook rose up from our left into our peripheral vision. It tilted its wings and soared by us to join its mate.

The crow is the trickster's bird. It is comfortable in the borderland between the hot and cold swirling winds of developing weather. It is close to the heart of mystery and knows its way in and out of the shadows. It scavenges in secret places and tracks fresh mud from ancient sea beds.

The crow often presages changes.

My partner and I sat cupped in a small cave in the face of the rock and talked of signs. The raven streaked once more across the face of the cave. Seeing us over its shoulder, it flipped into an abrupt landing under the lip of the cave entrance. Four times it hopped up above the lip, cocking its head to look us each in the eye.

The eyeball-to-eyeball contact with the raven brought an immediate and powerful response of excitement and joy from me and my friend. That spontaneous rush, that passionate flash, was the longed-for missing ingredient in our daily lives.

On reflection, it carried a sense of being rescued from some empty fate. Not that the bird saved me magically by altering my future, but that my energetic response to synchronicity dissolved a dim view of things and strengthened what had been a weakened sense of belief that things can be okay, even though life is painful. The moment revealed that the wheel *is* turning and that I can feel whole and in grace again.

I came away from the encounter with a refreshed faith in the possibilities of my own future. However difficult at times, I am still on my own unique path, and it still holds mystery and growth.

—*Rand DeMattei*

THE CARETAKER

I am an "animal" person. There are people who love their creatures, treat them decently, and think of them as pets. Then there are those of us who have a deeper soul-connection with our furballs. We treasure their lives and mourn their deaths in the same way we would that of a best friend. All of the animals I have shared my life with have been unique, but Napoleon was undeniably special.

Nappie was a big, beautiful, indomitable long-haired tabby cat. He was part ancient-souled curmudgeon, part sweet impish little boy. At times he could be quite superior, but other moments surfaced where you witnessed his vulnerability and realized he was feeling scared or hurt.

One of his most enduring qualities was his role as "The Caretaker." When I became sick, he would lie on my chest looking quite concerned, and stare straight into my face, as if to ask, "Are you OK?" He was my lifeguard and kept an anxious vigil by the bathtub to ensure I didn't drown. When my other cat had kittens, although incapable of being the biological father, Nappie still decided it was his duty to supervise their hygienic needs. A gigantic paw would gently pin a tiny head to the ground, and, despite loud and squirmy protests, the entire furry body would be thoroughly cleaned. We were together for many years, and like an old married couple, we understood and tolerated each other's idiosyncrasies.

Napoleon died recently following unexpected complications from surgery for a tumor that was compressing his heart. Over the course of four years, I had experienced and grieved a series of devastating losses, and I can't help but wonder if my caretaker adopted some of my pain. Mourning the loss of his incredible spirit was not that dissimilar to grieving the loss of my dad and the separation from my husband.

Shortly thereafter, I was suddenly forced to vacate my residence in Los Angeles. I needed to find a home in a relatively safe neighborhood that would allow animals and still be affordable. I scoured ads and showed up at open houses only to realize that decent homes rented in seconds, while dumpy places in dangerous neighborhoods still demanded top dollar. I panicked that I wouldn't find a place for my animals and me to live.

Time was running out when I spotted an ad that read, "PETS OK." I raced to the house, praying I would be the first prospective tenant. But others were already negotiating. My "Urban Guerilla" surfaced, and I literally bolted through the premises, saying, "Good neighborhood! Great backyard for my dog! OK price—I'll take it!"

"These people in front of you want it, too," was the landlady's response.

My heart sunk.

Resigned, I walked through the house more slowly, wondering what it would have been like to live there. I noticed the leather couches had deep scratch marks.

"Where is your dog?" I asked the landlady, who had been living in the house. She paused and fought back the tears.

"My dog died suddenly of cancer about six weeks ago. Every day I live here, all I can do is think about him." I felt badly for her. "I'm sorry," I said, "I lost my favorite kitty about six weeks ago from heart problems, and I know how sad you are feeling."

Before this moment we were strangers, but now we were sisters in grief. She showed me a picture of a handsome dog. "I miss Napoleon so much," she said.

I almost fell over. "I'm sorry, what did you say?"

"I miss Nappie so much, I can't stay here, I really have to move on. . ."

"But *my* kitty's name was Napoleon. . ."

I believe that in many ways our animals take care of us. A woman whom I had just met had lost her Napoleon at the same time that I had lost mine. She desperately wanted out, and I desperately wanted in. I can't help but wonder if our two Napoleons somehow collaborated or if my Nappie, always my caretaker, in a final gesture, found me this wonderful home.

—*Pamela DuMond*

THE BOOK

For years a book had gathered dust in my library—*The Starship and the Canoe,* which deals with the real-life adventures of George Dyson, son of Freeman Dyson, the famous physicist. The book describes how George built a replica of the ancient oceangoing canoes called *bedarkas,* which were used by the indigenous tribes of the Pacific Northwest, and it relates his remarkable adventures sailing the canoe up and down the coast of British Columbia.

When my wife and I were invited to speak at Hollyhock, a conference center on Cortez Island off the British Columbia coast, I finally decided to read this book. I felt it would reveal some of the history of the area and make our visit more meaningful. During our lengthy journey to the island, I became mesmerized by the account. I could not put it down, and by the final ferry ride to the island I was on the final pages.

When we arrived at the conference center, our host offered to take us on a walk along the rocky beach. A short distance above the high-tide line was a huge fallen tree, behind which a strange canoe rested upside down. I had never seen anything like it.

Suddenly I was stunned: I realized it was identical to George Dyson's *bedarka,* which I'd been reading about on the journey to this particular spot.

"What's that?" I stammered.

"Oh, that's George Dyson's *bedarka,*" our guide replied. "He parks it here on his trips up and down the coast."

Go figure.

—*Larry Dossey*

FIRST IMPRESSIONS

Once my daughter and I went to the airport in Charleston, South Carolina, to pick up a woman and her son from South Africa. We had never seen her before and I was not enthusiastic to be seeing her at this time. She was a woman that my husband had met on one of his trips. She had entertained him, and he had invited her to visit us if she ever came to America.

She was not difficult to recognize. She had the audacity to arrive wearing a khaki suit and pith helmet, and she walked about our little airport as though on safari.

When she marched into our living room, she stopped dead in her tracks, gasped, and shouted for her son to come immediately. He found her standing in front of a painting that my daughter and I had bought in a small village in southern France. We had fallen in love with it, but, because our funds were low, we had gone to lunch to think about it before making a decision to buy it.

The son could not believe his eyes.

He said, "This is the painting that my mother and I fell in love with in a small village in southern France, but, because our funds were low, we had lunch to think about it before making our decision. When we returned to buy the painting, we were told that it had just been sold to an American woman and her daughter."

They had settled for a lesser painting by the same artist, which they just happened to have a photograph of, showing the painting hanging in their living room in South Africa.

Of course, new friendships were cemented on the spot.

—*Ann B. Igoe*

BAND-AIDS

When I was about three years old, my mother and I shared a house with another single mother and her son, Chris. Chris and I were the same age and were like siblings during the year that we lived together.

One day, for no apparent reason, I decided I wanted a Band-Aid. I pulled a chair into the bathroom, so that I could reach the medicine cabinet and take one out of the box. Then I went out onto the front porch and sat down, waving the Band-Aid in front of my face like a fan.

Within a few minutes, my friend Chris came running up, crying. Blood was running down his leg from a wound just below his knee.

I asked him what had happened, and he said that the mean old dog next door had bitten him. So I handed him the Band-Aid.

It wasn't until that moment that I realized how strange it was that I had gotten it out in the first place. He thought it was weird, too, and stopped crying.

Then, since one didn't seem to be doing the trick, we both went into the house to get more Band-Aids.

—*Jennifer Brontsema*

SHIRLEY

A few years ago, I was struck with an overwhelming desire to know more about the Brontës: Emily, Charlotte, and Anne. It became an obsession without reason, as I was neither reading or viewing anything remotely connected to their works. My only scant knowledge had been through past literature classes taken in school.

At any rate, unable to shake off the inner urge, I finally went to the San Francisco Public Library and began pouring through their archives on the Brontës—though not knowing *what* I was looking for. After scanning countless numbers of pages, I spotted a brief phrase explaining that Charlotte had written a novel, little known in the States, that was intended to be her sequel to *Jane Eyre*. It was entitled *Shirley*. This was amusing, since Shirley was my name, but certainly not earthshaking. Although, oddly enough, after seeing that notation, my feeling of urgency disappeared. And I dismissed the situation as just another trick of the universe.

The next day, my boss—who belonged to a rare book club—handed me a list of classics that were available at a special price and asked if I was interested in ordering any of the books. In the middle of the normal day's rush, I just quickly glanced at the first few titles. Charlotte Brontë's *Shirley,* published in 1849, was on that list.

Out of curiosity, I sent away for the book. That very afternoon, during a lunchtime conversation with a colleague—a particularly well-read associate editor—the subject of animals came up. He was in the middle of editing a manuscript on the healthcare of dogs and cats, and he wondered if I had ever had a dog. After mentioning that I had a wonderful little Llasa Apso for many years, by the name of Phoebe (a name given by her original owner), he said, "Oh, Shirley was bitten by a dog named Phoebe in Brontë's novel, *Shirley*. Have you ever heard of it?" I admitted that I had only recently become aware of it and, in fact, had just ordered it.

That same evening, after returning home from the office, I received a call from a friend in London who had recently visited San Francisco. During our conversation, she suddenly interrupted with, "By the way, I've been meaning to ask you if you've ever read *Shirley,* a novel by one of the Brontë sisters?" She tried to remember what she could about the book, then added that it was a respected piece of literature in England and is often included as part of the British educational curriculum.

By this time, I was eager to receive the book. When it did arrive, I anxiously began reading—only to quickly lose interest and never finish! While I did see within the pages some uncanny similarities to names and dates in my own life, the heavy language of the period and the gloomy references to the Old Testament did not make for a lively read. And I could not sustain motivation to continue.

No insights, no revelations, no meaning—other than to suggest that I had simply and intuitively picked up on name associations that would be relayed by my friends. In other words, this experience and others, whether they are the result of precognition or thought transference, have always seemed entirely natural and comfortable. For me, they just serve to illuminate—if only for a moment—our true and eternal oneness.

—*Shirley Christine*

III. The Passing Strange

There are few persons, even among the calmest thinkers, who have not occasionally been startled into a vague yet thrilling half-credence in the supernatural, by coincidences of so seemingly marvelous a character that, as mere coincidences, the intellect has been unable to receive them.

—Edgar Allan Poe, *The Mystery of Marie Roget*

"She swore, in faith t'was strange, t'was passing strange..." wrote Shakespeare in *Othello*. Strange, a holy word. It points to something sacred, that which comes from another country, another world, often the underworld. That long, strong *a* in the middle of the word resounds like a deep bass note from a moaning cello in a dark blues club long past midnight.

Strange, too, is "The Rainmaker" story from China that Jung learned from Richard Wilhelm. Mysterious, as well, why Jung trusted so deeply in its powers to convey the uncanny power of one individual to transform the life force of the world around him that he told his biographer Barbara Hannah "never to give a course of lectures without it."

"Wilhelm asked him [the rainmaker] in wonder: 'So you can make rain?' The old man scoffed at the very idea and said *of course* he could not. "But there was the most persistent drought until you came," Wilhelm retorted, "and then—within three days—it rains?" "Oh," replied the old man, "that was something quite different. You see, I come from a region where everything is in order, it rains when it should and is fine when that is needed, and the people also are in order and in themselves. But that was not the case with the people here, they were all out of Tao and out of themselves. I was at once infected when I arrived, so I had to be quite alone until I was once more in Tao and then naturally it rained."

In Part III the contributors have endured something comparable to what mythologist Mircea Eliade described as "ordeal by labyrinth." The stories here are sudden encounters with the outlandish, the peculiar, the eccentric or erratic, either darkness, death, or the heartbreaking powers of the world. These are *eldritch* tales of the scritching and scratching at the doors of our hearts.

One of Jung's own numerous eerie experiences conveys the mood of this troubling territory. Returning from a lecture he had given, he had lain awake in bed for a long time, when: "At about two o'clock—I must have just fallen asleep—I awoke with a start and had the feeling that someone had come into the room; I even had the impression that the door had been hastily opened. I instantly turned on the light, but there was nothing. Someone might have mistaken the door, I thought, and I looked into the corridor. But it was still as death. 'Odd,' I thought, 'Someone did come into the room!' Then I tried to recall exactly what had happened, and it occurred to me that I had been awakened by a feeling of dull pain, as though something had struck my forehead and then the back of my skull. The following day I received a telegram saying that my patient had committed suicide. He had shot himself. Later I learned that the bullet had come to rest in the back wall of his skull."

Of this kind of disturbing telepathic communication, Jean Shinoda Bolen speculates we are being given "clues" or "singular events." She suggests an "Agatha Christie approach" to deeply unsettling synchronicities, in which people try to "see what the pattern of these clues points to suggests about the underlying meaning of these events." However, there remains the choice of seizing the soul moments, however painful, and interpreting them in light of our unfolding life journey or rejecting them outright, and bolting away. As the legendary black baseball pitcher Satchel

Paige phrased it in his inimitable syncopated, bebopping style, "When the world gets too *instanter,* I make myself *distanter.*"

What strikes me about the stories in this third section is miraculously echoed in a "found poem" by the author Annie Dillard in her recent innovative book, *Mornings Like This.* In this bold work she transforms passages from the letters of the anguished painter Vincent van Gogh to his brother Theo, into stanzas of luminous poetry. The first reads:

> At the end of the road is a small cottage,
> And over it all the blue sky,
> I am trying to get at something utterly heartbroken.

In the rigorous attempt to render a simple rustic scene, van Gogh simultaneously evokes two rarely connected emotions: beauty and sorrow. There are at least two as-yet undefined kind of synchronicities here. First is the meaningful coincidence of the expression of the artist's grief and the recognition of "something utterly heartbroken" in nature. Second is the poet's transmutation of the reader's preconceptions of the artist as only painter into the revelation of the hidden poet.

In these three lines we realize the bottomless depths of one man's vastly complex destiny. We discover him desperately trying to render his own heartbreak and that of the evanescence of life in a small cottage, and it's as if his and our vision *is thrown into the future.*

In contrast is this passage from Herman Hesse's classic book, *Journey to the East,* in which the narrator reconciles with the truth of what he had always felt was the failed pilgrimage of his youth.

"For our goal was not only the East, or rather the East was not only a country and something geographical, but it was the home and youth of the soul, it was everywhere and nowhere, it was the union of all times. Yet I was only aware of this for a moment, and therein lay the reason for my great happiness at that time. Later, when I had lost this happiness again, I clearly understood these connections without deriving the slightest benefit or comfort from them. When something precious and irretrievable is lost, we have the feeling of having awakened from a dream. In my case this feeling is strangely correct, for my happiness did indeed arise from the same secret as the happiness in dreams; it arose from the freedom to experience everything imaginable *simultaneously* [emphasis added], to exchange outward and inward easily, to move Time and Space about like scenes in a theater . . . as we conquered the war-shattered world by our faith and transformed it into Paradise, we creatively brought the past the future and the fictitious into the present moment."

One of my own startling and transforming encounters with the "passing strange" occurred many years ago when I dreamt of living in medieval France during the Plague. In the dream I was driving a *tumbril,* an old French cart, and sitting next to me was a woman friend of mine who, in real life, I had grown up with back in Michigan. We were fleeing our humble home in a walled town that resembled Carcassone, which I could see was being torched by brutal invaders as I ruefully looked over my shoulder again and again. Ahead of us was a line of wobbling carts, animals, and moaning peasants. I told myself I would look one last time behind at the smoking ruins of our home and when I did my blood ran cold. Behind me, piled high in the cart among our belongings, were burlap bags full of dead babies.

At that very moment I was startled awake by a phone call from a relative in Detroit. She had just heard from the same woman I had just been dreaming about who had called to tell her that she had just had her third miscarriage and was leaving home to start life over somewhere else. She felt her life was in ruins.

For weeks the story burned in my heart. Something inside me felt singed, as if the cross firing of dream and reality had caused an electrical fire. That crossover of a dream and a phone call, my inner and outer life, marked the point where I vowed to pay serious attention to anything dreamlike that ever came my way, from dreams themselves to sudden inspirations or remarkable synchronicities.

Our circumambulation of the soul of synchronicity continues. The touchstone words wielded here are distinctly darker: grief, curse, untimely, death, inexplicable, grueling, ordeal, peculiar, timelessness, involuting.

For Jack Kerouac biographer Gerry Nicosia, the peculiar appearances of the mysterious color yellow after the death of his close friend, Jan Kerouac, were like a "cross-contact" between the world of the living and the dead. Though unsure of the message or the meaning of the serial experiences, he admits to "certainly some kind of magic" happening to him.

To comedian and stuntman, James Van Harper, a freak episode of telepathic communication, vividly described in his story, "Red Asphalt," was so disconcerting he spent years trying to bury any feelings about paranormal or extraordinary reality. However, in recent conversations, he revealed how he has come to realize that the incident worked its way into him anyway, giving him a respect for strange encounters he had previously mocked or ignored. For Oakland, California, writer and naturalist, Anne Denton Hayes, the "Strange Plight" with her disturbed cousin in France several years back was marked by "twisted logic" and travel with "no destination." Her journey seemed only to be made worse by a kind of meaninglessness, yet, she sees in retrospect that the "chance event" became more, through reflection, a lesson proving to her that "lives are not simply linear." Moreover, in a splendid phrase that reveals one of the hallmarks of synchronicity, "the forces that bend" our lives often lie outside us.

In his deeply moving story, "My Father's Gift," Richard Beban painstakingly reveals "clues" to his grief with a blend of images that reflect his gift for imagery as both poet and screenwriter. The synchronistic intersecting of dreamtime and realtime at the end of the story conjures up the mystery of what the soul often must endure to find compassion.

Untimely deaths haunt Nashville musician and mountain man Richard Morris as well. His curious tale of Bob Dylan's near-demise on stage set him to brooding for years on the question of curses, chance, and coincidence. The guitarlike cadences of his reflections read like the stanzas of an old ballad pondering the eccentric habits of fate and destiny.

So too with actress and chef, Carrie Aginsky, whose deeply moving story about her mother's graceful death centers on the question of who will control our fate and the symbols that abound to those with "synchronistic eyes." Lesha Finiw's Borgeslike story about the sign her mother seemed to leave behind after her death, helps "transform [the incident] into a discovery of spirit and grace," while for Pamela DuMond, the death of her father became an unexpected "gift of heavenly wisdom" through the alchemy of synchronicity.

In "Two Patients," Brazilian physician Roberto Takaoka experiences the phenomenon of clustering, as well as giving a vivid example of what the French poet Paul Valery suggested when he once wrote that, "The deepest part of a person is the skin." In the charged words of Patricia Murphy, her encounter with thieves left her in a "trance of fractured attention" from which she wrested a healing "moment of grace." Finally, in the deceptively simple story of her father's death, Lois Nightingale provides a remarkable description of "divine order" that influences our lives.

No matter how sorrowful our path may be, there is a story from somewhere, sometime, that can help balm our wounded soul. This one by Idries Shah tells of the thirteenth century holy fool Mulla Nasrudin trying to plant a simple flower garden:

"He prepared the soil and planted the seeds of many beautiful flowers. But when they came up, his garden was filled not just with his chosen flowers but also overrun by dandelions. He sought out advice from gardeners all over and tried every method known to get rid of them, but to no avail. Finally he walked all the way to the capital to speak to the royal gardener at the sheik's palace. The wise old man had counseled many gardeners before and suggested a variety of remedies to expel the dandelions but Mulla had tried them all. They sat together in silence for some time and finally the gardener looked at Nasrudin and said, "Well, then I suggest you learn to love them."

THE YELLOW CAR

I've experienced synchronicities long before I knew what they were called, but then the psychic and visionary world has always been as real to me as the world of things that so many people seem to think is all there is. In the last few years, as more and more of my friends and family die, these synchronicities often take on the semblance of some form of communication from beyond.

Recently I was very troubled by the death of my friend Jan Kerouac, whose estate is almost in as bad a tangle as her father's was—and by her will, Jan has requested that I be one of the people to disentangle it. This has put me in the unhappy position of having to tangle with her heirs in order to do what she wanted done with her papers and literary rights.

The other thing you need to know to make sense of this story is that my mother, eighty-five, had a stroke a little over a year ago. It affected her speech greatly. She does not talk much at all anymore, and, when she does, it is usually just simple sentences like, "I'll have more milk." But sometimes she gets nouns wrong; she'll substitute a totally inappropriate noun for the one she really means. For example, she might say, "I want Missouri" when she means "milk." And then sometimes she says things that are so surrealistic, so out of context, that I have thought, at times, that being so close to death herself, she can now hear whispers from the dead.

One day, as we sat out in front of her nursing home, she said to me, "I thought we had a yellow car here. What happened to the yellow car?" No one in our family has ever had a yellow car, and she has never said such a thing before or since. I was so struck by it that I wrote it down on one of the slips of notepaper that I keep in my breast pocket.

Often, I stop for coffee at a place called Java on my way back from her nursing home. This day I could not park where I usually do, and so I went home down a street I don't usually take. Suddenly I spotted the most glaringly yellow car I have ever seen in my life. The name of the street was Monte Vista, the name of the street Jan Kerouac lived on in Albuquerque in recent years.

During the next two or three days, it seemed like my life was besieged by yellow cars. One got stuck coming by mistake down our dead end street and had to turn around right in front of me. Needless to say, I felt somehow Jan was trying to contact me, but what on earth was the message I was supposed to get?

About the third morning, our house was unusually cold. We're in the middle of construction, and the whole top floor is open. It was summer, but there was one sweatshirt lying around for me to grab and put on. It happened to be the one that publicized the benefit I had put on for Jan a year before. Suddenly I saw, and remembered, that she had signed the back of each one in yellow paint—"Thanks to you all, Jan Kerouac." Simultaneously I recalled that Jack Kerouac, Jan's father, had said the root of their name was the Celtic word "Carr"—the same as in the name of his friend, Lucien Carr, whom he always claimed an ancestral relationship to. The "yellow Carr"—none other than Jan herself! Pulling the note out of my pocket that I had originally written my mother's strange remark on, I realized that it was the blank sheet of paper I had taken as a souvenir from Jan's own archive in Albuquerque, which I had gone down the week before to begin inventorying.

The next morning I walked around to the back of the yellow VW that was again parked head to head with my car. For some reason, though registered in California, it had no plate on the front. The plate on the rear read: 2AYU991. I sounded it out: It sounded like "to aid you." 209 had been her street address in Albuquerque; 1991 the year she'd had kidney failure, which had led to the resumption of our friendship after a hiatus of several years.

Perhaps some people will think I'm crazy, or just have an overactive imagination; but I'll never be able to see a yellow car again without thinking of Jan Kerouac—and there is certainly some kind of magic in that.

—*Gerry Nicosia*

RED ASPHALT

In the football season of my junior year in college, I found myself one of the co-captains in a game for our Open Week. It was a Thursday night game; I caught a couple of passes and made a few good hits. Nothing memorable, other than hurting my ankle.

The next day during varsity sports—the last period of the day, the class was a combination of study hall, P.E., and goof-off period for athletes—the class was required to watch one of those graphic scare-teenagers-into-driving-slowly films called *Red Asphalt*. Somehow, I had already seen the film and didn't want to watch it again, so I volunteered to wash towels with the team quarterback, Bobby Lord. As we washed them, we heard the sound of cars crashing and injured kids crying and yelling. I turned to Bobby and said, "I don't know what I'd do if one of my friends got killed in a car accident."

At that moment we heard a loud voice scream, "Bob! Bob!"

We went out and asked who was yelling Bob!

The class was busy watching the film and didn't know what

we were talking about. Nobody was screaming the name on the film either. So we shrugged and went back to our scrubbing duties. I took the bus home with my girlfriend-of-the-week since I couldn't drive my VW due to my injured ankle.

As I reached home, my mom nabbed me at the door and started crying. I started taking my shoes off and asked her what was wrong. She didn't answer. She just kept crying.

I asked, "Is it Granny?" since my grandmother was dying of terminal cancer.

"No," my mom answered. "It's not Granny."

"Is it Dad?" I then asked.

"No, it's not your dad."

Then she said, "Bob was—"

I cut her off, saying, "*Killed?* Killed in a car wreck?"

"Yes, how did you know that?"

"I, I don't know, Mom. . ."

At the time I was living in Pensacola, Florida, and Bob, my best friend, had just moved to Milwaukee, Wisconsin. His sister called to let us know. Nobody in my hometown knew Bob. In Milwaukee, Bob ran with a wild group of kids, and that night he slipped outside to go joyriding in a friend's new car. I later found out that the kid's car drove into a tree, and Bob went through the windshield and died on impact.

The driver went into shock, screaming Bob's name over and over, "Bob! Bob! . . ."

Later that night, that kid, who was only seventeen years old, became a father; his girlfriend went into labor and gave birth to a baby boy. It was only a few hours after Bob's death. I heard that they named the baby Robert, but I'm not sure.

I tried to bury my feelings about this for a long time, but I never quite managed. I went on long walks in the woods or on the beach trying to find peace or make sense of the situation.

I don't know how this incident changed my way of thinking or my feelings, other than I don't like to talk about plane crashes before I fly or talk about death on the highways before I leave in my truck to go on a drive. I don't know what to make of this actually. Does God have a sick sense of humor?

I guess I keep my guard up more. That's about it.

—*James Van Harper*

STRANGE PLIGHT

When I was eighteen, I traveled to Paris alone. I had no plan; I had a place to stay and I wanted to discover the world. Most of all, I wanted to be far, far away from the town where I'd grown up.

My first port of call was the home of an old friend of my mother's, an American woman who'd married a French man. They lived in the *banlieu,* the suburbs, west of Paris.

With this woman's help, I enrolled in a couple of classes at different schools in Paris, and it didn't take me too long to begin to establish a few friendships. It was probably about four weeks after I had arrived that I went out for the first time at night. It was a Friday night.

I can no longer recall where I met my friends, two young American men, but once we'd joined up, one of them suggested we have a drink at the bar of the George V, a swank hotel off the Champs Elysses. We entered the lobby, and there in front of us was my cousin Mark, seated on a circular sofa, wearing a trench coat, smoking a Dunhill cigarette.

The last time I'd seen Mark was in San Francisco. In the

interim, he'd become schizophrenic. I didn't know he was in Paris—but he knew I was. He went to Europe to find me, and fate saw to it that he did so quite easily.

I met Mark again the following morning at the Gare d'Orleans. I bought him a train ticket to Zurich, where he said he wanted to go next. As I left the station, I felt as though a weight were being lifted from me, as if a heavy coat that I'd been wearing had been taken from my shoulders. I was relieved. *Goodbye,* I thought. *I'm glad that's over.*

But it was not over. Mark returned to Paris for me—it was obvious later that he needed me because he needed money. At the time, though, through my own innocence, ignorance, and egotism, I was persuaded by my cousin's delusions into believing we were both in trouble. I again put on the coat of psychosis, and we fled Paris.

Mark began to call me Moneypenny. He was James Bond, and, in the twisted logic of his semicoherent hallucinations, I was his sugar baby. I awoke from this bad dream five days later, on an empty road under sullen November skies. We were on foot, walking out of the border town of Mulhouse, France. We had no destination. When I realized Mark didn't know where we were going, it became clear to me we had been acting out a fantasy, a falsity.

"It's not true," I said. "All those things you've been telling me; they're not true." We were two very uncertain children in a foreign land, a land with no sympathy for us and no recognition of our strange plight.

Mark grew angry with me and we parted ways. He walked one direction and I walked the other. I went back into town and took the train back to Paris. I don't know where Mark went. He eventually resurfaced in Paris and returned to the United States. I do not know whether he is dead or alive.

This small odyssey was spawned by a chance event. It was not all that unlikely an event. I ran into my cousin. Nonetheless, it changed my life. The aftermath of my experience with Mark was painful, but it left me with a very useful disbelief in the seemingly solid, rational world. If our lives are trajectories, they are by no means simply linear, and the forces that bend them often lie far outside the realm of our normal perceptions.

—Anne Denton Hayes

MY FATHER'S GIFT

It was February 1986. My father was dying, slowly, from the metastasizing lung cancer that had now invaded his brain. We had been estranged for much of the prior seven years at my instigation, because of my constant complaint that his alcoholism had warped the family gravitational field, the way no light can escape from a black hole. But we had a rapprochement in May 1985, when I took him to Paris for two weeks. He had been a Sunday painter when I was a child, and I could not let him die without seeing the art in the Jeu de Paume, the Louvre. I wanted him to live, even for a moment, in a city where the streets are named for artists.

After that trip, we saw each other more regularly, and other family members sighed with relief that the emotional siege between us was done. I visited him and my stepmother in Rohnert Park, forty miles north of San Francisco, where I lived, and we would simply spend time together, at his house, driving to the seashore, doing an errand, whatever.

On these visits we communicated as we did in Paris, shoulder-to-shoulder, the way, as James Hillman puts it, "in which you walk through the same ground, your shoulders maybe touching. You don't talk a lot, but the connection of those two male bodies touching each other, and working together, does a healing for the son." When we did talk, he steadfastly denied he was dying, and the final fiction was all right with me, if it was easier for him to live with.

In early February 1986, he and my stepmother drove to San Francisco to see my sister, a cabaret singer, perform, but he ended up not feeling well enough to attend. I sat with him in their rented hotel room while my stepmother went. While she was gone, my father could not stay still; he was suffocating, unable to breathe comfortably, despite using an apparatus that guided a steady stream of bottled oxygen to his nose.

On the 17th of February, I awoke out of a sound sleep at about 5:30 A.M., crying. I did not know why. If it was because of a dream, I could not remember the contents. So I went to the computer to consult the keyboard, hoping, through writing, to uncover a clue to my grief.

In short order a poem emerged, a great surprise, since I had no inkling I would ever write poetry. My feeble college attempts years earlier had resulted in an incomplete—a compromise because my teacher felt badly about flunking me. Nonetheless, a poem emerged that morning. It read:

Marks
I sit,
arranging words
on paper
like charms
    against death.
My father, spindly, frail,
paces in agitation.

Afraid to sit still.
Afraid to lie down.
Each of us has left marks upon the other.
He rests now,
breathing with a machine.
We are on the eleventh floor.
I look to the window,
    will him to jump.
Compassion?
He is smaller than I am.   Finally.
But the desire to make him pay is gone.
I want to hold him.
Breathe for him.
Something of me goes with him.
I don't know what.
Each of us has left marks upon the other.

Just as I typed the final line, the telephone rang. It was my father's sister, who said he'd had a stroke earlier that morning and was in a coma in the hospital nearest his home. She and my uncle were coming to pick me up. Without the medical heroic measures he had already refused, his brain-dead body hung on another eight hours, long enough for the family to gather from all over Northern California, despite the area's worst rain and flooding in years.

Then he stopped breathing.

I suspect that he woke me hours earlier to say good-bye.

—*Richard Beban*

CURSE OR COINCIDENCE?

In the Robert Mitchum song, "The Ballad of Thunder Road," a moonshine runner eludes his pursuers from Harlem to Asheville to Memphis with apparent ease, but

Blazing right through Knoxville, out on Kingston Pike . . .
they made the fatal strike. He left the road at ninety,
that's all there is to say.
The devil got the moonshine and the mountain boy that day.

There's something that rings true in that old story-song regarding Knoxville, Tennessee, my hometown. True about people making their runs through Knoxville, and especially true for certain musician composers.

In February 1943, Sergei Rachmaninoff held a concert performance in Knoxville. While here he stayed at the Andrew Johnson Hotel. The concert turned out to be his last. A few weeks later in Los Angeles, the great classical composer died unexpectedly from what was discovered to be cancer of the spine. His protege, Vladimir Horowitz, believed Knoxville had somehow cursed Rachmaninoff, because he had played his last show there. Horowitz would refuse to ever perform in Knoxville.

Ten years later, Hank Williams rolled through town on New Year's Eve en route to a show in Canton, Ohio. He too stayed at the Andrew Johnson Hotel, where firsthand accounts say he was carried out and put in the back seat of his Cadillac when he and his driver left town on January 1, 1953. A few hours later, some two hundred miles up the road, the "Father of Modern Country Music" was declared dead of a "severe heart attack with massive hemorrhage."

There has always been some mystery about the untimely death of Hank Williams at age twenty-nine. The use of narcotics has been suggested, as well as the possibility that he was already dead when he was carried out of the Andrew Johnson Hotel.

In April 1993, Bob Dylan and his band played at the Civic Auditorium in Knoxville. I don't know where Dylan stayed the night, but the Andrew Johnson had been relegated to office space by that time. During the show, as he sang the song, "Everything Is Broken," a large stage light with a "barn door" shutter apparatus fell from high overhead and crashed to the stage floor, just missing Dylan and his bass player, Tony Gaurnier. The coincidence of this occurring during that particular song aside, there was nothing planned or spectacular about the incident. I watched it from side-stage and saw how stunned and upset the soundman and crew were. Dylan may have blinked, but he kept singing and the band didn't miss a beat.

The following night in Asheville, I watched again from side-stage as he played that song, and as he sang "Every time I stop and look around, something else just hit the ground," he quickly glanced up and to either side before cracking a classic Dylan near-smile. Perhaps he is a man used to such synchronicity, as well as sidestepping death. Still, I can't help but consider the repercussions of what could have happened had Dylan taken a direct hit. He would have suffered great personal injury at the least, and most likely death. After the untimely deaths of Elvis Presley and John Lennon, one can barely imagine the cultural reception that Dylan's death on stage would have received.

In the inevitably brutal and speculative light following his tragedy, the curse that Horowitz claimed on behalf of Rachmaninoff would no doubt resurface and resound with a terrible circumstantial evidence. Three of the most original and influential figures in the pantheon of modern music would have become part of an odd synchronistic death sequence.

I cannot help but consider all this, as well as my thoughts and feelings regarding it. Do I believe in such a thing as a curse? Did Dylan hold his mouth just right and manage to dodge it? Does this mean that one does have the ability to alter apparent destiny? Are willpower or some personal power major components in shaping such life forces—or do they allow synchronistic forces to take shape? Do certain people attract some force of synchronicity or are they endowed with the ability to affect that force? And specifically, are traveling acts dealing with some crazy form of Russian roulette by touring Knoxville—especially the more prominent acts?

In the end, I believe it all, or I find myself giving credence to there being some truth to all of it. But I am not at all sure of the exact nature of that truth. It is an inexact science; it is no science at all. It is a phenomenon of an elusive nature and one cannot, seemingly, be of certainty.

So, as I go forward playing music, working within the creative process, and living in general, I have to carry this with me, both as an uncertainty and a faith in the patterns and powers in life, as well as my involvement therein.

Sometimes one has to *feel* more than *know,* and this approach seems most appropriate.

—*Richard Morris*

WHEN THE LEAVES GET RESTLESS

I want to tell you a story of my mother, Natalie's, passing.

When I brought her to our home from the convalescent hospital, it was clear that she wouldn't last long. She was barely eating and was talking a lot about being ready to go. When the weather was sunny, I would wheel her chair out onto the deck where she would sit smiling at the leaves of the wisteria vine turning yellow and falling on the deck. Every day I'd sweep up the fallen leaves, and we'd talk about the passing of the seasons and the cycles of the years and of our lives. Even in her befuddled mental state she had real moments of clarity and spoke on essential issues. One day, as the wind was blowing the leaves around her, she smiled at me and said, "When the leaves are gone, I'll be gone too."

Three weeks later she passed away.

There was one leaf left on the vine.

It fell.

That my mother should predict the time of her passing was not surprising to me but a great relief. She had always said that when the time came that she could no longer care for herself, dress herself, or clean herself, she didn't want to live anymore. But the years had passed, and, with the loss of her memory, she had forgotten that, too, and, as each level of independence fell away, a deeper level of forgetfulness descended. She was ninety-two years old, and, besides being frail and demented, she was basically healthy and could have lived on and on. Her only control over her fate was to stop eating and that was precisely what she did. And like the leaves falling from the wisteria vine, she went lightly and with grace.

She was happier in those last few weeks than I remember seeing her in years. Never having been a religious person, she began to speak of being surrounded by angels. All of us who cared for her were also her angels. After years of wishing to die and saying she didn't know how, here was knowledge, if unconscious, of how to die on her own terms.

Was this acausal that only one leaf was left when she finally let go, or was this a causal willing it to happen? I don't know.

Is destiny something that happens or do we create it ourselves? If synchronous experiences are not noticed, destiny moves in from exterior happenings, but recognition and wonder and destiny emanate from the heart. I do know that all through my life there have been inexplicable events that have served as milestones for me, the memories of which serve to guide me on my path.

—*Carrie Aginsky*

THE STRANGE BUBBLE

My mother died very suddenly of a heart attack just before Thanksgiving in 1994. Of course, we were all in shock to lose her without warning and were coping in whatever way we could. I had worried about attending the wake. I thought it would be a grueling ordeal and wasn't sure how I would hold up. But it turned out quite differently. There were so many people who came to share their feelings. I couldn't believe how many people told me, "She was my best friend." Each one of them would lean closer to whisper in my ear, so that others would not hear and become jealous.

Back home, while washing up after the wake, a single, tiny bubble appeared in the kitchen, then floated from one person to another in the room. Believe it or not—it changed directions two or three times.

Finally, it hovered over an empty chair and dissolved.

You may say that there's nothing unusual about a soap bubble popping up, especially when the sink is full of bubbling foam, but we were all mesmerized. The fact that it was just one bubble, and the way it moved, seemed quite extraordinary, as if to acknowledge each member of the family. We took it as a sign of our mother's presence. You might even say that we ourselves caused the changes in direction, just with our breathing, but I swear no one wanted that bubble to disappear, and we all held our breath until it was gone.

After the funeral, we mentioned the story of the dancing bubble to a number of people, who indulgently nodded along with our recitation, perhaps more touched by our wish to believe in this sign than by any belief on their part in its reality. But there was one person for whom this story took a more serious turn. I told it to Genya, just as I tell it to you. But Genya did not nod or smile or pat my hand. She burst into sobs.

It was Genya who found my mother dead. Genya had been my mother's hairdresser for almost forty years. That morning she came over to give her a new perm. My parents were coming to Boston for Thanksgiving, and, of course, my mom wanted to look her best. Genya came in the side door, which is always open when we're at home and called for my mother, Mary. When Mary did not answer, Genya called again. Still no answer. Genya went through the dining room to the bedroom, still calling and looking for her.

Then she saw my mother, lying on the bed, as if peacefully asleep. But when Genya once more spoke her name, Mary did not respond. Genya ran to touch her. Mary's hand was cold. She wasn't breathing. Genya called out the window to my father, who was working in the yard. As he came running in, she noticed there was a single, tiny bubble on the corner of her mouth.

As we talked, it was clear that Genya blamed herself for not being able to do more for my mother. She kept saying that if only she had come earlier, they might have been in time to revive her. My mother was her best friend. If only, if only . . .

We had already reassured her that it wasn't her fault, but Genya was distraught. She couldn't get over what she had seen. She hadn't mentioned the bubble to anyone before, but it was one strange detail that stuck in her mind. So it meant a lot to her to hear about the light, entrancing dance of the bubble in our kitchen.

Our story seemed to help change the meaning of the bubble for her. No longer was it locked in the image of her mortifying discovery, but transformed now to another—of my mother Mary's spirit continuing to grace us.

—*Lesha Finiw*

CAMERA MOMENTS

I feel grateful that my father, John Lewis DuMond, has always been my best friend and mentor. He taught me the importance of living life with integrity, honesty, and a positive mental attitude. Through him I know the power of laughter and love. He was my touchstone for truth and throughout the years my biggest fan. Unlike many people, I grew up knowing and being loved by a parent who freely gave his wisdom, time, and love. My dad died suddenly and mysteriously on June 9, 1993, at the age of sixty-eight, most likely from a combination of heart disease and irreversible hospital error. We buried him with a phone that had a twenty-foot extension cord, and before the casket was closed we reminded him, "Dad, wherever you go, phone home!"

As a child, I traveled extensively with my family. Every place we visited, I watched my dad open his heart and connect with strangers through what I call "the camera moment." He'd spot a tourist pointing the camera at their travelling companion and feel badly knowing that when the prints returned, the photographer would not be in the picture. This inspired a lifelong mission in which he zealously approached hundreds of tourists and offered to take their picture *together*. The funny thing was, the people he cornered were always grateful! My Dad would laugh and reply, "This is how I acquired my fine, expensive camera collection!"

By this small gesture, he touched many lives.

When he died, I had already been coping with an overwhelming series of life-transforming losses. His death devastated me, and I became paralyzed with grief. Shortly thereafter, my husband and I separated. I found myself spiralling down through the darkest time I have ever experienced, literally living my most primal fears and terrors. Severe anxiety struck, and for the first time in my life I developed panic attacks.

One day I was lying on my office floor, crying and praying for help and guidance. Seemingly from nowhere, thoughts and advice began pouring into my head: ideas about how I could help myself and others by teaching what people can do to begin to help themselves, and eventually to touch our earth. It was as if the floodgates had opened, and in that moment I was given a gift of heavenly wisdom.

When I finally sat up and dried my tears, I said, "OK, Dad. Are you helping to send me these messages? Are you nagging the powers that be to help me out? I've never asked this of you before, but I need a sign, and I need it to be obvious, and I need it *now*!"

The Third Street Promenade in Santa Monica, California, where I work is bustling with tourists from all over the world. That day I was hungry and decided to walk down the Promenade to buy lunch. I was completely lost in my thoughts when two Japanese tourists broke though my daze and stopped me. The man said haltingly, "Please, will you take our picture? *Together?*"

I have practiced therapy in this location for four years and have walked this street hundreds of times. This was the only time anyone has requested this favor.

I thanked my dad for his help and thanked God for a moment of healing intervention that gave me hope. I realized that the very lowest moments of one's life can also be the most transforming and healing.

—*Pamela DuMond*

THE FAMILY CIRCLE

Synchronistic events occur with some frequency in my life. Often when they happen I just acknowledge that something has happened, and then continue on with my life, but some events are so amazing that I recall them.

Both stories I want to share here are about death. I have always felt surrounded by spirits and/or angels. I also feel a very strong connection with animals, plants (particularly trees), rocks, bodies of water, air, and fire. I was in fine health and fit as a fiddle when I awoke one morning with a dizzy feeling. Strange, I thought, as I knew I was not ill. Therefore, I got myself up and dressed and off to work. Work at that time was student teaching at Marina Junior High School in San Francisco. Both my classes were team taught, so as I felt the need to lay a little low this morning, I did so. I continued to feel dizzy.

Finally, after first period, at around 9:00 A.M., I simply could not continue. I was nearly in a stupor. I asked the other teacher to please carry on and soon found myself wandering down the hall. The vice principal came along and escorted me to a room with a cot. I lay down. I was facing the wall. The dizzy feeling had become a fierce headache on the left upper side of my head. I could barely open my eyes. I felt like I was in a trance. I felt like I was dying. Or, rather, I knew I felt like I was dying, but I didn't think I would actually die.

At this moment, two junior high girls came into the room and started to chatter, thus breaking my concentration. I was so far gone that I could not roll over and ask them to either be still or leave me be. Anyway, I tried to get back into it and figure out what was happening.

Soon it was noon, and the feeling faded. I went out to my car, lay on the seat for a few minutes, then drove myself home and went to bed. When I woke up, it was dark outside. I lit a candle, went to my bookshelf, pulled down *Trinity* by Leon Uris, and the book fell open to the grandfather's wake. I read about the wake.

Soon after my father called. My paternal grandmother in Yucaipa, California, had awakened with a dizzy feeling. (She had been taking some type of chemotherapy for a malignant melanoma.) She was being transported to the hospital around 9:00 A.M. when an elderly woman pulled in front of her speeding ambulance. Grandma was thrown against the ceiling and suffered a head injury to the upper left side of her head. She died around noon.

We were about 500 miles apart.

• • •

I was very close to my maternal grandfather. Grandpa was Irish and Catholic. One of his favorite stories involved his mother running about sprinkling holy water throughout their little house in Rock Island, Illinois, as a big midwestern storm thundered down upon them. Although I seldom knew him to attend mass, in his later years a lay woman from the local parish came once a week to pray with him.

When he became very elderly, I cared for him. At a certain point, he was in a very nice board and care facility. He had his own apartment, and it was very homey. He was very happy there. He had recently turned ninety-four. We were joking about going for 100. Grandpa was so goal-oriented!

The past few days he had not been eating his normal three square meals, and he had declined to take his morning walk. He always left at 9:00 A.M., walked along the Palisades, watched the ocean, breathed the beautiful morning air, and then returned home at 10:00 A.M. Not eating and not walking were very much unlike him. He was fiercely independent and always insisted upon getting out and taking a morning walk with the salty morning air.

He lived his life in a very ordered manner. He had grown up on the Mississippi. His first job as a fourteen year old was as the "timekeeper and water boy" for a construction crew on the Rock Island Railroad. He always woke up around 5:30 A.M., dressed, and then sat in his rocking chair.

One Friday night as I said good-bye to him, there was a certain look in his eyes, which I had never before seen. Saturday morning when I awoke I thought I should go over right away to see him. When I got there, I sat beside him. His hands were folded neatly upon his chest. I was sitting beside him admiring the beauty of the skin on his hands. The skin was thin and nearly translucent. I was thinking I would like to hold his hand, but he was still sleeping. His breath was rhythmic and low. It was about 8:30 A.M. I then felt the room was too close. I went over and opened a window. His apartment faced the ocean in Santa Monica, so a beautiful breath of morning salt air came into the room.

I sat down again beside Grandpa. I was admiring his hands. At that moment he stopped breathing. I cried out to him: "Grandpa! Grandpa!" I rocked him in his bed. He breathed one more time. The ocean air was circling all about his bed. I looked out his window. Two Catholic priests were coming up the front walkway. I went out and told them to come into Grandpa's apartment. They did, and they gave him the last rites.

Only then did they tell me that they had come to visit someone else. I then realized that in the three or four years my grandfather had lived there, I had never seen nor heard of Catholic priests visiting. The priests were Irish, as was my grandfather.

For me both events are most synchronous and meaningful. Regarding the link in my mind, it is between them and my mother. My mother died most tragically. At the time there was discord and exploitation in our family—a major rupture. The family circle was broken. One of my mother's deepest desires was to find a way to renew and strengthen the love and the union in our family—to renew the family circle.

My mother and I were very close. People who knew her often remark on how much I seem like her—my manner, my voice, and so on. About a year after my mother died, she came to me. From a deep sleep I awoke to find her standing near the foot of my bed. She was like an apparition. She spoke to me, but I did not hear her with my ears, but rather with my heart. She told me that she was all right, that she would love me always, that everything would be all right, and that I should not worry. After her presence faded, I made certain I was awake, and then promised myself no one would ever convince me that this had not occurred. From that time forward, I have always felt her near me.

Regarding my grandma, my experience of her death was extraordinary. I think that my mother was with her, and together they called to me. My role, I think, was to work toward renewing and strengthening the family circle with my mother and grandmother, and to give my grandmother strength as she died. Regarding Grandpa, my experience of his death was extraordinary, also. My grandfather was very orderly, with a strong emphasis upon time. When he knew he was going to die, he arranged himself nicely in bed (hands folded on chest), he waited until morning, somehow I was called to be there, and I went. I was then directed to open the window, which I did. With the salty morning sea breeze, Grandpa was called by the spirit of the waters, and he went out. He "left" just about the time of his usual morning walk. Instead of walking in his physical body, he went as a spirit. In fact, I feel he still strolls along the Palisades. The arrival within three minutes of the Irish Catholic priests was extraordinary.

Since earliest childhood, I have had prescient dreams. For me the challenge is to find a way to bridge the outer world with the inner world and to meet whatever challenge this requires. These experiences did, I suppose, reinforce my belief in my own inner guidance.

—*Anonymous*

SECRETS

It was a bitter cold February. My mother had been in the hospital for a prolonged period of time. I was going to her house three times a week to feed the cat, Ti, and water the plants.

I stopped in one morning to find the apartment very cold. Tapping the thermostat did nothing, so when I got to work I called the super.

The next day, I stopped by to find my mother's apartment a shambles and her cat lying dead in the snow on the patio. We surmised that the super had not bothered to show up, knowing my mother was in the hospital, and in the bitter cold night the pipes froze. Everything was soaked with water, plants were knocked over, pictures on the wall were askew. Probably the cat trying to escape the steam.

The super later admitted that he had thrown the cat's body out into the snow, but hadn't known who to call.

All I could think of was how to tell my mother her cat was dead and most of her belongings were destroyed. Driving to the hospital that evening, I went through a series of ideas and finally decided I would try not to say anything. But it is very hard for me to keep secrets from her, especially ones that directly affect her.

I walked into her room and normally she would be lying listlessly on her pillow, giving me a weak kiss and wanting to go back to sleep. This evening she sat bolt upright as I entered.

"Guess what?" she said. "When I awoke from my nap this afternoon, Ti was sitting over in that chair staring at me."

I felt the color drain from my face, and through my tears I broke down and told her the story. For some reason, she patted my hand, shrugged it off, and said we would never mention it again.

If I learned anything, it was that I simply couldn't keep secrets from her, she'd find out the truth somehow.

—Jeanie Quinn

TWO PATIENTS

16 November 1993, Sao Paolo, Brazil

I saw a patient in my office for the first time. She was a twenty-six-year-old woman named S, the daughter of an owner of a Japanese restaurant my brother goes to, and who was referred to me by him.

She had a strange skin condition. White spots on the skin resembling a skin disease called *Pityriasis alba,* but it was hard to diagnose and treat. She told me she'd been to other dermatologists before coming to me. I explained to her that her case was not serious and gave her my treatment.

22 November 1993

I saw another patient, also her first visit. She was also a twenty-six-year-old Oriental woman also named S, who was the same age as the first woman (indeed their birth dates were only eight days apart). She was referred to me by my brother-in-law's sister. So the two patients don't know each other and have no connections, whatsoever.

Strangely enough, she had the same skin condition. I also had difficulty giving her a precise diagnosis, but definitely the two patients had the same condition.

Later, I discussed their cases with other colleagues and found out that they also saw similar cases of the same disease. It's not serious and also not contagious. In the medical field, this phenomenon of seeing patients with a very rare disease successively, is known as "Velpeau's Law."

Don't ask me how this can happen. Just coincidence? I definitely have to do some more research. I haven't seen these patients for a long time. All I know is that one of them is living in Tahiti now.

—*Roberto Takaoka*

NO COINCIDENCE

I spent ten years participating in an organization where we were taught there are no coincidences. Of course, at first I did not believe it—but there was much that felt good and right about this place and these people, and I have a very curious mind. So I kept watching, watching, and it soon became clear that it was true—and had been true, even before I noticed it. Since then, there have been many wonderful noncoincidences in my life—and many upsetting ones.

But the one—or series—which completely changed my life was the manner of my participation in my mother's death. I had been able to come to terms with my old issues about her well before my brother-in-law called me to say she was dying. When he did call one Saturday morning, I immediately booked a compassionate fare flight to Chicago to be with her. She had been able to arrange hospice care, and she was at home in her little house next door to my sister and her kids. My one thought was to make sure she would not die alone.

When I got to Chicago, my mother was already involuting, turning inward and preparing for death, although I did not know that. I knew nothing, then, of what it means to make that enormous transition from life to death—but I sensed she had all she could deal with in any case and didn't take it personally. That night, I helped her into bed as the hospice nurse hooked her up to the morphine pump that was the doctor's compromise between what she wanted—to go, easily, peacefully, and quickly—and what he needed to feel right. My mother went into the fetal position as soon as she lay down—and I didn't know what that meant either. Then, when the nurse left, I sort of half sat and half lay on the bed—puzzled at the feeling of being torn between wanting to hold her and the residue of a lifelong inability to hug or be close to her.

I eventually lay on the bed sort of hugging her from behind and tried to bring her peace in the otherwise empty, silent room. I had no idea whether she would awake again that night, or ever. At about 11:00 P.M., I decided to go to bed—certain in a deep and utterly serene way that I would awaken when I needed to be there for her passing. I fell asleep easily with no trace of fear or anguish. About 6:00 A.M., while it was dark and still, I awoke for no apparent reason. I went into her room to give her another, *extra* dose of the morphine—as my sister and I had promised. As soon as I walked the few feet to her room and did so, I could tell the end was near.

I lay there on her bed and watched and waited. Her breathing became shallower and shallower, and soon I could tell she was not really breathing. Her lungs were filling up, but I don't know if I knew that then or if I guessed or if I have found it out since. In any case, I lay there in a state of awe as her breathing became, clearly, a mere reflex of the medulla. It felt as profound as I hope it sounds—and the feeling I had was one of profound, still, and utter peace. The only thoughts I remember having were of a different nature than any other thoughts I have ever had—it was as though my mind were completely and almost eerily quiet. And yet thoughts did form, and one was that I was where I was supposed to be, doing what I was supposed to be doing, probably for the first and only time in my life. There was no fear and no pain, only a pervading sense of profound, numinous awe and serenity.

As she drew her last breath, I looked calmly at the clock by her bedside to be able to tell the proper authorities the time of death, and I picked up the phone to call next door to tell my sister and brother-in-law. I don't remember much of what happened right after that—it's sort of a blur—but I believe without even the faintest doubt that it was no coincidence that I had awakened when I did to be with the last moments of my mother, Marjorie W. Price.

I have since learned many other things about the act of dying, including the fact that most people die in the wee hours when their relatives have left—apparently because the relatives are holding to them, and only thus can they go in peace. I doubt that it is a coincidence that I was in the right spiritual place at the right time to be able to provide a loving transition to my mother, with no fear or holding or trauma for either of us.

—*Carroll Strauss*

THE STOLEN JEWELS

Back in the '60s, when I was braless and raising organic horseradish in a rural California community, my partner and I and a good friend of ours were scraping by making handmade silver jewelry. We had been accepted to a local but prestigious craft fair, nestled deep in the California redwoods, having passed muster by submitting slides to a jury. We worked hard for a few weeks with hammer and torch, then took our handcrafted wares and offered them for sale.

Not having a display case at that time, we laid our work out among rocks and crystals on a beautiful cloth supported by a low table, in our allotted space in the fragrant redwoods, along with fifty or sixty other craftspeople selling their wares: etchings, fabric paintings, musical instruments, weaving, sculpture, pottery, and the like. The smell of hot falafel, apple cider, and other fair food wafted our way. There was a confident elation among the three of us friends. We sold a few things and were generally pleased with ourselves.

At one point in the early afternoon of the second day, I don't remember exactly when, we had slumped into a kind of trance of fractured attention. It was the '60s, and we were partly lulled by the fair atmosphere: the bright sights of tie-dye, glimpses of marvelous things, soft notes of a dulcimer, and the rising and falling of mingled children's and adult's voices and dogs barking or whining. Perhaps we were following our natural ultradian rhythms or perhaps it had been the couple of jovial fair goers who offered to pour a little rum into the coffee. We would rouse from the atmosphere only when a would-be-buyer would directly engage one of us about the techniques used to make, say, a hawk ring, or how we etched the silver to create a watery effect around a whale bracelet.

Then, in one important moment, V realized the display table looked practically empty—that a number of our pieces had disappeared, they'd been stolen! Shocked and sickened, we tallied sales and found about fifteen pieces missing.

How could it have happened? Had we been asleep? Naive? Incredulous, we rummaged through the possibilities. No leads appeared. Reality was hard: We were poor, and we had been ripped off. Sobered, we deputized ourselves, sadly walked among the fair goers in turn, suspiciously gazing with sly, determined looks at fingers and lapels, casting an eye for our stolen work. It was the only remedy we could think of.

The good thing had been ruined. There were few pieces left to sell and not much spirit among us. People ceased to respond to our empty table. Prospects seemed dim; when V suggested we pack up and leave, we agreed. In mid-afternoon, taking our losses, we set out on the winding coast road home. We didn't speak for the first miles, all staring at the road. The radio seemed out of tune, no comfort, and each sank into his own thoughts, silently.

V's mind, always a little different, suggested we celebrate. Celebrate a loss? It went against my grain. Unbeknownst to us, he had bought a bottle of champagne. Lacking alcohol awareness, we did the unadvisable and opened the bottle and sipped it driving in our colorfully decorated International Harvester van with the ocean on our left, the preceding events falling behind us.

Ten or fifteen miles into the trip, we came on two hitchhikers in the dry brush by the roadside, and again, against my grain, V stopped (he was driving) and offered them a ride. Three more burst out, laughing, almost menacing, from behind a bush and piled into the truck, which had ample room for all. We went on our journey down the coast road, and then the amazing thing happened: We noticed that they were all wearing our jewelry!

All of us were equally stunned. They were trapped in our moving truck, and, after a few exchanges of stricken looks, they returned the jewelry, and we celebrated with the remaining champagne. We were still missing two or three things but got almost all of it back. They got out at the next big town, and we all made our way back home.

I have never forgotten this experience. For me, it was V's attitude that taught me something. It was to celebrate and share, no matter what your circumstance. It was a way of sticking to the high road. I had gotten all wrapped up in the situation. Had I not agreed to celebrate, I would have remained angry and melancholy, isolating myself to lick my wounds, which was a low road for me. V was detached, ready to move on; it was one event, a learning opportunity for him. There was nothing more we could do; we needed to move on.

He broke the cycle. Celebrating ended it. He refused to be dragged down by the circumstances. Since the other two of us participated, we came full circle by being willing to participate in that reality. What are the chances of this happening, I ask myself?

The thieves were equally shocked. I have always wondered what they made of it, or what lessons they took from it. In that moment, we were all just people, confronting a situation. It reminded me of stories from the Bible; it was a moment of grace.

—*Patricia Murphy*

I REMEMBER

I remember the magically lyrical sound of the red-winged blackbird, a sound I have never heard outside of the north Rio Grande Valley area of Albuquerque, New Mexico. Its cadence has a liquid percussive quality, much the same as that of the sound of running water over small, smooth stones.

I remember the fat, puffed-out roadrunner sunning itself on top of the old stump at 7:00 o'clock in the morning. Steam rose from its back, as well as from everything else around it as the sun stretched its long, warm fingers through the previous night's chill. Eventually, the roadrunner would shake itself, take a long, graceful jump to the ground, and streak its way down the road next to the field of Johnson grass.

It was in that field where my cousin Teresa and I almost lost our lives.

We were about six years old, playing in the grass that was much taller than we were. We heard my father circling the field in the tractor. Mounted on the front was an eight-foot row of steel cutting blades. He was mowing the field! Unbeknownst to him, Teresa and I thought it was fun to play hide-and-seek with him.

The noise of the tractor got louder as my father's circular path got smaller. He finally had only a small patch of grass left in the middle of the field when something told him to stop.

He shut off the tractor and looked at the remaining grass: our hideout. All around the field lay the cruel remains of a once-majestic forest, our childhood jungle now slashed and dying, the air pungent with the milky bleeding of the thick Johnson stalks.

It was all we could do to suppress our giggling. We were virtually unaware of the possibility that the bleeding in the field that day might not be only white.

My father called out our names. We were discovered! The game was over. As we sheepishly emerged from our hiding place, he must have died a thousand deaths realizing what could have happened in that field.

Thirty-nine years later, because my father paid attention to an inner voice, I am able to sit here and write, "I remember. . ."

I have always admired the sixth sense that women seem to have, such as their innate connection to their children. My father proved that day that men have it, too. We just need to be a little more grounded to be in tune with our feelings and to listen to them.

—*Stuart Balcomb*

PREMONITION

During my studies to be a psychologist, I took course work and personal training in hypnotherapy. Toward the end of a session, as I was coming out of trance, I remarked to my therapist, quite unrelated to the issues I had been working on, that my father's death would coincide with the ending of my marriage. (At the time my father was well and I had no intent of divorce.)

Many years later, after I had completely forgotten about the session, which I had discussed with no one else, my husband and I did separate.

Several days later, and one hour before my thirteenth wedding anniversary, I received a call from my mother.

"Your father is dead," I heard her voice saying through the phone.

My father and I had always been very close, and I felt confused and abandoned at this time during the loss of my marriage. But, when I remembered the premonition I had shared with my therapist years earlier, I felt a sense of peace knowing that my father knew I had attained some resolution in my life.

Also, I experienced a strong conviction that there is an all-knowing divine order to the events that affect our lives.

—*Lois V. Nightingale*

FOR THE BIRDS

Recently, my cousin Rob died on the Isle of Wight where he lived. He was a keen countryman, having a particular interest in bird-life, and loving nothing more than the sound and sight of geese which inhabit the island.

His cremation took place on the mainland at the town of Aldershot, Hampshire, in the south of England. A large gathering of the family emerged from the service to chat and greet each other on the lawns.

Then, with immaculate timing and joy to Rob's widow and the family, a flight of geese flew directly overhead, apparently honking their farewell to an admirer.

—*Nick Charrington*

IV. The Grace of Great Things

A young woman sits near a fountain in the Botanischer Garden. She comes here every Sunday to smell the white double violets, the musk rose, the matted pink gilly-flowers. Suddenly, her heart soars, she blushes, she paces anxiously, she becomes happy for no reason. Days later, she meets a young man and is smitten with love. Are the two events not connected? But by what bizarre connection, by what twist in time, by what reversed logic?

In this acausal world, scientists are helpless. Their predictions become post-dictions. Their equations become justifications, their logic, illogic. Scientists turn reckless and mutter like gamblers who cannot stop betting. Scientists are buffoons, not because they are rational but because the universe is irrational. Or perhaps it is not because the cosmos is irrational but because they are rational. Who can say which, in an acausal world?

In this world, artists are joyous. Unpredictability is the life of their paintings, their music, their novels. They delight in events not forecasted, happenings without explanation, retrospective.

—Alan Lightman, *Einstein's Dreams*

For as far back as we know, human beings have sought out signs, omens, augurs, and patterns for a glimpse into the hidden order of life, a hint of the future, and more specifically, their own destiny. The gloriously unpredictable stories of people's lives have captivated audiences from the early cave fires to today's biographies in print or on film because they dramatically reveal the entire arc of a single human life, which allows us to see the myriad possibilities for the journey of the soul. Within the pages of our favorite biographies are an accumulation of details that can reveal the very workings of fate and destiny. Often, their lives, in retrospect, reveal a series of tantalizing coincidences that suggest how a life can be linked together. One of the most emblematic episodes of this kind concerns Abraham Lincoln, and is retold here by Ira Progoff in his study, *Jung, Synchronicity and Human Destiny*:

"One day a stranger came to Lincoln with a barrel full of odds and ends. He said that he was in need of money and that he would be much obliged if Lincoln would help him out by giving him a dollar for the barrel. The contents, he said, were not of much value; they were some old newspapers and things of that sort. But the stranger needed the dollar very badly. . . . Lincoln, with his characteristic kindness, gave the man a dollar for the barrel even though he could not imagine any use that he would have for its contents. Some time later, when he went to clear out the barrel, he found that it contained almost a complete edition of Blackstone's *Commentaries*. It was the chance, or synchronistic, acquisition of these books that enabled Lincoln to become a lawyer and eventually to embark on his career in politics."

This mysterious faculty at work in the world has long dazzled human beings. The Persian poet, Mevlana Rumi, indisputably one of the great voices in all world literature, in "One-Handed Basket Weaving," tells the grisly tale of a man who is accused of stealing and so loses one of his hands to the chopping block. However, he goes on to defy fate by learning to weave with one hand and becomes a master basket maker, prodding his neighbors to wonder about the presence of the invisible helping hand.

As with many Sufi stories, Rumi's tale is a parable of the "prepared soul" (in contrast to the "prepared mind" of the traditional scientist), one who is able to recognize the unfolding possibilities of fate and destiny in each moment, and be aware of the hidden forces that are there to help guide us even through calamity. Recently, mythologist Joseph Campbell, in conversation with journalist Bill Moyers in *The Power of Myth*, described the miracle of the "helping hands," phenomenon, that mysterious appearance of allies in the world who help us when we stumble on the dark path through the forest of life.

Another version of this ancient story of being helped by unseen forces comes from the creator of the legendary *Twilight Zone* television series, Rod Serling. It seems that Serling was gravely wounded at the end of World War II and was hospitalized for many months of recuperation. As if a plot point in a movie script, the U.S. Army offered the wounded soldier either basket weaving or creative writing to take his mind off the war and distract him from his pain, and, who knows, possibly prepare him for the future. Serling picked the writing class and began to write himself back to life. The rest is history, at least in that "fifth dimension beyond that which is known to man," as he eerily wrote as the opening to his legendary show.

Then there is the destiny-driven story scripted for Broadway but never produced, then sold for a pittance to the movie studios. This war-time melodrama about a bitter expatriate exiled in a remote African country who opens a bar and prepares to drink himself to death. One night, as he's mooning over the woman who left him in Paris for another guy she coincidentally walks into his bar—"of all the gin joints in all the world."

Everybody Comes to Rick's, better known by the celluloid version, *Casablanca,* is regarded in poll after poll, year after year, as the greatest American romance movie ever made, prodding two generations of film critics to ask *why?* And two generations of audiences to resist analysis and bask in the romance. "The long arm of coincidence" reached out and touched the project from beginning to end.

On the very day that FDR asked for a declaration of war, an alert story reader at Warner Brothers became intrigued by a timely play set in Casablanca and helped transform it into a script. The Hungarian director Michael Curtiz, as chance would have it, was a war refugee himself, lending him a special affinity for the exiled characters who frequented "Rick's." One of the writers happened to remember a song he'd heard several years before, "As Time Goes By," and chose it to be the theme song for the movie and a metaphor for the existential stance all the characters take on. In the revelation scene between the husband, Viktor Lazlo (Paul Henreid) and our (anti) hero, Rick Blaine (Humphrey Bogart), the resistance leader reveals his knowledge of Bogie's love for Ilsa (Ingrid Bergman), inspiring Bogie to say, "It seems that destiny has taken a hand." Then on November 8, 1942, Allied troops seized the city of Casablanca from the Vichy French, the first significant victory against the Nazis since Hitler's invasion of Poland in 1939. Suddenly the name Casablanca was everywhere, a fortuitous twist of fate for the production. Then, several months after its wildly successful release, in early 1943, as if blessed by the gods, Roosevelt and Churchill met in Casablanca for one of their historic wartime conferences.

A multitude of chance happenings had combined to create around the script, the actors, and the popularity of the movie, an aura of destiny.

The splendid stories in this last section reverberate with comparable transformations of happenstance into destiny. They display the kind of conviction that Ernest Becker called for in his book, *The Denial of Death*. Objective creativity, says Becker, is the only answer to the problem of life. "Who knows what form the forward momentum of life will take in the time ahead," he asks, "or what use it will make of our anguished searching. The most any one of us can seem to do is to fashion something—an object, ourselves—and drop it into the confusion, make an offering, so to speak, to the life force."

The common theme was beautifully articulated by the French sculptor Auguste Rodin to his then-secretary, the German poet, Rainer Maria Rilke, that if one does the work proper to one's true vocation, "the grace of great things" will come naturally.

In one of the most powerful stories in this entire collection, the legendary Lithuanian mountain climber Vladas Vitkauskas passionately describes how he "chanced upon" an unmistakable "sign of destiny" when he noticed a "strange coincidence" between his life and that of the first man to climb Mount Everest, Sir Edmund

Hillary. His ability to stop and take notice of that single detail eventually led to his maverick career as climber of the world's seven highest mountains, upon which he planted his newly revived country's flag. What to others may have been "mere chance" turned into a profound synchronicity, the sudden realization that "Everest was my destiny and meaning of life."

In Alexander Eliot's story, we find a particularly pithy phrase, "a greater present moment," that signals the atmosphere of synchronicity, a place where, as Terrence A. Taylor, writes, "Things were re-solving themselves." For Leila M. Reese, her event reveals a "great part of the mystery of life," what transpires "when souls communicate." In "God Moments," by Betty Rosen, the value of synchronicities in her life is how they become learning devices, a place where one connection leads to another and "everything unfolds"—if she pays attention. The series of coincidences that led Elisabetta Orlandi to her dream job shine for her like a web.

Other telltale phrases and key themes include the sudden realization, in Pohsuan Zaide's story that "something was telling me there were deeper things," and that she should allow herself to be guided by her heart and soul.

To Judy Issac Conley, her remarkable encounter on a flight to Europe was heart-opening, a phenomenon, she writes, which "engendered wonder."

We conclude with two of the most stirring stories in the collection, from two of our preeminent writers, Tess Gallagher and Huston Smith. In Gallagher's remarkable story, precognition combines with a poet's artistic vision. Two visions overlap with deadly accuracy, so moving she allows them to guide her to a trembling new discovery about her own imagination. As she writes elsewhere, "There is so much we must be witness to." In "Lost in Africa," a story that he has said in conversation is "very dear to my heart," Smith confirms my long-held suspicion that the true heart of the mystery of synchronicity lies in the realm of human connection, not how and why, but when and where. His humble tale of being lost on the Serengeti Plains, spying the bones of other dead animals and seeing his own impending fate there, then being saved by a dozen rollicking Masai warriors is a tale for all time, and reaffirms, as he writes, "the unity that binds us."

Again and again, what emerges in this last section are vivid testimonies to the vital difference between the times when, as Jung said, "chance strikes out of the blue," and the true experience of synchronicity tends "to happen to people when they need it. . . ."

MY MOUNTAIN, MY DESTINY

The world's tallest mountain in Nepal, Chomolungma, Tibet, is known as Sagarmatha to the natives and as Mount Everest to the rest of the planet. It measures 8,846 meters in height. The way up to the summit of Mount Everest is different for each climber.

My climb started in May of 1953, on the day I was born. By a strange coincidence, it was also in May of 1953 that New Zealander Edmund Hillary and Sherpa Tenzing Norgay won the race to be first on Everest's summit. It continued forty years later, in 1993, when I became a part of the second Lithuanian expedition to attempt to raise the national tricolor at the top of Everest, which I had grave doubts about taking part in. But I had chanced upon Tenzing's book about Everest, which I vaguely remembered from my childhood, and I saw the light again. When I read his book I understood it wasn't just his life, but it was my life also.

These coincidences are yet another sign of destiny. I always believed that the age of forty was an important milestone: You must achieve something before this age. So forty years after his own ascent, in the small Himalayan village of Khumjung, Sir Hillary wished me luck in my attempt to scale the mountain. His farewell words came true: After a month, on May 10, 1993, I reached the top of the world. At the height of nearly nine kilometers I left a Lithuanian national tricolor, a handful of ambers from the Baltic Sea, and a photo of my Latvian friend, Aivars Bojars, who had died three months earlier on Elbrus (5,633 meters high) in the Caucasus. Together we had been planning to top Everest, but after Bojars' death I had to make all the preparations alone. Seven weeks were spent in exhausting work and acute tension: four weeks in Vilnius, Lithuania, and three weeks in Katmandu.

Money was what I needed most of all. Many climbers have to

pay $40,000 or more to participate in an Everest expedition. To me, this sum of money seemed preposterous. I, however, never lost hope. Having secured a loan of $5,000 with the help of my friends in Vilnius, I headed to the Himalayas and joined a Nepalese women's team as a photographer. I was twenty days late, therefore, a loner's fate awaited me in the mountains.

Unaccompanied, I walked from one camp to another, crossed crevices in ice walls, battled the fierce winds of the Himalayas, and suffered from high-altitude sickness. It was very hard, but I was ready to face any and all difficulties that arose. I had spent twenty summers in the Caucasus, Tien Shan, Altai, and Pammir. In the autumn of 1992, together with Bojars and nine other mountaineers from Lithuania, we made an unsuccessful attempt to reach Everest from the northern (Tibetan) side. However, I never stopped believing that Everest was my destiny and the meaning of my life.

Finally, the mountain accepted me. Surrounded by snow and glaciers, I merged with the mountains and the cosmos. I felt vibrating links with my homeland, Lithuania, and with the people who had helped me, prayed for me, and were waiting for my safe return. The gear no longer cut painfully into my shoulders, I did not feel the severe beating of my heart, and the strain of my tired muscles was gone.

Time stopped, and I realized that it was impossible to conquer the mountains. They had no mercy for those who came here to become victorious, famous, or rich.

After seven hours of climbing, I reached the summit. Imagine stairs leading to the sky, without a rail or a wall, hanging on a flying aircraft. Stairs covered with ice, plus a concentration of poisonous gases and a lack of oxygen. Each time I wanted to rest, I had to solve a dilemma—shall I remain standing or shall I sit down. If I sit down, I'll have to get up again. After each step, not bigger than one-half of a foot, I had to take four breaths before I could make another step.

On the summit I felt no euphoria, although I had expected some relief. Every movement—taking out the camera, taking off the cover—required enormous effort. The only moment of relaxation was when I saw the Lithuanian flag flying, for me a symbol of Lithuanian freedom. It looked beautiful. I knew there were people back in Lithuania who were praying for me and waiting for me. I almost saw the stream of their energy, like a silver band in the expanse. Later and only after a good night's sleep did I start returning to my real self.

I wasn't sure I could go back down the mountain. My real quest had been to reach the summit. I feared that I might not come back; I don't know why except that it might be fear. After reaching the summit I understood. I had a lot of problems. The climb down was very dangerous. Twice I fell on the ice into crevices. I was able to stop from falling not for materialistic reasons, but because of the power of the world, God, and of nature; that helped me. I think I lived because I thought of my children living without me, their father, so I was able to put my arms out and stop my fall of 300 meters down the mountain.

During the three weeks on Everest's flanks, I witnessed the deaths of Pasang Lhamu, leader of the Nepalese women's expedition, and one of her team guides, two South Korean climbers, and the nephew of the first-to-Everest Sherpa Tenzing Norgay. In this seemingly cruel realm of the mountains, I once again came to understand that human life was not measured by the day. We are still unaware of our possibilities. Their materialization depends on our insight, belief, and effort. Each person can have his or her own Mount Everest. And it does not necessarily need to be the highest mountain peak in the world. If you want something very much, nothing else has any importance.

Now I tell children about the mountains and see the light of dreams in their eyes. It may encourage them to seek higher peaks, in life as well as in the mountains; that would be the most significant result of my flag march to the seven highest peaks on the five continents, both to me and to Lithuania.

—*Vladas Vitkauskas*

FATE

I returned to Sarasota, Florida, in July 1982 after nearly a year of working as a showgirl/dancer and lion tamer in a traveling Mexican circus. I felt that I had experienced every emotion known to human animals during that time in Mexico.

And then there I was, back in neat, clean, predictable Sarasota with a huge question mark hanging over me: What next? I could go back to school, but that thought left my inner self feeling limp. Sitting in a classroom once again after I had experienced so many other worlds a world away felt impossible, ludicrous.

In the middle of my panic, I was offered a job working with twelve Bengal tigers in a circus act permanently established in Orlando, Florida. At first, the thought was scary. I was afraid that if I did not turn my back on circus work and close that door, I could get caught up in animal acts and show business forever. I wanted to do something that meant something to me. I started getting severe headaches. I was sick to my stomach with confusion. Deadlines for applying to graduate school had arrived. The circus wanted a yes or a no.

On the day I had to make a decision, a letter arrived in the mail with a Belize postmark. The letter said,

I know you know who I am, and I know who you are. We have a mutual friend in Chuck Hettel. I am in desperate need of a film assistant, because the woman who had been working for me went back to Australia. I know that you have worked with animals. I know that you have been in Belize and know what to expect. I am only asking for a month's commitment from you. Enclosed is a round-trip ticket to Belize.

Sincerely, Richard Foster

It was an incredible coincidence. I knew Chuck from a dive operation two years prior, when I worked at a marine biology lab that was located in a cave off the mainland of Belize. Chuck mentioned the filmmaker Richard Foster to me during that time.

I put my belongings in storage and left to work on a film project for a month, which turned into two months. When the film was finished, Richard was sent to Borneo to complete another film for the parent film company in England. I was left behind to be the caretaker of his property and to find homes for the animal film stars, because there were no funds to care for the menagerie.

Sitting alone one night, a guy named Big John from Alaska happened by to pay a visit. He saw that I was not getting rid of any animals and that I was putting up a sign to charge anyone a dollar who stopped in to see them. People from the nearby British army camp who knew Richard would stop by for a "lovely day out."

Finally Big John said, "You could always start a zoo!"

And I did.

We now have more than thirty acres of land with 100 species here, including jaguarundi, tapir, ocelot, exotic birds, and an anteater who's become the national animal! It changed the way the people of Belize view the animals of their country. Sometimes I wonder what Belize would be like if the zoo had not been born then, in January 1983.

I would have to say that the intrigue of watching connections happen within the human mind regarding the understanding of the natural environment has fueled me through the difficult years of running the zoo. From the beginning of this project, I was excited to provide the connection between the wild facet of Belize and its people. That initial idea has metamorphosed into an education effort of grander proportions: providing the resources for the comprehensive understanding of the natural environment of Belize to the people living here, who are so eager for this knowledge. This is accomplished through a very thorough training course about the country's natural history, a course designed and implemented at our Tropical Education Center.

The incident helped confirm for me that the dream world is the world of imagination. The world of imagination is the theater where creativity is born. The creative spirit is destined for impact only if it leaves the arena of its creation and enters the world for its effect. The zoo, and the evolution of our environmental education programs, expresses the concept of the growth and evolution of creative idea over time.

—*Sharon Matola*

GOD MOMENTS

Your blue might be gray
Your less might be more
Your window to the world could be your own front door
Your shiniest day might come in the middle of the night . . .
That's just about right.

—*Jeff Black*

What others call synchronicity I have come to name *God Moments.* I began to notice them early on in my life. "Pay attention," as Ken Kesey says, "Look! They're everywhere!"

The most recent is a series of of new beginnings, which took place at the Penland (North Carolina) School of Crafts. Penland is precisely where I learned the value of a series of synchronicities as a learning device, a way to persist and to see an idea through. The background story includes glassblowing, shadow artistry, the music business, an ancient Jewish prayer called the *shehechyanu,* and a seven-week-old puppy named Scout.

For a few years now, I've been increasingly and intensely dissatisfied with how I am spending most of my time. It's a pure hot white anger. It's not that I hate my job; it's that I fell in love with another one. Yet, the commitment to the craft of blowing hot glass seems to require more than most craft hobbies; it seems it can no longer be a precarious promise.

The tools for glassblowing are not as simple as easels and watercolors or even a photographer's darkroom. The process is challenging, requiring travel, megaheat, electricity, light, annealing ovens, furnaces, blowpipes, and the same style of benches and metal tools they've used everyday for centuries. It's collaborative, dangerous, immediate, and fiercely hard.

My work in Nashville, running a music publishing company, seems to be the antithesis of glassblowing, with its long-term gains. Publishing has its long-term gains, but rarely a sense of immediate progress. Most often it's a solitary process with uncertain rewards. In my job I'm an enabler, and a damn good one on my good days. I've discovered the source of the hot white light in all of this. The problem is that no matter how creative my input or contributions, the outcome is not *my* work.

On my list of things I'd hoped to do at Penland, marble-making was the one item left in my journal without a line slashed through it. So, when I recently read that one of the largest international Marble Festivals was going to be held in nearby Smithville, I felt lured. When I saw that a demonstration was scheduled for Friday afternoon at the Craft Center where I took my first "Hot Glass" workshop, I wanted to go.

But as luck would have it, work engulfed me, and by six o'clock Thursday night I felt sorely tested, then finally decided I couldn't break away, though good friends kept insisting that I go.

That night I called my cousin, Mark, a healer, who helped me after a horrid car accident several years ago. He was getting married for the second-and-a-half time, so to speak, and I wanted to tell him personally that I couldn't be there and also ask for his help with our aunt who was having back pain.

We chatted for a while, and he asked me if I knew the English translation to the prayer, the *shehechyanu*. I told him I didn't but that I'd call my rabbi the next morning for a translation and fax it to him. I couldn't remember the significance of the prayer, so I asked Mark why he chose the *shehechyanu,* and he answered with a story about a man who said a hundred prayers a day. When he was finished with all of his prayers, the man had forty left. He then said forty *shehechyanus:*

> Blessed art Thou, Lord our God, Creator of the universe
> who has kept us in life and sustained us and enabled us
> to reach this season.

When asked why he said them, the man said it was because this prayer blessed new beginnings. He said that he recited the *shehechyanu* forty times a day to help him appreciate each new moment.

On Friday morning, I was repapering Scout's new digs on the floor, in the back room, with the newspaper I'd copped from the local coffeehouse since I don't subscribe. I opened one spread of the paper and laid it out on the floor. Staring back at me was a review of the Marble Festival complete with directions and details of the demonstration at the Craft Center.

Fine, I thought, a nod in the direction of Smithville. Coincidence. But at the moment I'm not making a connection or remembering the *shehechyanu* or blessing new beginnings. I'm cleaning up after a seven-week-old Labrador-spaniel mutt, stressing out over it, and thinking, *There's not enough time to do it all and who the hell am I to think I could be a glass artist? Just go to work, damn it, and be grateful for the steady paycheck from someplace at least involved in the arts. . . .*

I grabbed another clump of newspaper. Feeling pissed off, scared, and confused, I knelt down on the floor and opened the pages. What lay before me was the exact same article—the same feature about the Marble Festival—revealing itself once more.

No longer pissed, I laughed out loud!

One God Moment was not enough for me. It was the *series*, I tell you.

The drive to Smithville was gorgeous.

At the glass blowing demonstration I reconnected with my first two glass teachers and firmed up plans to assist them. I got names and numbers to buy a microwave kiln, as well as the number of a woman who runs a gallery in Italy that I hope to visit one day.

One connection led to another.

In essence, the half day I spent there has kept the glass rolling in my life. It gave me momentum and inspired me in my new-found art. It celebrated my new beginning.

So now, as I wrestle between music and glass, I feel as if I'm negotiating for a new life and making baby steps toward the next precarious leap of faith. I have the *shehechyanu* to remind me to celebrate each of these new moments, whatever the path.

When I continue to believe and act as if I am an instrument of God, everything unfolds itself to me. If I pay attention—especially pay attention—to the newness of things and the awe of the newness of things, my fear subsides and I am welcomed.

I don't know if I will become a glass artist or a published writer, or if I will continue to be a music publisher, but I hope that by paying attention to the God Moments presented to me I will be of use to the universe, be able to use my skills, and will see the world through the eyes of an artist.

Gratefully, it's not all for me to decide.

—*Betty Rosen*

THE SWEET SMELL OF SYNCHRONICITY

David Grogan first contacted me in the late spring of 1995. Being a lively conversationalist, he grabbed my interest immediately with the rendition of his life-altering collision with the Campbell material. He ended with a dignified plea for more Joseph Campbell books, though, being a book addict myself, I could detect the near panic of one who realizes he's near the end of his "supply." With the instinctive compassion of a fellow sufferer, I asked him if he'd read *The Flight of the Wild Gander*. Finding that he had not, I pulled a copy off my shelf and sent it off with a note saying, "My favorite chapter is 'The Symbol Without Meaning.' In that chapter is the sentence that I find to be the most provocative in the entire book, but you'll find your own favorite ideas, I'm sure."

Imagine my astonishment when several weeks later, David called to thank me for the book and said, "Let me ask you something, Rebecca. What do you make of Joe's statement on page 189 of Wild Gander where he says, 'I believe there is a precise relationship between the format or stature of the psyche and the quantum of immediate experience that one is capable of sustaining and absorbing, and that the training and shaping of the mandala-conditioned psyche of the incomplete man of the agriculturally based societies has simply unfitted him for the reception of the full impact of any mysterium tremendum whatsoever.'"

This was the very same sentence I had underlined three times in red in my personal copy!

Even given Joe's propensity toward very long sentences, there have to be thousands of them in that chapter; hundreds of them so compelling and poetic in content and in style as to warrant being underlined in triplicate. Yet the fact is that David selected the same one. It alerted me to the fact that we were on similar tracks of consciousness.

This recognition prompted me in early 1996 to write to David with a proposal that he join me in a research project combining the works of Campbell with those of his long-time friend and associate, Ira Progoff. When David quickly agreed, I called Ira's son John and had him ship a set of books to David.

By this time, I was aware that David had removed himself from his former role as Protestant minister and was working and living in very humble circumstances—as a salesman in a local department store—so as to be able to further his burning curiosity for things of the spirit. In late spring, I called David with an exciting discovery of my own. While researching an entirely different project, I had uncovered an intriguing reference to Progoff in a biography of Emmanuel Swedenborg. In the same conversation, David floored me with what has to be one of the more astounding synchronicities in my memory: "Rebecca, let me ask you something. . . ." (David's favorite preamble!) "Do you know that reference to a Mr. Belk that Joe makes on page 246 of *Bakesheesh and Brahman?*"

I confessed I had no recollection of that name at all.

"Well, Rebecca, the footnote says that this Mr. Belk owned a chain of department stores in the South prior to becoming interested in parapsychology, and I know it sounds wild—the man who owns the store I work in is named Mr. Belk. Of course, he's too young to be the man named in Joe's book, but do you think I should write to him and ask?"

Of course, I heartily encouraged him to do so, already convinced that with his "mythological luck" it could be no other than the same Belk family! Sure enough, within another few weeks David called back in a tremendous excitement: Not only was *Joe's* Mr. Belk the grandfather of *David's* Mr. Belk, current chairman of Belk Store Services, but Mr. Belk II had sent David a copy of his grandfather's book, *A Cosmic Road Map and Guide Analysis,* which contained references to both Campbell and to Ira Progoff. In fact, Mr. Belk had an entire chart devoted to a comparison study of Progoff, Jung, and Hinduism!

A final cap to this delightful tale—as we ended our phone conversation, David lamented that he had run into a dead end trying to find a book on the poetry of Robinson Jeffers, Campbell's favorite poet. Everything was out-of-print, and in such a small town there was no likelihood of finding a copy in a library. Later that day, as I was walking in my hometown of Evanston, Illinois, I was suddenly drawn to enter a used bookstore I'd never frequented. (Evanston has a dozen of them, but I patronize only three or four.) I wandered randomly down the aisles and found myself (you guessed it) in the poetry section, where, standing nobly alone, was a handsome, hardback edition of the complete poetry of Robinson Jeffers. It was even marked down to half price!

I could smell a sweet synchronicity here, so I promptly purchased the book and sent it off to David, a man charged with the irrepressible good fortune of those who leave the beaten path and forge into the unknown, fired only by their deep conviction that the mythic life is the only life worth living, and that if you walk through the door that the universe has opened you will undoubtedly find your bliss—not to mention an endless supply of good books!

—*Rebecca Armstrong*

BORN FOR BOOKS

Cold November night. First time in Paris. I was walking along the Seine, smelling Paris, and letting my eyes be filled up by mobile shadows and lights still living in the sky and town. My boyfriend was with me, and I was trying to describe to him what Paris meant to me.

"You know," I said, "I feel there is a kind of strange link between Paris and me. I've never been here before, but I feel exactly as if I had already spent a part of my life right here on the Rive Gauche, as if I already knew sights, colors, sounds, streets, scents, people, and moods. Maybe I read about them somewhere. But where? and when?"

Suddenly, the words took form on my lips: "But this is how

Paris was in the early days, when we were very poor and very happy."

Movable Feast. Hemingway. A book read some years before that windy Parisian night, lent by a cousin I used to meet maybe twice a year. I had loved it. I had learned Paris by it, and I had almost forgotten it.

We went back up onto the main street, crossed it, and totally by chance found ourselves in front of Shakespeare and Company Bookstore. We went in. I was astonished. A castle made up by books! Books, books, books, everywhere! Nothing but books.

I wandered in that paradise for about two hours and finally I sat upstairs, in the children's corner, where only fairy tales are allowed to talk, and when they do they tell about elves, fairies, and magic. I let my hand run over hundreds of books that live up there. It stopped on one of them, what I thought was a collection of fairy tales. It wasn't. I had in my hand a copy of that *Movable Feast,* that same book that had moved in me the desire of coming to Paris and living there years before. I started reading, devouring it. But the bookstore was closing. So I went out. Ten steps and back, quickly to buy my copy, which was the last one in the shop. I spent that night going all over my book, and the following day going all over Paris, following Hemingway's eyes and his senses.

I was as happy as you are when you meet an old, beloved friend. I needed Paris, and I needed a place to stay when I came back from my home in Venice (because that's what I had to do; don't ask me why). But it should have been a very special place, between earth and sky, near the clouds, so as to see all Paris, and nearby the place where Hemingway used to rent a room to write: Rue Descartes, in the fifth *arrondissement.*

I told my dreams to a friend of mine, who was working at Shakespeare and Company Bookstore. And he answered me,

"Well, I know somebody living there. She had a room and she used to give hospitality to my friends. You could ask her if she can help." I went to her apartment, but she was not there, so I went home to Italy. She was in Paris, however, when I returned in May with my friend Pamela to spend a holiday in the wonderful town we had dreamed about since we were at primary school. Pamela met the mystery woman with the apartment, and they became friends and promised to accommodate us in the wonderful room we were dreaming.

The following autumn the two of us moved into her room on the Rue Descartes, under the roof and near the clouds and the wind and the wonderful sky of Paris.

I could go on telling you the story of my last year in Paris, a story that is maybe incredible, because it is made up of strange, wonderful facts, last but not least my getting a job at Shakespeare and Company Bookstore! I feel it as a web of shining, perfect little stars, linked up together like notes of a harmony, which is maybe written somewhere but not completely played. Not yet.

I just move (or am I moved?) from one shining little star to another, knowing I can't explain. I just live and believe.

—*Elisabetta Orlandi*

DESTINY

During the Iraq-Iran War in the mid-1980s, I was counseling an Iranian college student, who was very worried about his family. They had to leave their home, which was in the war zone.

Over a few sessions I searched for a way to ease his emotional pain. Thinking I could bring some spiritual flavor into the sessions, I showed him the book, *Autobiography of a Yogi.*

He reached into his satchel and, to my amazement, pulled out the same book. We were both practically on the same page.

This synchronicity seemed to bring a calm to the student. He knew that destiny was controlled by an essence greater than ourselves.

—*Rolf Gordhamer*

THE DEFINITION

One day, at the Jung Institute in San Francisco, about twenty years ago, the analysts were having a "family meeting" with the candidates, as analysts in training are called at our Institute, to discuss issues that had arisen in the training relationship. There was an anxious subtext to this experiment in direct confrontation: many of the analysts and quite a few of the candidates seemed unsure if the meeting itself was really a good idea, given that one group was charged with evaluating the other and had always conceived of the training experience as an initiation. The thought was that it was better perhaps to honor the relation of this 'initiation' to the traditional mysteries (in which the initiates were actually called mystes) by keeping its own group process somewhat in the dark.

Nevertheless, here we were, facing each other in the name of consciousness-raising, trying to get into the various problems that from the candidates' side, seemed to be asking for an airing. The meeting had just gotten underway when the telephone rang. As this was a Saturday, there was no receptionist at the Institute to answer, and so one of the candidates, Bill Goodheart, got up to answer the phone, which was in another room.

When he came back into the large meeting room in which we were all sitting in a circle struggling to encounter one another, Bill said to us, "You're not going to believe this: there's a woman on the phone asking for a definition of synchronicity!"

Jo Wheelwright, one of the founders of the Institute, and a strong believer in psychological democracy, spoke up. (I should mention that Jo, who was then about 70, had long established himself as the Jungian world's incomparable comedian.) "Tell that woman," he intoned, in his most authority-arrogating prep school nuisance voice, "madam, we are having a meeting. You have called in the middle of it. That is the opposite of synchronicity."

Everyone in the room laughed a long time, and I really think that after that, no one among us could seriously doubt that we ought to be meeting.

I never found out, though, what Bill actually told the lady on the phone.

—*John Beebe*

THE TASKS

I had the wrong job. It was 1986. I was supporting my writing by selling real estate. I loved meeting new people, hearing their stories, the treasure hunt of matching person to perfect place, but I hated financial and legal paper work.

I lived in a modest cottage with a heavenly view in Santa Fe, surrounded by federal land. Because I could walk all day in the arroyos and pinon-spotted hills around my home, and see no other human being, I decided to do a vision quest. I would walk and meditate for three days, seeing no one and making no phone calls, until I'd chosen a new career.

By the second day, I'd narrowed the choice to three possibilities: 1) teaching myth at St. John's College in Santa Fe, 2) being a forest ranger (the solitude would give me uninterrupted time for writing), and 3) being a traveling art dealer. (I'd always felt close to painting and artists. My sister and I had made books by hand as children; I'd write the stories, she painted the illustrations. I'd been to many art museums in Europe and America.)

On the third day, I decided that being a traveling art dealer would suit me perfectly. I was a natural agent; I believed in the value of art over almost everything; and I loved to travel. It would also bring me new experiences as a writer.

As I headed back to my house at dusk, it occurred to me that there were several obstacles in my path: namely, that I lacked a degree in art history, had no financial backing, and knew no art dealers. Also, I was not interested in being a shopkeeper, either in starting my own business, or sitting all day in someone else's gallery.

As I turned the key in the front lock, I heard the telephone ringing. It was my best male friend, a gifted painter named Richard.

"Hi," he said, "I just had a flash. This will sound off-the-wall to you, since I know you love your job. But I was just thinking about how you're the only person I know who talks about my paintings like a poet, and it occurred to me that the owner of my gallery has been looking for six months for someone to go on the road to sell paintings for the gallery. I don't know if this is something you've ever thought about, but I think you'd be perfect for the job."

"Richard," I said, smiling in wonder, "can you get me an appointment with her tomorrow?"

"Call you right back."

Moments later he called to say she'd meet me for lunch at noon the next day.

Ten minutes into the interview, she offered me the job.

My first client was the art curator for The Valley National Bank in Phoenix, Arizona.

"How strange that you should call right now," she said, "I'm in a big bind. I've curated two collections of art at one of our branches. The manager hated both of them. I'm afraid I'm going to lose my job if I don't find something to put in his bank that he likes. Can you meet with him this afternoon?"

Could I! After a conference with the man, I knew he wanted neither the on-the-edge experimental art she'd selected, nor any of the array of figurative and abstract art I carried. He wanted solid representational Western art—cowboys, Indians, and desert landscapes.

I made calls to artists and galleries in Santa Fe, and delivered the goods. The curator was so grateful, she invited me to fill two banks in Arizona with art, which I happily did.

The whole experience reminded me of the tale of Psyche and Eros. When Psyche is given seemingly impossible tasks by Aphrodite, she despairs, but various magical helpers come to her aid, and miraculously—to Psyche's surprise—the tasks are accomplished.

—*Kaaren Kitchell*

Direct Assistance

After eleven years of spiritual awakenings as a result of my recovery from alcoholism, I find there are still some amends to be made in my life. One especially has haunted me for a long time.

Last year, following a series of dreams, it became clear that it was time for me to find Vincent. We had been friends and lovers during the early '70s. We shared much love and a profound connection. I remember once we had what I feel was a cosmic experience *seconds* before what almost became a major car accident. There was a brightness surrounding us as we became aware that we had gone to our deaths together in another lifetime. We both felt this extraordinary experience, although the other two passengers in the car saw or felt nothing.

During our time together, Vincent and I experienced other similar phenomena, but my substance abuse ruined our relationship. I was always sorry and shameful about hurting him and losing his friendship.

But where would I begin to search? The last I had heard of him was that he got married and moved to Florida, but that was twenty years ago. I tried calling information in Florida, but there was no listing for him. Old friends who might have some ideas came up empty. I tried to find his brother and his father with no results. So I took it to a higher authority: I prayed. I even prayed to Vincent's mother, who had passed away when we were friends. For two weeks, I continued to pray and to look for my old friend.

One afternoon at work, I noticed a card at the back of my telephone message pad. It lists all the area codes for the United States. There were four area codes alone for the state of Florida. Suddenly, I found myself dialing information. I gave the operator Vincent's last name and oddly enough, she simply gave me his phone number. I sat there amazed. How could he *suddenly* be listed?

That evening I decided to call the number in Florida that information had given me. A woman answered. I explained who I was and why I was calling. She knew all about me and was very gracious, so we spoke for awhile. She was Susan, Vincent's wife.

When Vincent came home, he was quite surprised at finding me on his telephone! He got on the line and we talked for a long time, laughing and reminiscing. He was still the same sweet Vincent. It felt as if not a single day had passed between us. He was polite about my desire to make amends, but he didn't think it was necessary. We exchanged addresses and I promised to send him some photographs and music I still had of his.

Finally, I began to tell him about my search, my prayers, and, curiously, how that afternoon I got the telephone number from directory assistance.

He said that was impossible. For as long as they had lived in Florida, they were unlisted. An astonished Susan picked up the extension and told us that exactly two weeks before she had listed them in the directory, then promptly forgot to tell him.

The three of us felt a supernatural sensation about the two week coincidence and my answered prayer. I guess Vincent and I still have the spiritual connection, only now Susan is part of it.

—*Linda Ranieri Melodia*

FINDING SYNCHRONICITY'S TRAIL

Flashing back on the year 1983, I am sitting in a Venetian cafe around the corner from the Bridge of Sighs, contemplating a Renaissance horizon and slipstreaming into a conversation with two fellow travelers exploring futures beyond the force-fed American corporate culture we were trained for. My wine-soaked conversation revealed that I had a hidden desire to make *something* related to the ecology of ideas contained in a rather strange book I was carrying at the time, Buckminster Fuller's recently published, *Critical Path*. Now I had a goal but no idea how to bring it about.

A few days later, I found myself rambling through the maze of epicurean Europe on my own peculiar version of the Grand Tour. In Paris, I was invited to a dinner party and while there tried to listen to a radio show called "Here and Now." Unable to under-stand the din of languages at the party, I pulled out my copy of *Critical Path* to gander at while waiting for my first real French meal. Across the table was a multilingual Frenchman, who was intrigued by the book title and struck up a conversation with me about Fuller. Eventually he became my mentor in my developing interest in design and a collaborator in my first post-collegiate project, cross-fertilizing Silicon Valley educational software into the Euro market.

Flashback to 1989. I am dreaming of other worlds in a History of Alternative Film class at New York University. After the much too theoretical class, I'm riding the elevator, still carrying my copy of *Critical Path,* and bump into another guy in the class, Brian Dannitz, who notices the book. We strike up a conversation because he too has long been fascinated by Fuller and his work.

Soon, we became filmmaking partners. Once we jointly con-ceived of making a film dealing with the pattern of ideas Bucky brought forth, the road of delectable synchronicity unfolded again and again.

That summer I noticed a description for a class at the New York Open Center by Phil Cousineau, who had co-written *The Hero's Journey,* a documentary film on the life and work of mythologist Joseph Campbell. I attended the class and was intrigued enough by his ideas to invite him out to dinner that night. Over drinks Cousineau told me that Campbell and Fuller had actually taught together several times—on cruise ships of all things! Campbell would lecture in the morning; Fuller in the afternoon; then at night they would convene over dinner and discuss the parallels in their work. For Campbell, Fuller's conception of the Geodesic Dome was a marvelous counterpart to the Hindu image of the Net of Gems, where everything in the Universe is interconnected, and where it connects is a shining gem. Furthermore, Campbell thought that Bucky's colorful metaphor of the "critical path" that modern people find themselves on was an equivalent for his own "hero's journey."

Flashback to 1991. I'm driving north with Dannitz on Route 101 toward the mythic hills of Northern California. Beside a rambling brook I come upon a short, rather gnomelike man named Jay Baldwin. It turns out he has been following Fuller's "Critical Path" for years, studying with him, writing about him, and living a life based on his designs. Once we settle into his California bungalow, he then proceeds to gently guide us through a labyrinth designed, science-infused Universe of fun and form. After three days of receiving enthusiastic wisdom, we leave spellbound, blustering forth with newfound direction for our film project.

For the next few years we set out on the hero's journey of filmmaking, which, it turns out, is an adventure in the synthesizing of imaginations. The everyday and the novel are props for further inquiry into the truly worthwhile. One thing leads to another, from single thoughts to scenes to the collective dreaming. One idea leads to another; one interview to the next. It's a bold adventure, but the magic name of "Bucky" opened the door again and again, like the code to a safe of advanced design knowledge. To invent what we truly desire is a way of evolving and unfolding a meaningful life in a place that expresses my guiding heuristic during this time, which came from Goethe, "Whatever you can do, or dream you can do, begin it. Boldness has genius, power, and magic in it."

Synchronistically, our film, *Ecological Design: Inventing the Future,* was finished in time to appear at the 100th anniversary of Bucky's birth and appeared at the celebrations of his life and work in San Diego, California.

—*Christopher Zelov*

HOUSEHUNTING

My husband and I had lived five hours apart for the one and a half years of our marriage; I in Baltimore, he in Lynchburg, Virginia. When we married in 1987, I stayed in Baltimore so my son could graduate with his high school class. Now that he was in college, the housing market was slow and jobs in banking, my field, were hard to find. My husband had not found appealing work in Maryland. We seemed to be on hold.

Then my entire department was eliminated in a bank merger. After the initial panic, I realized this was a signal to move.

We set up a weekend of househunting with a Lynchburg realtor. Nothing we saw seemed right. Saturday afternoon, the realtor announced that he had to go to a suddenly remembered meeting. Another realtor, quickly located, showed us a house that would not officially be on the market until the next day. It had everything that was important to us, even down to the sound of rain on the skylights, almost the same as rain on a tin roof, which I had always loved. We made an offer that afternoon.

Sunday, we went back to check details of the new house. The owner pulled me aside and said, "I'll bet you're surprised to be buying so quickly. We're surprised to be selling." She told me that three weeks earlier, she and her husband had both had the same dream, the same night, of buying a new house farther in the country. Two days later, a realtor called them unsolicited, with news of a country house. They bought the day before an open house. We had bought their house the day before the open house.

"I'm not superstitious," she said, "but I don't think you'll have any trouble selling your house in Baltimore." In fact, I *was* worried. In 1989, houses often languished on the market for months.

Two days after I went home, I found a letter in my mailbox with a return address I didn't recognize. "This will seem very strange if you're not selling your house," it began. A neighbor had told the letter-writer that we might be moving. She had always liked our house and asked to look at it. She bought it, and for the price we had hoped to receive. I had not seen the neighbor who told her about our house for months, until I ran into him just before my trip to Lynchburg.

We found the house in Lynchburg only because the first realtor was unavailable Saturday afternoon. Later he told us that he had been mistaken about the date of his meeting. The final synchronous event, I later realized, was settling into the new house two days before my severance pay ran out.

I am convinced now, for many reasons, that we were intended

to be in Lynchburg. This incident has made me more aware that God moves and directs our lives, if only we are willing to let ourselves be guided.

—*Naomi W. Caldwell*

MERLIN, GANESHA AND MONKEYS OF CIRCUMSTANCE

The year was 1976, and our son Merlin had turned seven while we were in Sri Lanka. My wife Robin was studying Oriental Sacred Architecture for her doctoral work; one day, as we inspected and meticulously described stupa enclosures, Merlin ran off into the trees with a rough band of temple monkeys—big blackfaced langurs that we learned were very dangerous. We bought him his own monkey that day, his birthday: a kind of midget macaque babysitter.

Our little family unit became a traveling circus, as we moved around the countryside in Sri Lanka and India, with crowds of hundreds (no exaggeration) watching with ill-concealed mirth as Robin and Merlin attempted to put diapers on something with hands on its feet. (It is difficult to housebreak monkeys because of their arboreal, "live and let fly" attitude.) Merlin called him "Spider Man," and they became an outrageous and inseparable duo.

The monkey accompanied us into some of the most magnificent temple complexes of the subcontinent—scampering along in the great subterranean galleries of Ellora, riding nobly on the bow of our boat as we passed the burning ghats on the Ganges. Eventually it rode the rice trucks with us through the Nilgiri hills and on to Katmandu, where we settled into a little garden room in a guest room with a tree right outside the window.

Then we were going to Solo Khumbu in the Himalayas to photograph a Tibetan Buddhist temple and its once-a-year magical ceremony. We would be spending most of our three weeks above 14,000 feet, and we were told the little tropical monkey would almost surely die. We searched the local community of Westerners before finding enthusiastic—and we thought trust-worthy—monkey-sitters: A young German couple at a nearby guest house.

Alas, when we returned from Khumbu, the German couple had moved on, taking the monkey with them and leaving no for-warding address. Merlin was absolutely disconsolate.

Now Ganesha is the elephant-headed deity especially beloved by children all over India, and Merlin had bonded with him with our very first night in India when we beheld an eerie torchlit parade in which an effigy of an elephant-headed deity was carried in an overstuffed easy chair by an ecstatically chanting crowd. Merlin sat on my shoulders in rapture—this was much more fun than Sunday school. Now he had a new religion; and we began to collect little Ganeshas. Merlin would do his own little Ganesha-pujas (ceremonies), when he—or we—needed something. It was disconcerting for us to see how efficacious they were. Ganesha is actually the deity in charge of synchronicities; obstacles and their removal. Those who have lived in India have a sense of just how full of obstacles everyday life can be—especially if the indigenous bureaucrats are involved. But Ganesha seemed to be opening all kinds of doorways with his long trunk!

To help Merlin feel better, we would take him to a famous Ganesha temple in Katmandu which also had about 10,000 rats as devotees, rats being sacred animals in the temple. (Rats are to Ganesha as Timothy is to Dumbo, Merlin pointed out, apprehending the archetype to be larger and more ancient than Disney!) In this extraordinary power-place Merlin made a broken-hearted seven year old's prayer to tubby, lovable Ganesha: "I hope those (German) people crash their Volkswagen bus and my monkey comes jumping back into my arms!"

"Now, now," we said, fearing the efficacy of the childish prayer which inadvertently becomes a terrible curse, "just leave out the accident part." "Ok, Ok!" said Merlin. "But I want my monkey jumping back into my arms!" We were faced with the vast immensity of India, and the irresponsible disappearance of the monkey-sitters. Merlin stayed depressed and began to succumb to the fever he had come down with from the Himalayas. We were worried.

A week or two later, we flew the several hundred miles or so to New Delhi. We were almost out of money, and I was to pick up my penultimate sabbatical-leave paycheck that would allow us to stay in Kashmir and Afghanistan for another month. It was sweltering in New Delhi, and Merlin's fever grew worse. We knew we had to get to cooler Srinagar right away. But when we went to the designated bank that was to receive my check, we faced a smoking rubble in a pool of water. The bank had burned down the night before. Aghast, I faced the consequences of being broke, with a family, in India. I said to Merlin, "Now we really need the help of Ganesha! Pray!" A well-dressed man walked past, and I told him of our plight. He turned out to be a bank officer of the burned down bank. I tried to persuade him to go with me into the ruin to try and find our check. He finally agreed—but would not let me accompany him.

As we waited on the street by Connaught Square, a New Zealand mountaineering friend we had met in Nepal walked by. He asked about the monkey, and we told him what had happened. Soon after the bank officer emerged, jubilant. He was holding the check, which he had miraculously found! But how could we cash it? A friend of his from a still intact bank was so amazed at the story that he immediately cashed it for us. Hooray! We would be out of the heat, with our sick child, the following morning at 7 A.M., and on to Kashmir.

The phone rang at 3 A.M. "Who the hell knows we're in this seedy hotel in Delhi?" I grumbled. It was our New Zealand friend. "I've found your monkey!" he said. "It's out at Hanumayan's Tomb, at the edge of the city, but it's escaped into the trees and I don't think the Germans can get it back." "Holy cow!" I said. By 4 A.M. I was in a motorized tricycle rickshaw buzzing my way out through predawn streets, while Robin stayed in the room with the feverish Merlin.

I had never been to Hanumayan's tomb, and found it suitably eerie for such a strange mission. I saw what I thought was the German's VW bus in a campground by the tomb. I halted the rickshaw and told the driver to wait. I sat down on a log beneath a banyan tree and began luxuriously to peel a banana I had brought. Suddenly he was there—Spider Man himself. He just came down from the tree and got on my shoulder. I fed him pieces of banana and then clipped the leash to his collar. I woke the monkey-sitters up and told them I had repossessed the monkey. They returned the basket we carried him in on airplanes and his "fuzzy," the "transitional object" he loved to snuggle.

Just at dawn, I turned the key in the lock and pushed open the door of the hotel room. The monkey, peaceable enough until that time, suddenly dropped his fuzzy and bit me—I dropped the leash in astonishment. Merlin sat up in bed, wide-eyed. The monkey bounded once—and jumped into his arms! Six hours later we were all drinking lassis and cooling off on a houseboat in Kashmir.

Merlin's health improved—and we were finally to diagnose

and successfully treat his Gardia, for such it was, in Zurich, our point of departure for the Asian journey. The Swiss authorities told us they would destroy the monkey if we tried to bring him into the country and so we placed him with a nice family with lots of children and a courtyard garden in Athens. Merlin has turned out to be a climbing guide with an uncanny skill on the rock. And every now and then I wonder if that is his simian Totem or is it the ghost of Spider Man on his shoulder?

—*Stephen Larsen*

ACTS OF GRACE

It was in the 1940s, during World War II. My husband worked on aircraft as a mechanic at Hill Field, Ogden, Utah. He was sent to Detroit for some special training and took me along. We went by train, stopping overnight in Chicago to visit an aunt and uncle.

Before leaving home, I'd received a letter from Wally, my brother, who was in the navy. He said he was being transferred to Chicago on assignment. He didn't give me the exact date nor the name of the new station.

We had arrived on a Saturday and stayed overnight. Sunday, we had time for a little sightseeing before our train left later that day. Being near Lake Michigan and hearing there was a naval base close by, we went looking for it. We thought we might be able to find out about my brother.

It was a sunny, warm day. We walked toward the blue lake, which we could see a block away from us. There were few people out and about. My husband suddenly grabbed my arm and said, "Isn't that sailor across the street your brother?"

It was!—and so we called and rushed over to him. I was thrilled and so was Wally. What luck it was, because he was on a seventy-two-hour pass before he officially had to report for duty. He was just out walking around. Even if we'd found the base, we would have missed him.

I felt sure at that moment someone was watching over us. Now, so many years later, I believe synchronistic events are part of the great mystery of life. Sometimes it is easy to see they are acts of grace. As souls are able to move in different dimensions, perhaps synchronicity is when our souls communicate with each other.

—*Leila M. Reese*

A TALE OF SEVERAL CITIES

These tales of multiple synchronicities revolve around four central characters, including myself. It all began at a New York airport while I was waiting to board a much-delayed charter flight bound for England. A young man attached himself to me. Jim was his name.

The plane was scheduled to leave at 8:00 P.M. that Saturday evening. That hour became a ubiquitous *leitmotif* in an unfolding story. Nine hours later, the aircraft was ready to board, from where it was docked at the far end of the runway. Jim quipped, "They want us to walk to Logan Airport (in Boston) to catch the plane." Neither of us could see the future, but his offhand comment proved ironic. One year later, I moved to Boston to teach at a local college there, and some years after that, Jim would spend the last night of his life in the Boston area.

COINCIDENCE OR DESTINY?

Jim had a loyal girlfriend in New York, Elaine, who, much later, became one of my best friends. For part of my stay in England, Jim appointed himself my tour guide and found me charming lodgings in London. I was not interested in him romantically, but we enjoyed our burgeoning friendship, and he was a knowledgeable traveling companion.

One Saturday evening, while staring at the ocean on a high cliff overlooking the sea on the Isle of Wight, we encountered a local couple. "We come up here every night at 8:00 P.M. to *hear the silence,*" the woman imparted. Then, after a poignant moment she added, "I wouldn't give a tuppence for London."

The following day, after a rushed journey back to London, we had dinner with Jim's best friend from the States, who was also traveling abroad. The moment I met Paul, we were instantly attracted to each other. We planned to get together once we were each back in our respective states, a distance of three hours by car.

Each of us was to go our separate ways the next day. We bid *adieu* after dinner. For the remainder of his European vacation, Paul was to stay in Switzerland. Elaine was to join Jim for a well-planned biking trip throughout the South of France. I intended to remain in London.

One week into socializing with my English friends and ecstatically enjoying long walks through London, I summarily sent a telegram to a Parisian friend. On a whim, I asked her if the next day would be a good time for me to accept her longstanding open invitation to visit. She immediately replied that she would meet me at an appointed railway station at 8:00 P.M. the following evening.

It was 9:30 P.M., soon after my arrival in Paris, and the Latin Quarter was engulfed with throngs of people. As a couple departed from their curbside table at a busy sidewalk cafe, my Parisian hostess and I deftly slid into their chairs and marveled at acquiring such a unique placement in that location at that hour.

"Madeline!" a voice exclaimed. "What are you doing here?" Looking up from my seat, I saw Paul towering over me. He was talking excitedly. Paul, who was supposedly in Switzerland, was amazed that I was not in London.

Scarcely a few minutes before spotting me at the cafe, while crossing the Pont de Saint Michel, which was only a few hundred yards away, Paul had suddenly met face to face with Jim and Elaine! They were supposed to be cycling in the South of France, but had changed their plans, too.

We had all gone to our prearranged destinations and each one of us had peremptorily changed plans and arrived at the same time, practically at the same spot, in a city uncharted on any of our itineraries. Even amidst the pulsating masses of people, Paul noticed his friends in the crowd.

The next day, Paul and I took a boat ride along the Seine, lazily gazing at the sunbeams dancing on the water, and pretended that we were in love. We shared ice cream cones alongside the river at twilight and reveled in the astonishing encounters the previous evening and the confluence of our intersecting lives.

Back in New York, I become friends with Jim and Elaine, and had an on-again-off-again, out-of-town relationship with Paul. At our last meeting, I had peremptorily suggested that he view a deeply personal experience of his from a different perspective than he had chosen. My advice was unsolicited and unwelcome. His reaction was understandable, especially since I had spoken without forethought and without first sensing the boundaries of his willingness to review the circumstances. Painful memories are difficult to revisit for most people, even if they consciously choose to venture into that emotional territory for healing purposes. This was not the case for Paul at the time.

Three years later, as I was absorbed one evening in reading nothing particularly important on my couch at home in Massachusetts, where I now live, my thoughts drifted to the incident over which Paul and I had differed. I felt a profound moment of compassion for him, and then forgot about it.

The following evening, at approximately 8:00 P.M., my phone rang and a guest at a house party I had created for "spiritual musicians" answered the phone. He handed the receiver to me. It was Paul. Somehow he had managed to locate me. The purpose of the call was to say that the night before, he was suddenly faced with the poignant memory of the episode over which we had contended, three years earlier. He said that all the pieces of the puzzle suddenly fell into place, and he felt he had to tell me that my interpretation was correct and to thank me, for it helped tremendously to see the truth.

I did not need to be right but was sincerely happy for him, so I told him I appreciated his call. Even more, I felt astonishment and awe at the unexplainable circumstances of two people recalling the same traumatic incident, a considerable distance from each other in time and place. For the mutual recollection had occurred simultaneously the previous evening.

As I gasped out loud at the conjunction of internal events, the friend who had originally answered the phone, intoned, "Don't you know? When one tree blooms on my street, all the trees bloom at the same time." His cryptic message was incomprehensible to me at first. He softly repeated it as if enunciating, "Madeline, all the trees bloom at once, not one and one only."

After a moment's reflection, I felt as if I had been zapped by a Zen *koan,* an inscrutable statement or question for the rational mind, which, once heeded, informs the questioner with its seeming illogic. Translating the synchronistic events into Eastern wisdom, I relaxed into a vague understanding that nature itself is synchronistic. Even if we attune ourselves to individual similarities and compare only what is immediately apparent, we are glimpsing an important piece of the harmonious natural flow of events.

"All the trees bloom at once on my street. . . ."

—Madeline Nold

THE SIEGE

My story involves my marriage, the Civil War, and expensive wine. My eleven-year marriage had never been good, but this last year looked like it was near its end. Last Christmas was particularly difficult. As a begrudging holiday gift, my wife gave me an expensive bottle of wine, Opus One. I set it aside and didn't open it. I silently promised myself that I would only open the wine to celebrate the happy resolution of our problems, or to acknowledge that the marriage was over.

The Civil War is part of this story, because several years ago I began to see America's great and tragic conflict as a metaphor for my relationship with my wife. Since I was trying with every ounce of my strength to get her to live up to what I felt were her marital obligations, I actually saw the marriage as "The Siege of Vicksburg." I was the persistent, unrelenting, overpowering General Ulysses S. Grant. My wife represented the intransigent Southerners. I never told my wife about this, but this past summer I made a visit to Vicksburg as part of our summer vacation, just when our emotions reached their lowest ebb.

Later, even though things were resolving themselves in a positive way, it didn't occur to me to open the bottle of Opus One.

But I did, for some reason, have a desire to listen to a tape of Civil War historian Shelby Foote reading his story of the Battle of Gettysburg. I put the tapes on at work. It took me several days to listen to the entire story.

On the day I finished listening to Gettysburg, I took my wife out to a new Birmingham restaurant, where we planned to have dinner and then listen to a performance by jazz singer Nancy King. After dinner, while we waited for the music, we just relaxed and talked. At the table next to us was, apparently, one of the owners of the restaurant. He was entertaining a group of friends and was kind enough to send us each a glass of dessert wine. We enjoyed it and thanked him. A few minutes later, as we listened to the music, he reached over and filled our empty glasses with a different wine. He showed me the bottle. It was a sherry bottled in 1863, the year of the Battle of Gettysburg, which "I" had finished that day.

There was no need to open my expensive bottle of wine to celebrate the resolution of my marriage. I had been given a glass of wine that itself was worth ten times what my bottle was worth.

—*Terrence A. Taylor*

LO AND BEHOLD

I was twenty-two years old and graduating from college in upstate New York. I had lived for almost the entire four years with my boyfriend, Matthew, in a very intense relationship. We had met as freshmen, fell immediately in love, and had a number of strong nonordinary experiences, particularly when making love—we left our own minds and bodies, merged psychically with one another, and then we merged with the All. Such experiences convinced us that we were soulmates, but he often bemoaned the fact that we had met when we were so young, before he had the chance to sow his wild oats.

This was the mid-'70s when open relationships were popular, and so we decided to try explorations with other people; Simone de Beauvoir and Sartre were our models. We found it excruciatingly hurtful, Matthew so much so that he felt he could never be involved with me again, even when I offered to end my other involvement. It seemed that our relationship was over. We both planned to set out on cross-country trips, but separately. No travel agendas. He would go with a male friend, I with a man in whom I had no romantic interest.

When Matthew and I said our tearful good-byes, I literally thought I was going to die. I felt as if I were exploding inside, and all the molecules in my body were flying off into space. I could not conceive of living without him. To comfort me, he held me close and whispered that this was not the end, that we would see each other again.

As we went our separate ways, I felt inconsolable, and yet was desperately trying not to show it to this new beau of mine. He and I packed a tent and sleeping bags into a car and set off from upstate New York at the beginning of September. By mid-October, after criss-crossing the continent to Arizona, I was exceedingly sick of sleeping in a tent and was convinced that I had made a major mistake in hooking up with this guy. Every place we visited I would look for Matthew—in passing cars, in stores, in campgrounds—all the while reprimanding myself for acting crazy!

"Two hundred million people in the country and you expect him to show up!" I would mutter to myself as I continued to look.

Then one day, two months later, we were driving down a residential street in a poky little town outside Tucson, lo and behold—there was Matthew, casually walking down the street with his buddy!

The upshot of the story is that both of us saw this as a sign that we really did belong together. After several months of working through the hurt, Matthew and I got back together for another three years, and, when it was *truly* time for us to move on, we did, remaining best friends to this day, twenty-five years later. And we both feel we still are soulmates, just ones who live with other people.

—*Anonymous*

It's in the Stars

Beginning in 1982, I was ill with a prostate infection that lasted a year. I was in constant low-level pain. After several months, it became emotionally debilitating. I was tired, depressed, and totally uncomfortable.

One Friday night, I was alone watching TV, trying to distract myself from the pain. As I channel-surfed, I ran across a public television docudrama about a wonderful artist who spent most of his time as a recluse working on an island off the Gulf Coast of the United States. But I never caught his name or where he worked.

Nearly ten years later, I had recovered from my infection, made a career change, and enrolled in the M.F.A. program at the University of Alabama to learn how to make handcrafted books.

I had to decide what to do for my M.F.A. project: I decided to print a book that featured the work of an artist whose work I had seen years before, but I didn't even know his name.

One day I was chatting with a woman student from Mississippi, who had become a very close friend. For some reason, it suddenly occurred to me to ask her if she had any idea who this artist was. I described his work, and she went pale. She took my hand and said that not only did she know who he was and where he worked, but she had a friend who lived a few doors from the artist's daughter.

The artist was Walter Anderson. He had died in the mid-1960s. My friend introduced me to Anderson's daughter, Mary, who gave me permission to use her father's drawings, invited me into her home, and helped me select the work to appear in my book.

A few months later, while I was preparing to go to New York for a summer internship, I was standing at the Xerox machine at school when a professor friend from another department walked up and asked me what I was going to do for my M.F.A. project. I told him about the artwork of Walter Anderson, but that I didn't know what I was going to do for text.

The professor asked if I was aware that there was a poet on campus who had written a manuscript of poems about Walter Anderson that hadn't yet been published. He gave me the poet's name. I contacted him in New York, got the manuscript, and selected some poems. The result was a very successful book called *The Stars Undone*.

—*Terrence A. Taylor*

ANCESTORS

Casey and June met during World War II. Casey was an American soldier stationed in England, where June was volunteering in an American Red Cross canteen. June said that she noticed Casey the minute he walked through the front door. She pointed him out to a friend, saying, "That's the man I'm going to marry."

They were, indeed, married a few short weeks later.

Their first baby was born with an extremely rare error of metabolism and died only two weeks after birth. The identical genetic problem was diagnosed early in the second child, who survived. The physicians told Casey and June that the disease could only be transmitted genetically. Casey and June, however, adamantly proclaimed the impossibility of a genetic link. They wanted to have more children.

Casey and June decided to investigate their ancestral lines and heritage. In so doing, they discovered that three generations removed, their two families had lived only a few miles apart in County Cork, Ireland.

They were, undoubtedly, related.

A framed homily in their kitchen reads, "You are my happiness, my sorrow; my yesterday, my tomorrow."

—*Anonymous*

A CHAIN OF COINCIDENCE

In 1989, during the research for my novel on Bert Stiles, I visited the Stiles' home in Denver. I introduced myself to the Marion family who now resides there and discovered that they had purchased the house from Mrs. Stiles, Bert's mother, when she moved to a rest home in the mid-1960s. Mrs. Marion introduced me to her fifteen-year-old daughter who, after I told her I was writing about the former resident of the home, responded that she had presented in high school just that week an oral paper on the author and war hero, Bert Stiles.

That afternoon, Mrs. Marion told me another coincidental happening involving her son. He had been home from college the previous summer and had read Bert's book, *Serenade to the Big Bird*. He'd wanted to read the book written by the former resident whose bedroom he was sleeping in. The son returned to his Ivy League college for his junior year and found himself meeting a new roommate.

"Where are you from?" the roommate asked young Marion.

"Denver," was the response.

"Hmmm, all I know about Denver is what I picked up from a great book I just finished. It was an autobiography by a Denver native named Bert Stiles. He described his tree-shaded neighborhood and home so well that I feel I knew it. He lived on South York Street—know where that is?"

"That's my neighborhood, my street, and my house," the stunned Marion boy responded. "The same house Bert Stiles lived in just before the war."

Later that year, I traveled to Monroe, Wisconsin, a rather small town in the north-central part of the state. I went there at the invitation of Dan Bauer, a magazine writer who'd written about Bert Stiles two years earlier. Bauer had gone to Denver to interview friends of Bert's—and subsequently wrote a lengthy article with numerous photographs for the May 1987 issue of *Air Classics*. I'd wanted to talk to Bauer because of his extensive knowledge of Bert and also to select photographs that he'd gathered during his own research.

We talked about Bert for two nights and part of the day in between. He told me of a "coincidence" the previous year. While in Denver, probably in 1986, he'd known of, but had not been able to meet, Dr. Frank Stiles, Bert's first cousin. Bauer returned to Monroe and finished his article, while Stiles retired and moved out of Denver. A year or so later, Bauer's daughter Lindsey, about ten years old, became seriously ill late one night. For some reason, the hospital was not an immediate option. Dan's wife suggested they call the new doctor she'd heard had moved in down the street. The doctor got dressed and accompanied Dan to his home, where he examined and treated young Lindsey. "Now," Dan told me, "I have no question that he saved Lindsey's life by his quick and accurate diagnosis and treatment."

The doctor, of course, was Frank Stiles. He and Bauer became good friends. Frank Stiles died in 1989, a few months before I arrived in Monroe to talk with Dan Bauer.

These three incidents, all occurring in the same year, strengthened my determination to complete the book and do so as clearly and forcefully as I was capable. It amazed me that my protagonist, Bert Stiles, a young man who died forty-five years earlier, was still a force in the lives of people not yet born when he wrote his only book.

—*Bob Cooper*

Right Here at the End of Everything

At the end of the summer of 1995, I had come to feel discouraged, dispirited, and hopeless about my life. The last few years of shouldering the weight of a bitter divorce, trying to make ends meet, working and going back to school, and parenting two young kids had caught me off guard; life was caving in on me. I felt impoverished, more so than I had ever been in my life. It was a personal hell; I felt utterly alone and profoundly lost.

Then, within a two-week period, a whirlwind of amazing events constituting prophetic dreams, peculiar stories told to me by my friends and strangers, and coincidences swept me off my feet and on the way towards a personal journey of reclaiming hope, courage, and lost dreams. Catapulting experiences hurled me forward, especially when I discovered a brochure in the package from an author in San Francisco. It was a four-page flier with a figure of a dancing goddess advertising a "Myth in the Mediterranean" tour—to be led by the author himself.

I immediately recalled a dream I'd had of going to a free lecture led by a famous mythologist whom the tour leader had worked with. Loving the coincidences, I toyed with the idea of going on this trip—but then thought, Who was I kidding? I was over my head in debt, without a job, and could think of fifty other reasons why it was out of the question. Which only plunged me deeper into depression.

Then a dear friend told me two stories that helped. Several years ago he was at a difficult phase in his life. It was Christmas and he wanted to give a grand dinner for his friends, a non-traditional seafood feast. But he knew he couldn't afford it. Yet, something in him was moved to hold on to his faith, a kind of "knowing" that the Universe would provide for him. He made a decision there and then that he was going to give this seafood dinner no matter what it took.

Two days later, as he was coming to a stop at an intersection in his pickup truck, a delivery van suddenly and violently swerved around the corner and sped away in a screech. The door of the van flung open and a wooden crate fell out. Something in my friend told him to quickly pick up the crate (before the other person at the intersection who had seen what happened and was eyeing it as well). He pulled it into his truck and saw there was no address or any identifying marks. The van had left too quickly for him to have caught sight of any information about where it came from or even a license plate. At home, he opened up the create to find that it contained a magnificent assortment of seafood! Frozen prawns, fish steaks, lobster, caviar, enough for a feast! Suffice it to say, they all had a fabulous—and non-traditional—Christmas dinner. For me, my friend's synchronicity story hinted at the importance of decision making and *commitment* to follow through on decisions.

Within hours of hearing his story, another friend I hadn't talked to for months called me up. We exchanged updates on our lives. I told her I was tired and depressed. Out of the blue, she said, "I hear Greece is a lovely place..." Another synchronicity. But still I could not figure out how to go.

The first few days of September found me not sleeping well. I would wake up at five or six every morning. One morning, I went for a long walk along the beach about six thirty. I jokingly asked the universe for a fairy godmother. About half an hour later, as I was sitting on a bench sipping my take-out coffee, I glanced over at the bench next to mine and heard a woman telling stories to a young man while simultaneously weaving a mat from strips of newspaper. Twenty minutes later, this flamboyant, sixty-ish woman came up to me, or more accurately, breezed over. She wore two cloaks embroidered with sequins and of the color of rainbows, psychedelic spandex leggings, and a big purple hat. She smiled, revealing a gold, star-shaped filling on the front of one of her incisors. She said her name was Orunamamu, meaning "Morning Star" in Nigerian. She was a storyteller from Berkeley, on her way home from attending a festival in Alberta. She asked me if I was interested in hearing some stories. I said yes. She said, "Before I begin, let me say that life is about making decisions and sticking to them. You gotta chart your own course, for ain't nobody do it for ya."

Hmmmm, okay, I thought. Then she continued dramatically, "If you see a feather, a pretty little feather, a soft, white, little feather, if you see a feather, pick it up! Pick it up and put it in your pocket. For you see, a feather is a *letter* from a bird!"

This could be fun, I thought to myself. And this was only the prelude to three special stories that Orunamamu told me that morning, which I jotted down in my journal when I got home. Not until much later did I see how powerful and meaningful they were to become for me.

For the sake of expeditiousness, I shall tell only the first one in detail. Once, a long, long, time ago, and far, far away there was a tailor. He was a penniless fellow. In fact, you could say he was flat broke. Whatever he made from his sewing had to be put back into the business. One day, this tailor decided that he ought to have a new topcoat for winter was fast approaching. He had no money for new fabric, and fell into despair. Then he had an idea to go to the weaver's shop. There he gathered all the tiny scraps of discarded fabric from off the floor and took them home, working throughout the night, cutting and stitching until morning came. Out of those scraps he had made a new topcoat of the most incredible colors and textures. With great pride he wore his coat everywhere he went, receiving much praise for it. He wore it and wore it until it was all worn out. But when he laid the tattered coat on his cutting table, he saw that there was enough there to make a tunic! Again, he sewed all night, and in the morning he had a beautiful multi-colored tunic! When the tunic was worn out, he made from those scraps a vest. From the vest, he created a scarf, and from that he fashioned a button. When the button was falling apart, he saw that he had enough left to make a story. And that is the one I have just told you.

(Later on, I realized that the message of this story for me was to *be creative, go to the sources of your creativity, to your deep self because from that place you can make much out of the smallest shreds. . . .*)

At end of the story, I bought Orunamamu a coffee and asked her why she carried around a jar of purple dye in her pack. She told me that a long time ago purple was a royal color. Only those of royal blood were permitted to wear purple. That was the law. Those who broke it had their heads chopped off. Therefore, she carried purple dye to remind herself that *her* head was still on, and that she was *alive!*

All this advice helped me see that the trip was inevitable. I made the travel arrangements, asked for an extension of my credit card limit from my bank, and wrote to my family for help. Within days of my departure, I received a check from my brother for a nice sum, and a stunning loan from my ex-husband. Some dear friends gave me a touching send-off party along with several hundred drachmas. I was on my way.

Greece was a marvel-filled adventure. A collection of astounding sights, sounds, smells, moments, and stories galore! Many transformations happened for me during that trip, a journey that heralded deeply personal revelations and painful realizations. Traveling with strangers offered me the unexpected opportunity to "return to myself," reclaim lost parts, rediscover the stuff of which I was made. In Greece no one asked who I had been up to that point and I didn't tell. I could just be whoever I wanted to or imagined I could be. Not anyone's ex-wife, mother, lover, friend, or therapist. No demands were made on me; I had only to let myself be carried along by what unfolded, and to be enchanted by even the most ordinary things. So I reveled in the magical moments, drank in the blue of the Aegean Sea, and my hungry soul feasted.

Upon my return, I was welcomed by friends and neighbors who were enchanted by my stories and pictures. It was as if they too were inspired by my experiences. Friends of friends who had heard of my adventures began to tell me their own life-shaping synchronicities. I had been given the gift of what James Joyce describes as seeing *how deep was the place from which my life flowed.* I began to view my work not so much as creating solutions for people, but as teaching them to bear witness to their own lives, deeply honoring their hearts and souls.

My life is still fraught with uncertainty and chaos. No steady work, little money, and anxiety about the future. But I know that what has happened to me over the last year has made a profound impact on my life. It has given me the courage of my convictions to live from my own depths, guided by heart and soul, and affirmed my unshakable belief in the existence of *something far greater than us all.* It is a force that guides us, if we but pay attention. I know that there will be many more portals to cross, many more roads of trials to endure. There will be more to learn, much to contribute. But I know I can make it because I have come home to myself.

—*Pohsuan Zaide*

THE CHINA CONNECTION

In 1979, when I was twenty, I went to Germany to attend a foreign language school for two months. After the course, I found that I had fallen for my instructor, and he for me. He was quite different than anyone I had ever dated. He was thirty years older than me. He was from a different culture, of a different religion, and his native language was obviously German. It was as if two people from two separate worlds were drawn together, and we began living together in Germany.

And as anyone can imagine, not too many people—including my family members—approved. I guess, as they say, opposites attract. I did not see myself as rebellious. Naturally I wanted my family to approve, and yet somehow I could live without their approval. This man was very educated. He had written several books and had traveled all over the world, usually to teach German at foreign language schools in foreign countries. His most recent trip had been in 1978 to China, and he had Chinese artwork all over his home, as memories of his trip. At that time, in 1978, China was not yet open to tourists or even business people. In fact, the only Germans that could go to China were those who had been invited by the government—and they were few and far between.

Well, to get on with the story, the relationship with this man did not work out. I was devastated, and it took a long time for me to get the pieces of my life back together. I returned to the United States and did not date for about three years.

Near the end of that period, I found someone who seemed worth spending time with. I met him while I was working in Los Angeles for German television. This man was on a business trip from Germany and was meeting with my boss. This man and I had dinner together, and I found myself very interested in him.

Over time, with many trips back and forth to Germany, our relationship developed. It was during one of those trips that I noticed something kind of eerie—he had the same type of Chinese artwork on the wall of his office as my former boyfriend had had in his home. It was at that time that I found out that he, too, had been in China. I, of course, noticed that he had some other things in common with my former lover: He was older (only twenty-three years this time), German, of a different religion, and traveled all over the world. We began living together after about another three years (1987), at which time we became engaged.

I had not seen nor heard from the first man since the end of our relationship. I heard through mutual friends that he was still writing, still traveling. As a matter of fact, in 1987 he had just written a German grammar book and was looking for someone to translate it and adapt it for the English-speaking market. Through these mutual friends, he inquired whether I would be interested in doing the translation. He felt, since I was now attached to someone else and so was he, that our working together would not stir up any pain for me or for him over our past. I was very excited about working with him, but I did not want to do the book without my fiance's approval, because I did not want my old relationship to stir up any feelings of discomfort for him. So with my friend's approval, I arranged for the three of us to meet.

We met in a restaurant in Munich, and the situation seemed somewhat awkward. The two men both appeared somewhat uncomfortable and had difficulties engaging in conversation. My old boyfriend did not know that they had both been to China, so I brought this up, knowing that it was a wonderful experience for both of them. They found out that they both had been there in 1978 on business by invitation of the Chinese government, when China was just opening up to the West.

It turned out that they, in fact, had both been to Beijing. And they had both gone at the exact same time, for the same period. The final surprise came when they discovered that they had both stayed at the same hotel.

I am an American. I grew up in a different world, with a different culture, religion, and generation, and yet I ended up with two men, who in many ways were the same. It was as if some higher being had said: Judy, you will meet an older German man, who has been to China, and you will fall in love with him and marry him.

And then, after meeting the first one, it was as if this higher being said, "No! Not that German, Judy. The other one!"

With sixty-two million Germans at the time, and with 240 million Americans, I still wonder how in the world these three people's lives could come together and be so entwined.

If that isn't synchronicity, what is?

—*Judith Hime-Everschor*

COINCIDENCE OR DESTINY?

In the summer of 1989, a group of people from around the United States gathered in Paris to participate in a Bohemian Paris art and literary tour and to celebrate the Bicentennial of the Independence of France.

On the third day of the tour, Martha Fletcher, a dancer from San Francisco, joined the group as they boarded the houseboat of an American writer, Mort Rosenblum, living on the Seine near the Pont d'Alma, under the shadow of the Eiffel Tower.

It was over a table covered with wine, cheese, and bread that she met John O'Brien, an artist from Greenwich Village. The sparks continued to fly through the tour until good-byes were said and they returned home to opposite sides of the continent.

Several months later, when Martha was moving into a new home, she discovered that an old photograph she had had on her bulletin board since grade school was of a painting of a houseboat on the Seine at Pont d'Alma with the Eiffel Tower in the background.

The following summer, John moved to San Francisco to escape the hot summers in New York and to paint. With him he brought a painting of a ballerina with long red hair that he had painted ten years before. The ballerina looked exactly like Martha.

They spent the next summer together in Paris with John painting and Martha dancing. On one of their many excursions, they spent a day in Moret sur Loing, a beautiful and charming little town outside of Paris. At the end of the summer, they once again parted, only this time John would return to New York, only to pack up things to move out to California. In the process he discovered an old photo he had been saving for years of a painting of the little town of Moret sur Loing, exactly where the two of them had traveled and taken photos.

A year later, John and Martha were married on the day they fell in love. One year after that, when Martha was sorting through old boxes to make room for a nursery, she discovered a diary she had kept when she was twelve. Browsing through the pages, she came upon an entry that read, "I wish I could be Michelle O'Brien," referring to a ballet dancer she admired at the time.

Two months later, she gave birth to Michelle O'Brien, born to the music of Swan Lake.

Coincidence or destiny?

—*John and Martha O'Brien*

THE RENOIR CONNECTION

It was two years after the painful end of my first marriage. I was relatively happy but ready to find someone to love again. I went on vacation for a week and left my house in the care of a female friend from the church I attend. She was given free reign to spend as much time there as she wanted.

The first day back in church after my vacation, a woman in the congregation named Kathy approached me. I had never spoken to her. She said that she was good friends with the woman who had watched my house and had been in my house several times during my absence. Her reason for approaching me was to tell me how much she liked my house and how it was decorated. She particularly wanted to compliment me on the Renoir that I had hanging on the wall. She had the same print in her house. I was amazed.

Several years before, I had been looking for a piece of art to decorate my house. I ordered a print of a Renoir painting from the Metropolitan Museum of Art in New York. It was a painting of a bowl of fruit, and I had it nicely framed and placed over the fireplace.

I have never seen that print before or since.

I cannot say exactly why, but in the moment that she told me she had the same print, Kathy began to glow for me. I fell in love with her. I don't know if it was the print or mutual tastes or what. I prefer to think it was the Great Mystery at work.

Today, Kathy and I are happily married. Both prints hang in our house.

Thank you, Renoir. Thank you, Met. And thank you, Great Mystery. All of you helped bring us together, and it is right and good.

—*Art France*

THE AWAKENING OF WONDER

Having chosen to engage in life by consciously accepting and working from the rawness and vulnerability of my own Achilles heel, I have been stunned by the many synchronistic experiences, and the many awakenings of wonder I have subsequently found myself absorbed in. In keeping with the pulse of the psyche as it speaks through particulars, reflections, and moments of wonder, I am moved to recount an experience in which I directly experienced the interconnectedness of life, and which to this day serves to link my life to the life of an individual who, in all probability, I will never meet again.

In January 1996, Phil Cousineau was the Saturday guest speaker for the Humanities and Depth Tradition class I was taking at Pacifica Institute in San Francisco. During his presentation, he showed a film clip based on a story written by James Joyce, called *The Dead,* which addressed, in part, the great abyss which may, paradoxically, cleave a marriage, the union that is seemingly the most intimate of relationships that can exist between a man and a woman. The intensity of the depth of communication I had experienced during my weekend of study at Pacifica, and our speaker's passion for the multifarious voice of soul, buoyed me invisibly on my airplane journey home to New York. Arriving at my Los Angeles stopover, I scanned the waiting area at my gate, looking for a seat.

I had disembarked, the latest wayfarer. I was simultaneously sized up and disregarded by a sea of staring, detached strangers. I had yet to carve a boundary that would initiate me, by way of separation, into this holding camp. By ordinance of the unwritten and unspoken code of the road, the seat I chose became my space, my boundary, my acceptance by the other pilgrims, into this liminal domain. I toyed with my luggage, then shuffled books, sweaters, and tickets, settling in to the space that delineated my body and my territory, from connection to any other soul.

Beside me, a man's voice penetrated the invisible partition I had erected. "Do those things really fit into the overhead compartment?" The question pertained to my suitcase. "They do if you don't stuff them as full as I have stuffed this one," I replied.

It was a relief to smile, to connect, to become somebody again. The conversation started like many conversations of the road: Where to? Where from? Then came subsequent acknowledgment and validation of one's hometown, one's life.

What ensued, continues to sustain and affirm my affiliation to life, and will, I imagine, forever stir my heart with a bittersweet sense of wonder.

The gentleman's name was Shay Duffin, and he spoke with a heavy Irish brogue. He was an actor, he said, and he was on his way to New York to work a one-man show on Broadway, a show that he had written over the course of the last three years, *Confessions of an Irish Rebel,* the story of the late poet and playwright, Brendan Behan.

This Irishman had just come from a tour of Canada, he said, singing Irish folk ballads that his mother had written, sung, and recorded before him. He even showed me her picture and that of his children and of his grandchildren. He dreamed aloud about his wife, "the spitting image of Eva Gabor," as he described her. She had passed away in her early forties, a victim of lung cancer. "She'd been a heavy smoker," is all he said.

My story was about Pacifica, and I enthusiastically inquired of Mr. Duffin if he had heard of Phil Cousineau or of the documentary film work he had done. I told him about Cousineau's portrayal of soul and showed him Cousineau's recent book, *Soul: An*

Archaeology, and mentioned, for the sake of conversation, the film clip from *The Dead.* Shay Duffin had not only acted in *The Dead,* he had been born and raised in Dublin, the same town as its author, James Joyce.

At this revelation, the energy between our bodies heightened and tensed. I remember an acute sense of knowing that we could talk all night. Time stood still. The rest of the world became a mere backdrop. We were vibrant amidst a grey manic blur of movement, light, and sound. Synchronicity had exploded linear time with a "riot of emotion," as Joyce had written in the story, and the awakening wonder between two strangers now closer than the estranged lovers portrayed in the movie.

"Without the nourishment provided by the ability to rest in uncertainties, mysteries, and doubts, the soul begins to starve," as Alan Jones has written. I have carried this story with me, and I have offered it delicately to nourish certain dialogues in which I feel it would be warmly received, for this experience dwells in a protected space in my heart. There are those for whom this story would not be well received—those who must defend against wonder and the contemplative availability to reality that opening the heart engenders. For such impoverished individuals, wherein lies their soul?

And indeed, does such a life yet have a story?

—*Judy Issac Conley*

THE BASS NOTE IN MY LIFE

Synchronicity has always played the bass note in my life and has echoed through all my major rites of passage. When I was fourteen and was first attracted to boys, my friend Anne Sattenspiel and I took out the Ouija board and asked about the most popular fellow in the ninth grade class. It spelled out his name: "Steven Lerner." Of course, we knew him from afar. He was at the head of the class academically and had the lead in the school play. She asked for his phone number and as the Ouija board responded with seven digits, I said, "Let's dial it."

We did, I asked for Steven, and a voice said, "I'll get him. He's in the den watching television."

"Is this the home of Steven Lerner?" I stammered.

"Yeah."

I froze for a minute then said, "Hmmm, this is a marketing survey . . . We just want to know his favorite TV show. . ."

• • •

I made many close friends when I worked at *Time* magazine in the 1970s, among them a couple named Web and Gale McLeod. Web was a man about town, who knew all the literary figures; he was about twenty-five years older than me, and he was a suave and debonair figure. He and Gale had a dinner party and fixed me up with my first husband, Paul Hale.

Twenty-five years later, after my divorce, I moved to California and became engaged to an elegant older man named Fielder Cook. Fielder worked in television in New York and used to live around the corner from me on Lexington Avenue. Yet we'd never met in our New York incarnations. One day Fielder showed me the picture album from his first wedding. I recognized the best man.

"God," I said. "That's Web McLeod."

"You know Web?"

"He introduced me to my first husband."

"We went to school together at McCallie," said Fielder. "And he introduced me to my first wife."

For the next five years, we wondered how our lives would have been different if he'd introduced us to each other.

• • •

In the 1970s, after I left *Time* magazine to freelance, I spent two hours on the phone everyday with an artist friend, Tom McKnight. He painted mythological scenes of nymphs and satyrs and the lost world of Atlantis, and we often talked about the occult. We both read voraciously. One night I told him about a passage in Jung's autobiography, *Memories, Dreams and Reflections,* that particularly excited me.

"Did you read the part when Freud tells Jung there's no such thing as the occult?"

"Not yet. What happens?" Tom asked.

"Well, Jung scowled at him and must have looked like a furious old sorcerer. Then, suddenly, a very loud crack emanated from the bookcase. 'See,' he said, 'and just to prove my point in another ten seconds there will be another crack in the bookcase.' 'Not very likely,' Freud scoffed. Ten seconds later, there was another noise so loud it could have been a gunshot. And Freud fainted dead away."

"Oh sure," said Tom, teasingly. "You're telling me Jung made it happen?"

"Of course!" I responded vigorously. "Don't you believe it?" At this exact moment, the built-in bookshelf on my living room came crashing down.

"Geez," Tom said contritely. "What the hell was that?"

A year later, Tom and I were having one of our long, late night telephone discussions about the work of Carl Jung, in particular his last book on UFOs.

"You know we used to see the strangest lights over the meadows, where I grew up in New Jersey," I ventured. "My mother was convinced that they were spaceships. She used to sit in front of the living room window for hours waiting for them to come and pick her up.

"Maybe they were looking for you, too," Tom said as if trying to bait me. "Maybe they're out there, trying to find you now."

My West End Avenue apartment overlooked the Hudson River, and in the distance I could see a green light hovering on the horizon.

"Tom, let's change the subject. This is getting kind of eerie."

"What's up?"

"There's a glowing object in the vicinity of Gutenberg, New Jersey. . ."

"I'm right. It's coming to get you . . ."

"I'm hanging up. You're going to make me a nervous wreck."

Finally, I went to bed, convinced that I had imagined everything.

The next morning the paper carried a small item that read, "Odd sighting last night near Gutenberg, New Jersey. Doorman reports unidentified flying object . . ."

• • •

Other times, synchronicity has been related to my dreams. At *Time* magazine, I worked with a wonderful Englishwoman named Elaine. We lost touch over the years, then out of the blue I dreamed of her. I was in her suburban house, when all of a sudden the dream went from full-color into black-and-white, the room turned upside down, and her husband, Bob, was hanging from the ceiling.

The strange thing was that there were bars on all the windows. I couldn't tie this into anything that was happening in my own life, and so I dismissed the dream. Later that week I heard from a *Time* colleague and talked to my friend.

"Didn't you hear?" she said. "Her husband was arrested for embezzling. He tried to hang himself and then went to jail, and they had to sell the house."

• • •

My most recent experience of synchronicity has to do with dating. At mid-life you get a chance to do things differently, to make sense of your past loves and past mistakes. I had just met a man I was very interested in. It was a strong attraction, but I wanted very much to change my way of being in a relationship. All this had to do with my missing father and with the compromises I made, early on, to ward off abandonment. I kept thinking, *Without divine intervention, I won't succeed in changing this.*

To adjust the programs from early childhood, you have to redo your basic wiring, so for two weeks I prayed, "Please, God. Help me change my hard drive."

Twenty-four hours before our next date, my PC went down. The main drive had been totally wiped out, as though God had come into the room and pushed a button called "Erase."

That night, I was so busy concentrating on how to restore the essentials of my life—my financial programs, the magazine articles I was writing—that I couldn't do my usual dance of pleasing and accommodating. It was significant, as well, that I'd wiped out all my journals and the chronicle of my last relationship.

Thinking of the role synchronicity had played in my life, I laughed, knowing that this episode was absolutely perfect: I couldn't have moved ahead in life without losing all my data, without this total clearing of the past.

—*Valerie Andrews*

The Transfer

As I sat, reading *Working on Yourself Alone,* by Arnold Mindell, waiting for the bus, an elderly black man approached. A white plastic grocery bag was swinging low in his left hand. I looked up from my book. Our eyes met. We nodded to one another. His right and free hand began to move, rising toward his chest pocket, reaching, slowly. I flinched. My eyes went down, meeting the page again.

I felt myself hiding. Something in the moment—something altogether unknowable—told me that this gesture was for my sake. I knew this without knowing this. And I was afraid. What could he possibly have for me as one stranger to another?

I felt him opposite me, crossing my shadow. I looked up. His right hand was down again, held out before my eyes. He was shaking a ticket at me.

"Take it!" the gesture said. "Take it! It's yours!"

It was a transfer. I took it without thinking. My hand was there holding his ticket before I knew my hand was holding his ticket. I thanked him.

Nothing. He didn't turn. No words. Just walking, walking on. A black man hobbling down a city street with a white bag brushing against his leg. A simple mosey. A Sunday morning stroll. No Mass today.

I examined the ticket. It was still good; there was still time on it. It hadn't expired. I was still so afraid to trust simple human kindness.

He continued walking, never breaking stride. He walked right on past the bus stop. So he wasn't coming to wait for the bus with the rest of us. Yet. he knew I was there waiting. He knew.

What was it in my sitting, in my reading, in my look that told him that I was waiting, that I was wanting something?

I looked after him feeling my distrust, my disbelief dissolve and transform into gratitude, astonishment. Where did such generosity come from? I wondered, watching him grow more and more distant.

Transportation. He saw the need in me for it, while he was just fine without it. He would get where he was going by handing out transfers along the way.

How close was I to myself, to my way? I asked myself. Where was I going, anyway? This ticket that I hold in my hand was it an edge or "channel," as Mindell calls it? Or was it an invitation to change, to proceed to the next terminus, the next level of consciousness?

I returned to my reading, feeling that I was not so alone within myself. As long as there are strangers in the world handing out free tickets for public transit rides, I can feel assured that all of us who are waiting or wanting will one day find our rite of passage.

—*Robert Martin*

THE LINES OF FORCE

I was a naval general duty doctor at Miramar Naval Air Station in San Diego. Because of a low service number, I happened to be the senior medical officer of a large dispensary and small partial hospital. It was peacetime; funds were, compared to now, plentiful. Filled with a sense of Presbyterian virtue, I had enlisted a group of eager volunteers who had helped train the enlisted hospital corpsmen to provide quick, courteous, efficient care to the 7,000 enlisted dependents assigned to Miramar. It became popular with the families, and we were able to provide high quality medical care in a busy but not overwhelmed place free of burnout. I was young, generally full of myself, and felt happy and conflict-free. It was, as I reflect, certainly the most naturally fulfilling period of my adult life.

The synchronicity vignette I am about to relate took place in a small wooden dispensary building that was adequately windowed with panoramic east and north views. In the winter months, after storms, a magnificent snow-draped view of the San Gabriel Mountains northeast of Los Angeles dominated the northern horizon. On this particular day in January or February, a storm had just passed through the area, leaving the local hills very fresh and green. It was, for a midwesterner recently dropped into southern California, magical.

The clinic was humming. The staff was happy. The patients in general were extremely grateful, and I felt really competent to be handling the practice that existed there. I had seen a number of children who had either viral pneumonia or bacterial pneumonia. They were fairly sick, and I remember the corpsmen being quite tender and careful with the preparation of these kids for my examinations. For a doctor, I was "in the zone."

I remember walking into an examination room and seeing this one baby about four to five months old lying on the table in respiratory distress, looking up at me with an ashen, pale look. He was accompanied by a struggling very young service mother who really didn't know what to do, obviously scared and overwhelmed. I remember looking at the child, with skin retracting between his ribs and his respiratory rate, and knowing that he had a pneumonic illness. This little fellow was not too toxic and having had a run of similar cases that week, I sensed his illness would pass with either antibiotics or proper supportive care, and I was confident he would return to being a healthy, happy kid in a few days.

I moved over to examine the baby, who would have been naked in a warmer setting. I put my hands around his tiny chest and rib cage and felt him breathing laboriously. I remember simultaneously looking out to the mountains, then without warning, I suddenly felt an immense sense of direct visceral contact with a line of force almost like a magnetic attraction: This line of contact connected me to those mountains, which had a specific linear direction flowing through the area of the dispensary and continuing on a west-southwest line to a mesa overlooking the ocean about seven miles away. Then, as I held this child (with an almost unconscious kind of awareness), I began feeling as if I were in a state of personal purity.

At that moment, I also experienced another line of force coming from the vicinity of Mount Queamaca, due east of where the military base is. I could "feel" that these two lines crossed on the mesa overlooking the ocean. It was a very explicit, clear feeling.

This all occurred within the twinkling of an eye and was associated with a quiet assurance of personal joyfulness. I had no frame of reference to make any meaning of it. It was just something that was experienced. I continued to take care of the sick child and others on that same day.

The day remains a mystery.

That evening, I put my young daughter, Caren, in the car and drove out toward the mesa as far as the roads would go—and then with her on my shoulders, we walked the area where the lines of force seemed to cross. I felt a heightened sense of both mission and of being in the right place at the right time with my own feelings and my own self. I was absolutely in full love with this little girl, and we were babbling and talking with each other. I had a clear feeling of self and direction.

As we walked and talked, I was *sure* I should establish a charity or low-fee clinic at that location and that it would be a place where kids could come and be healed. I was also convinced that the clinic should not be cluttered or corrupted by the fee-for-service model of care that was then driving the private practice of medicine. It was one of those extremely rare, absolutely certain moments, which, to my continuing grief, I did not follow.

Segue twenty years later to the late 1970s. I was taking a walk along the cliffs near Torrey Pines Drive with Dr. Jonas Salk, whom I had become friends with. I asked him why he had built his institute there.

"In February of 1959," he told me, "the March of Dimes awarded me a grant to build a medical center. These cliffs had long been a favorite place of mine, so I took a walk here and just felt that this was the place."

We happened to be standing about forty-five feet from the exact spot I had had my epiphany about constructing a clinic more than twenty years before. As if it wasn't already an uncanny coincidence, I tried to argue with him—or convince him—that his memory was off, but he didn't buy it.

Instead, he told me that he had had a kind of religious vision to develop a clinic, with two buildings, two halves on opposite sides of the road, symbolizing the two halves of the brain/mind.

I didn't know it then, but the land there had already been zoned for medical buildings. Now it houses the Scripps Institute and the University of California at San Diego.

Thinking back, I'm convinced that that *place* had everything to do with what happened there. In the years afterward, I read extensively about the phenomenon of ley lines and dragon lines, the "Old Straight Tracks" that are supposed to connect sacred places all over the world. I believe that there are lines of force, which are documented well in Europe, particularly Celtic Britain and France, that focus on healing. They operate whether we feel them or not. Where those ancient lines cross, there are now both temples of healing and cathedrals. The message of nature is available, if we listen; it is *there*.

At the time I had no conceptual framework for what was happening. I think it had to do with the state of purity that I was in at the time: I was doing what I like to do, I was raising my children, and I had a flourishing career. It was the right place at the right time.

If only I had had the right mentor, I would have followed through with my original vision and listened to the voice I heard. But I had no cultural context for the extraordinary power of the experience. I was entirely alone. I didn't tell anyone what happened for ten years. I talked to no one about it. It was entirely acausal.

One wonders if some of my later problems in life had to do with not being true to my original voice.

—*Stuart Brown*

MOTHERS OF CONNECTION

I was due to meet Phil at The Stinking Rose restaurant in North Beach in an hour. Leaving my desk at work, I couldn't help but keep thinking we were going to break off our relationship at dinner. We had been seeing each other for a few months, and I felt we had reached a roadblock.

Despite that, we had had a magical beginning, we loved all of the same things, and I was completely wild over him. I had doubts about whether I should stay with someone for whom writing would always take precedence. He has said that he was "over the moon" about me then but was in a funk about his writing life. I knew that staying together would mean sticking out a lot of rough times. Was I prepared for this? I decided I needed to look for guidance. I thought maybe I'd read my tea leaves after dinner.

Driven by doubts and looking for signs, I arrived at the restaurant famed for its liberal use of garlic in every dish. As we ordered our potent meals, we were simultaneously reminded of the saying, "Garlic is as good as ten mothers," and the conversation turned to our own mothers. I was reminded that his mother's name was Rosemary, like the herb and the flower (and our restaurant), and that she was just fifty-nine. Odd, I remarked, that he, twelve years older than I, had a mother the same age as mine. As our conversation progressed, we discovered that our mothers were born not only in the same year—but also the same day: February 28, 1932.

Exactly at the moment of our discovery, I mysteriously felt the nagging weight within myself disappear and a release of energy escape my anxious heart. I knew immediately that the timing was too uncanny, that the sudden lightness in myself was all the answer I needed about the strength of my commitment to this man. I knew at that moment that we would stay together. I didn't have doubts again.

Later, I did a few calculations. Knowing our ages, our mothers could reasonably have been born thirty-seven years apart (if his mom had given birth at forty-two and mine had at seventeen, plus the twelve years between our ages). And thirty-seven times 365 days in the year equals 13,505. There are 13,505 reasonable, potential birthdays for our mothers. That we found they are the same year and day has enormous meaning for us.

We also learned that our mothers had other things in common: Both married at nineteen to men five years older, and both had sons soon after. Each had a passion for flowers: Rosemary as a professional floral designer, Sue as a mad lover of cut flowers from her garden. Both divorced their husbands when they had teenage children, and each embarked upon new a life as a strong, independent woman who made her children awfully proud.

Today, six years later, Phil and I have grown quite contentedly together, and we're reveling now in the love of our young son, Jack Philip Blue, who seems as if he was destined to be. Neither of our fathers is living, and our mothers continue to be pivotal figures in our daily lives.

Somehow on the night it meant the most, we found a connection based in the past, between the women that brought us into this world.

—Jo Beaton

LOVE ON THE EDGE OF THE GRAND CANYON

I was seven when my great-grandmother reached ninety. She was a beautiful woman, with large violet eyes, exquisitely groomed white hair, and magnificent hands, veined and transparent, which she enhanced with antique rings. She gave me one, an oblong purple amethyst, set in heavy gold, which I love more and more as I get older. She wore brocade dresses with lace petticoats. The shoes on her little feet always matched her satin hair bands. She liked to talk to me. I loved to listen. She told me many things, once about a love affair she had years earlier "on the edge of the Grand Canyon." She was much younger then, she explained, only seventy-four.

"On the very edge," she repeated in her crystal clear, yet moss soft voice. "It was very romantic. I looked straight down the canyon walls—a thousand miles below. We were passionate then and unafraid, being young."

At the time, I had no idea what she was talking about. By the time I understood, I imagined my exquisite and delicate great-grandmother in a passionate embrace with a mysterious stranger on the very rim of the Grand Canyon, while a sunset of glorious oranges and golds spread across a darkening vastness.

Birds would have called to each other as they settled in their nests, their soul-filled evening songs as tender as any my great-grandmother sang to me. In my mind, the sky changed to green, then red and purple, finally settling on the dark blue of unpolluted night.

Meanwhile, a moon rose and shadows got darker. Single mesas were etched in silver, and the canyon rim itself was a rippling ribbon of black, silver, and sand, as far as the eye could reach. Mirror-smooth "a thousand miles below," a river reflected the moon and the stars, which came out, first one by one, then as if thrown by handfuls, until bucketsful were tumbled across the sky to laugh above the lovers. Holding hands, the lovers, I imagined, dangled their feet over the edge, rapt in the beauty. Then, when there was only black and silver and silence all around, they made love.

I believed the story, and so I always believed that life is extravagantly beautiful, slightly risky, and continuously love-filled.

Also precarious.

And a bit sandy.

Not for the faint-hearted.

In a word, *mythic*.

Many years later, I was on my honeymoon with Alex, driving across the West. Not being familiar with the speeds at which one could travel in those days, we had not planned upon reaching the Grand Canyon until the middle of the next day, but, by late afternoon, we found ourselves at the entrance to Grand Canyon National Park and decided to stay the night.

We followed the signs to the central complex, where a new hotel blazed in the center of what seemed to be a parking lot. Tall street lamps glowed down on the cars of many colors blocking off the late afternoon light. Coffee shops were already filled, the smell of fried food obliterating the fragrance of pines and cedars. People scurried with suitcases, calling sharply to children. No birds sang. Newly arriving travelers, all with reservations, crowded the lobby. The harried man at the desk was sorry, but there were no more rooms.

"I know that hotels always have an extra room for an emergency," Alex said. "Say a VIP arrives unexpectedly. Give us that room and we'll pay for it." Alex was in no mood to drive any further.

"Sir, that is not the case. We would give you a proper room if we had one. But we have only one room left, one we never rent anymore. It is in the Old Inn, and people don't like it, so we don't bother to show it."

"Sounds perfect," Alex said.

A bellboy called ahead and then, gathering our bags, led us over to the Old Inn. We followed him through its lovely old lobby and then down the corridors to the back of the building. We were quite disoriented by the time we reached our room—apartment, I should say, with rooms worthy of the Grand Canyon. The bedroom was the size of an ordinary ballroom, and the bathroom your run-of-the-mill living room. The tub itself was about seven feet long and four feet deep—a fitting object of sculpture.

Everything was ready for us by the time we got there: large towels in the bathroom, bed turned down, curtains pulled. A fire had been lit and was burning cheerfully. The room was large but had a cozy feel to it, green and white chintz and natural wood and wicker furniture. An antique silver mirror glowed resplendent over the dressing table. The bed was big enough for five.

"Nothing wrong with this," I said.

The bellboy silently accepted his tip, put another log on the fire, and left us.

The first thing was a hot bath. It took some time to fill, but soon the heat was loosening the tensions of the day. After a while, I remembered the sunset. The window was right there beside the tub. I hardly had to move to pull back the curtain and look out: sky, orange and gold, shot through with giant splashes of green and purple. A star. A half moon, green in the golden air. I looked over to the far side of the Grandest Canyon of them all. The edge was still visible. My eyes climbed slowly down to a silvery ribbon, running in the already black of the canyon bottom. I got up on my knees to see better and gasped.

Grabbing a thick towel, I tumbled out of the bath and ran into the bedroom. Our bed was set right against an enormous window. I jumped on it and threw open the curtains. Sure enough, the bed, too, was right over the canyon. I knew immediately that this had been Great-Grandmother's room all those years ago.

Speechless, I beckoned Alex. The pull of the dreadful height got to us. We lay on our stomachs to look. There was no rim on this side—nothing between us and the bottom. Only an awesome down. "Down a thousand miles," as my great-grandmother had said.

Alex looked at me, and I looked at him.

If Great-Grandmother could, we can; our eyes agreed.

We left the curtain open that evening on the very edge of the Grand Canyon.

—*Jane Winslow Eliot*

A FALL TO GRACE

If space/time is a reality, then doesn't everything happen in a greater present moment that only the unknown God could possibly comprehend?

Don't our personal experiences of synchronicity constitute vividly clear evidence for this?

One final question: Do people fall in love all that often? We may think we do, again and again, but perhaps the real thing is rare enough to qualify as synchronicity.

I was a sad, fat, smart-ass with a plush post: art editor of *Time* magazine. Hungover, as usual, I sat in my cell of Manhattan's Time/Life Building, that high-rise dungeon, staring at the catalogue for a Madrid exhibition. It was in Spanish, which I couldn't read, so I found myself in a poor position to write about the show.

"Not to worry," my researcher Ruth Brine said soothingly. "I'll go find someone who can translate."

Ruth returned leading someone new. I got to my feet, sucked in my gut, smiled, and stuck out my hand, while simultaneously gazing into the girl's eyes. I won't try to describe what I saw there. Life it was—and destiny.

Tipping forward I crashed to the floor.

The two girls stood over me, laughing. They helped me up and settled me back in my chair.

Time's music editor and sports editor, both pals of mine, occupied neighboring cells. Hearing the crash, they entered as the girls were leaving.

"What happened?" Chan Thomas asked.

"Gentlemen, I'm in love!"

"Seriously?" Marsh Smith wanted to know.

"Oh, yes."

"This is terrible," said Chan. "You must mount a hot pursuit."

"It's not as you imagine—" I began.

"Maybe not," Marsh put in thoughtfully, "but consummation is the only cure."

"No, I'll stay well away from her. I'm not going to even try and date the girl until I've cleaned up my act."

Six months passed, during which I tried hard to put my personal life in some semblance of order. When Jane Winslow Knapp and I happened to meet in the elevator, I silently stared at the toes of my shoes.

Finally, late one night, desperate, I could wait no longer. I looked her up in the Manhattan phone book, and called: "Jane, this is Alex Eliot."

"I know. I've been waiting for you to phone."

She'd known from the first moment, all along!

Twenty minutes later we were walking together in Central Park, hand in hand. The park was supposed to be dangerous at night, but not for us. We were also talking together, talking, talking, as we have ever since.

This went on for the rest of the night. We had breakfast at the original Reubens Deli on 59th Street.

Reubens is gone, but we haven't. We still breakfast together, daily.

—*Alexander Eliot*

THE WITNESSING

Sometime in late July 1995, I was drinking coffee at my sky house, which overlooks the waters of the Strait of Juan de Fuca between America and Canada. As I often do, I found myself staring at the water and rather letting my mind go blank. That morning a scene began to occur to me so strongly, however, that I had to go get my notebook and write it down. It was happening in Romania, by the Black Sea, where a woman on the last day of her holiday was staring similarly out at the water and found herself witnessing a drowning. I scribbled the scene down, not knowing what it might be attached to, feeling it was some fragment that belonged perhaps to something I had yet to write. I remember feeling very agitated and moved by the scene as I wrote it down.

Shortly thereafter, probably the next day, I began to write a story entitled "To Dream of Bears." The main character was a Romanian man, who was terrified of drowning. His mother had been responsible for instilling this fear. I suddenly realized that she was the one who had witnessed the drowning and had passed the scene on to her son. Thereafter he had an obsessive need to retell his mother's experience. Once the fragment had been imbedded in the story, I gave it to my secretary, Dorothy Catlett, to type in a working draft.

Some days later, I received a handwritten letter from Liliana Ursu, a Romanian poet, whose poems I had been translating with

Adam Sorkin and Liliana's help. In her letter, she wrote that she had been at a writer's retreat at the Black Sea. On her final day, she had witnessed a drowning. She wrote me in very moving detail how this tragedy had affected her. I recall I was quite stricken by the seeming coincidence of my vision of a drowning at that place a few days before, and how it now stepped forward into the real through Liliana's experience. I remember calling my secretary and telling her about the letter, being amazed and in a state of disbelief. Why had these drownings—written and experienced—conjoined so closely in time? Then I realized that the time period between Liliana's letter and my writing of the scene could indeed have allowed my writing to accompany her experience at the exact time of occurrence. Or at least it was so close in time as to shadow it, to blush against it.

The details of Liliana's experience were more exact than my own, and she had recorded the incident so poignantly that I went back to my draft of the drowning in the story and superimposed her version onto mine. I wrote and asked for her permission to do so, which I received. The final account is really a marriage of the witnessed and the transferred-at-a-distance images of the drowning, which unaccountably reached me far across the world at the edge of another body of water.

When such things have happened to me before, I've had a tendency to discount them. I didn't do so in this case. I seem to feel a responsibility to perfect and make live that drowning at the Black Sea, but also to remember and to tremble a little at the way I first received it. Perhaps, if my secretary had not already seen the account typed into the body of the story, the circuit would have been closed and I might have allowed the whole incident to float away without remark. But Dorothy's outside witnessing also gave me someone to call after I read the letter from Liliana. I remember remarking to her about the strangeness of what had occurred across time and distance. Then I dictated the letter to Liliana, asking for permission to use that passage about the drowning from her letter and acknowledging to her that what had occurred was also an important part of preserving the synchronicity of the event and our separate accounts. I haven't seen my friend since this correspondence, but, when we do meet, I know I will ask her to tell me the scene again.

We are both witnesses and I have the sense that we will stand together on the shore at the moment she tells me what she saw. I expect it will ignite my kindred vision and close distance and time. Maybe then I will take one step more toward certifying the extraordinary and unaccountable fact of my imagination, having discovered a linkage to the real so palpably and undeniably.

—*Tess Gallagher*

LOST IN AFRICA

"Where is the knowledge that is lost in information?
Where is the wisdom that is lost in knowledge?"

—*T. S. Eliot*

I was in Tanzania for a conference in the late '60s and didn't want to leave without a glimpse of big game in its natural habitat. There were no tours, so I found a fly-by-night car rental joint and took off in a rickety jalopy for the Serengeti Plain. There was no road map, but that was logical, because as far as I could make out there were no roads. I did encounter one road sign during the day, but I couldn't read it, besides which it had fallen over, so I couldn't tell which way its arms pointed.

A couple of hours into the desert, it suddenly dawned on me that I was completely lost and out of gas. When we rent a car here we assume the tank to be full. Not there. They give you about enough to get out of the lot, but I didn't know that and hadn't checked. At a total standstill, I couldn't think of a thing to do. The car was too hot to sit in, and there were no trees to shade me from the blistering sun. Giraffes were friendly; one literally looked over my shoulder when I had had to change a threadbare tire. There were other animals, but at that hour no lions. Dry bones were everywhere, though—portents of my impending fate. I ate my packed lunch, started rationing my last bottle of water, and tried to think of a plan of action.

None suggested itself when two figures appeared dimly on the horizon. I started toward them, but with every step I took, they retreated. I quickened my pace, making frantic gestures of distress, and they gradually slowed their pace to allow me to catch up with them. They were disconcertingly large and wore nothing, except spears taller than themselves and flapping cloths over their shoulders to ward off the sun somewhat.

What then to do? I was in human company, but without words to communicate. *Something* had to be done, so I seized one of them by the wrist and marched him to my dysfunctional car, his companion in tow. This seemed to amuse them, and why not? What had our move to a pile of metal accomplished?

The two of them conversed and then started to leave, but I seized my hostage's wrist again. Human beings were my only lifeline, and I wasn't going to let it be severed. More laughter and conversation between them, and then one of them started off while leaving his companion with me. When he returned he had in tow a small boy who knew a few words of English—"hello," "good-bye," and the like—so, pointing in different directions, I said, "school, school!" He showed no signs of comprehension, but after more conversation he and the man who had fetched him went off, leaving my hostage with me. In about an hour, the man returned with adult cohorts, and the sun set that evening on as bizarre a scene (I feel sure) as the Serengeti Plain had ever staged: a white man, seated at the wheel of his car, steering, while twelve Masai warriors pushed him across the sands. My propellers were taking the experience as a great lark. Laughing and all talking simultaneously, they sounded like a flock of happy birds. My first thought was, *who listens?;* then immediately, *who cares?*—they were having such a great time. Six miles across the plain they delivered me to the school I had asked for, which turned out to be Oldavai Gorge, where a decade or so earlier Louis and Mary Leakey discovered the tooth that "set the human race back a million years," as the press reported their discovery.

That encounter left me with a profound sense of human connectedness. There we were, as different in every way—ethnically, linguistically, culturally—as any two groups on our planet. Yet, without a single word in common, we connected. They understood my predicament and responded with a will and with style.

Beware the differences that blind us to the unity that binds us.

—*Huston Smith*

The Sly Winks of Fate

"I can't believe that!" said Alice.

". . . one can't believe impossible things."

"I daresay you haven't had much practice," said the Queen.
"When I was your age, I always did it for half an hour a day.
Why, sometimes I've believed as many
as six impossible things before breakfast."

—Lewis Carroll, *Through the Looking Glass*

A few years ago, an unorthodox scientist named Benoit Mandelbrot invented an innovative way of describing the jagged and fragmented shapes of nature, the unexpected order in chaos, patterns he called *fractals*, a word he conjured from fractured and fractional. His insight about a hidden organizing structure inside the strange shapes of nature was confirmation for him that the complexity of life is not random, not an accident. Then he went a step further and implied that those strange shapes carry meaning, and may even contain the secret soul of things. The implications about hidden patterns lurking in virtually every aspect of life have had staggering implications for geologists, economists, meteorologists and artists. As James Gleick has interpreted Mandelbrot's work, "Fractals also describe the way things cluster in space and time . . . Things wear their irregularity in an unexpectedly orderly fashion."

Unexpected order is one way to describe the fractal plots of Woody Allen's movies. To take just one coincidence-riddled, holy fool search-for-meaning masterpiece, *Annie Hall,* Allen pulls off a sleight-of-hand trick many of us have secretly wished for at one time or another. His relationship with Annie, his girlfriend, played by Diane Keaton, is in shambles. At a movie theater one night, they wait in line for a screening of Marcel Carne's movie, *The Sorrow and the Pity.* While they argue about their disintegrating love life, an insufferable bore behind them pontificates to his date about Fellini and Bergman, which sends Allen into conniptions. When the stuffed shirt cites the media maven, Marshall McLuhan, Allen tosses his hands in the air with an "I've-had-enough" expression and says to him, "You don't know what you're talking about!"

Then in a startling move, our discombobulated hero shuffles across the lobby and reaches into an office stage right, saying triumphantly, "I happen to have Mr. McCluhan right here!" With his trademark exasperation Allen drags the famous scholar from the shadows and into the conversation. Not one to suffer fools gladly, McCluhan confronting the self-proclaimed professor of media studies, "I heard you . . . and you don't know anything about my work. How you got to teach a course on anything is amazing to me!"

Smiling cagily, Allen steps forward and says into the camera and us, "Boy, if life were only like this . . . ."

It's one of those rare moments; triumphant, whimsical, daffy, romantic. With uncanny dream logic, this scene wonderfully recreates the incorrigibly human desire for timely, if not time-busting, coincidence. For one glorious moment the usually hidden movement and fantastic forces of fate (the old *deux ex machina* trick of ancient Greek theater) are transformed into synchronicity. Meaningless chance (McCluhan's mathematically possible presence in the lobby as they discuss his theories) turns into meaning*ful* coincidence right before our very eyes.

For a fleeting moment, we watch as our hero schemes to change the course of his destiny, or at least one of its subplots. The fact that Annie Hall herself barely notices the ruse only adds to the sweet anarchy of the moment. I suspect that this scene is evoked so often not only in film classes and everyday life because of our heart's desire for significant coincidence, but also because of the soul's desire for timely pandemonium.

"Humility is awed and wowed by meaning," James Hillman

writes in his essay, *Peaks and Vales,* "the soul takes the same events more as the puns and pranks of Pan."

In those unfolding moments at the significant crossroads and junctures of our lives, are the soul moments, the movement towards meaning and grace and wisdom that arrives with synchronicity.

To paraphrase T. S. Eliot, after all our exploration we've come to the end of our stories. But do we know the place, the baffling land of synchronicity, for the first time? Are these plangent scenes from myth, dream, movies, poetry, literature, and fables just random acts of imagination? Are these premonitions of earthquakes, romance, and death only wild spins on the wheel of fortune? Are these heart-racing meetings of lovers on a houseboat in Paris a simple case of how "happenstance twirls a kaleidoscope in its hands," in the brilliant image of the great Polish poet Wislawa Szymborska. What about the life-changing job offer to be a video stand-in for the guy you've hated being mistaken for (and who just happened to write the song called "Synchronicity")? A mere twist of fate? What about the sick child's dream-come-true in finding his lost pet a thousand miles from where he lost it? Only the opportunistic reach of the long arm of coincidence?

What can we make of the strange appearance of a soap bubble in a kitchen that reminds a family of the death of their mother? How do we explain the enigmatic vision of a Washington state poet that eerily mirrors the tragic sighting of another poet in Romania, half a world away?

Can we explain all this uncanniness as quantum events popping in and out of reality like subatomic particles in a cloud chamber? Describe it as time doing loop-the-loops like a World War I stunt plane? The soul bending backwards like a contortionist? The forces of the Tao running wild as a dragon in heat? The heart at a fevered pitch creating the majestic forces that pull another heart towards it? The gaping rabbit hole or magical looking glass beckoning us down and in?

But to ask *how* and *why* synchronicity *happens* is ultimately as exasperating as asking how a dream appears to us or why a mood comes over us, a long-forgotten memory returns, or an inspiration suddenly hits.

Instead, from the blue-lit stage of the Masonic Auditorium in San Francisco I hear the Irish bard Van Morrison moan, "It ain't why, why, why, it just is, it just is, it just is . . . "

And from the back of the quiet bookstore the poet Haydn Carruth whispers about "just the ordinary improbability that occurs/over and over, the stupendousness of life."

And from what Lincoln called the "mystic chords of memory" I remember my mother explaining her faith to me one time by simply and soulfully quoting Detroit's own Father Divine, "Can't you see the mystery? Ain't you glad?"

Four centuries ago the philosopher Giordono Bruno said, "To understand is to speculate with images," which is where we are now with the phenomenon of synchronicity. For "speculating" literally means to hold a mirror up to; and playing with images means to imagine, in our case what these stories *imply,* which is another way to say unfolding in our souls.

"Don't be satisfied with stories, how things have gone with others," said the twelfth-century Sufi mystic and poet, Mevlana Rumi, "Unfold your own myth." Nicholas of Cusa, writing in the fifteenth century, said, "Eternity unfolds in time." In the abyss

years between the world wars, the German poet Rainer Maria
Rilke, wrote ominously, "Where you are folded, you are a lie."
When interviewed by fellow physicist Renée Weber in a book
about the search for unity, David Bohm explained the implications of his theory of the implicate order for the ordinary individual, "You *are* your future, but not yet unfolded. You're still
unfolded."

What is most moving to me about the stories that have come
my way are the glimpses of *unfolding* destiny. To reflect that
spirit, this book offers up the soulful moments of synchronicity
as if they were story echoes of the medieval Cabinets of Wonder
that were the world's first museums. As David Wilson, the eccentric curator of the phantasmagorical Museum of Jurassic
Technology in Los Angeles (and modern Chamber of Wonder),
described the inspiration behind his work to the bemused author
Lawrence Weschler, "Part of the assigned task is to reintegrate
people to wonder."

So, too, these stories can be thought of as parables about reac-
quainting people to their wonder, or as fables that teach how the
soul, like the heart according to Pascal, has reasons reason does
not yet know about.

"And so one feels through such experiences that there is
meaning, that one is meaning, that one is personally, individually
meant," James Hillman writes in *Puer Papers*. "Let us call it meaningful discontinuity of the order of chance governed by fate, or
call it living from the principle which Jung circumscribed as synchronicity."

Time and time again, as if to say there's a time *after* time and
a time *beside* time, synchronicities suggest that when we seize the
soul moment something wonderfully *weird* is revealed. Then we

can "catch the sly winks of fate," in a memorable Hillman phrase from *The Soul's Code*.

"At first I thought this story was too weird to mention . . ." as one contributor wrote to me in her cover letter for this book. "Too weird. I didn't dream anybody would believe me, it was strange," another told me minutes after receiving my invitation letter.

So it goes with the polyfabulous, the many-storied phenomenon of synchronicity, the uncanny shaping of our lives that forces us to rethink the way in which we are connected to our own fate, the lives of others, and the world.

As it did ineffably and irrevocably for me early one morning in the spring of 1993. I had been up all night several nights in a row desperately trying to finish my opening essay for my book, *Soul: An Archaeology*. I was agonizingly stuck and in a near rage, savaged by doubts about what I was doing with my life, to say nothing of my book. Finally, I tried changing the music in my stereo, slipping in some Ray Charles and Nat King Cole, and then, as things began to flow, a CD of Van Morrison, for which I hit the repeat button for the song "Listen to the Lion." For the next hour I wrote as if in a trance and actually completed the piece with a brief description of witnessing Morrison singing the same mystic ballad at the Berkeley Amphitheater a few years before.

Unable to sleep, I dashed outside into the cold early morning air of San Francisco and headed in a huff to the Blue Danube, my local cafe, six blocks away. As I neared the door, I passed a figure who looked strangely familiar and, grudgingly, looked over my shoulder at Van Morrison himself with a woman friend on his way to the same cafe. I was stunned. What was he doing in my neighborhood?

Trying to look unfazed, I got in line and slowly figured out he had to be in town for a concert. I fought the urge to turn around and—what—ask for an autograph? Share the improbable coincidence that I'd just been writing about him a few minutes before— with a guy who lives as a Dweller on the Threshold, who writes out of the Celtic Twilight world where the past, present, and future coexist, and the Ancient Ones exist side by side with Blake, Yeats, Kerouac, and the bluesman Robert Johnson? What could I say that would mean anything to him?

Nothing, I decided. So I left as casually as possible, and dashed back up the street to my old Capri, and grabbed two copies of my own books out of the trunk, then pivoted and headed back to the cafe, signing them to Morrison on the run. When I arrived back at the cafe he was sitting down with his friend on the outside bench. Seeing me approach, he began a gesture with his hand that sure as rain in Connemara meant, "Leave me alone. Can't a guy enjoy a decent cup of coffee without being bothered—"

Out of breath from my mad dash, I gestured back, as if to say, "Don't worry," then actually said simply, "No, no, I don't want a thing. I just want to *thank you,* man. Your music has meant the world to me. Here's a couple of *my* books for you. What can I say? Thanks."

"Oh—you wrote these?" He said, genuinely surprised. As he took the books, something remotely resembling a smile began the arduous journey across his haunted face.

Nodding, I disappeared inside, ordered a coffee, and reemerged a few minutes later to sit at the far end of the bench.

For the next twenty minutes, I noticed out of the corner of my eye as he flipped back and forth between *The Hero's Journey* and *Deadlines,* while singing a soft bluesy harmony to the music on the cafe stereo, songs I'd been playing only a few minutes before, "What I'd Say" by Ray Charles and "Route 66" by Nat King Cole.

That night, my partner Jo and I snatched two of the last seats to Morrison's performance at the Masonic Auditorium. When two of his encore numbers were "What I'd Say" and "Route 66," I shrugged my shoulders and smiled.

I've rolled this story around in my mind for five years now and will probably wonder about it for the rest of my life. When I think about synchronicity the classic stories from Jung's work come to mind, as well as striking coincidences from the annals of literature and movies, and now from my own mailbag of examples from people around the world. But always I come back to my own experiences, the story of my father and "Two Years Before the Mast", the remarkable reunion with my nephew and his father, and the "Ballad of Van the Man".

Even though I'm sometimes bedeviled by a voice that asks *how* Van happened to be on the same street the same morning I was writing about him, and *why* did those songs string the day and night together the way they did, it's far less important to me than the joyous fact that it all simply *happened*. By no mere chance, as Robert Johnson notes in his opening essay, the word *happiness* itself derives from the very active verb "happen." So rather than submit to the soul-deadening reductionism of figuring out the odds or the "psi powers" that were activated that morning, the encounter taught me that an invaluable form of happiness is found by trusting what unfolds in my life.

This story hangs by a thread. That thread is soul, the vital force that somehow connects what is deepest and oldest in me with the rest of creation, with the immensity of life, in a "pattern out of time," as Laurens Van der Post has written in his autobiography, *About Blady*.

I can only say that in the fugitive minutes it took me to walk back up Clement Street to my apartment I left behind any doubts that I should be doing what I was doing with my life. Nothing I know *caused* the convergence at the cafe, and nothing *caused* the crystal clear realization that I was *meant* to be doing what I was doing with my life. In the end I simply felt graced to have the chance to express my gratitude.

These moments arrived, happened, unfolded.

Whether by chance, fortune, fate, destiny, accident, quantum leap, sun spots, or a tear in the space-time continuum, the strangeness that I happened upon reconnected me to my own life and revived my astonishment about the life I was immersed in.

"So much of the truth does not belong to the world of the clock and the calendar," Van der Post goes on to say about the life that comes out of the "the not-yet in the now . . ."

Indeed, these are, we should not be afraid to say, the "holy moments," in the deepest sense of the word, sacred and whole.

In his balm of a book, *Time and the Art of Living,* Robert Grudin proposes that what is needed "is a habit of looking not only at but *through* past and future events and of endowing present time with its past and future dimensions." Happiness, he writes provocatively, "may well consist primarily of an attitude toward time. Individuals we consider happy commonly seem *complete in the present:* We see them constantly in their wholeness, attentive, cheerful, open rather than closed to event. . . .

"One almost feels that their lives possess a kind of qualified eternity: that past and future, birth and death, meet for them as in the completion of a circle."

As if speaking to the influence of time on human happiness and the mysterious ways in which people find profound meaning in their lives, Marie-Louise von Franz said with riddlic power on

Dutch television in the early 1990s, that "The work that has to be done is the work with synchronicity."

The challenge will be to know what is trivial and what is meaningful, what is grandiose and what is genuine, in these maverick experiences called synchronicity. Suffice it to say they are more than chance, less than causality; more than magic, less than fantasy. More an enigmatic pattern suddenly detected, than a solid link in a chain finally proved.

• • •

Chances are you are wondering by now what your chances are that your life will be graced by synchronicity.

"Well, chances are," as Johnny Mathis sings, "your chances are awfully good."

And when your chances are as good as those we've seen in these marvelous coincidences from around the world, then chances are you'll notice the sly winks, the gemlike weirdness, the charming strangeness, and the mysterious blessings of the soulful moments of synchronicity.

Synchronicity, the blue guitar of the soul, making silent music at the crossroads of time, there in the quickening moments of our lives.

ACKNOWLEDGMENTS

First and foremost I want to thank Jo Beaton for first suggesting the idea of a book, then patiently allowing enough coincidences to accumulate in our lives to give me the time and space for it to unfold into a synchronicity.

Secondly, many thanks to all those at Conari Press for their patience in waiting for this manuscript to finally appear, especially my editor Mary Jane Ryan. Thanks also to Will Glennon, Brenda Knight, Ame Beanland, and all those in the art department, Suzanne Albertson for her wonderful design, Alan Mazzetti for his soulful cover art, and everyone else involved in the project who believe that Dame Fortune is smiling on us.

My gratitude also to all who shared editorial advice about the direction, format, and parameters of the project, including psychologist and mentor extraordinaire Robert A. Johnson, psychologist and film critic nonpareil John Beebe, and the godmother of synchronicity herself, Goody Cable. Salutations to Trish O'Rielly for her sage advice, and James Van Harper for his years of unflagging support and timely sense of humor. Many thanks also to Enzo and all my friends at the Steps of Rome Cafe and the great publican Myles O'Reilly of O'Reilly's Pub in North Beach, San Francisco.

Finally, heartfelt thanks to those marvelous contributors who sent in their stories from the soulful world of synchronicity. There would be no book without your trust and faith.

May your lives be graced forever by the heart and soul of synchronicity!

CONTRIBUTORS

KATE BULLARD ADAMS lives in Charleston, South Carolina, with her children Ben and Laura. When not removing whatever sticks may be in her head, she writes, reads, and runs.

CARRIE ROSE AGINSKY is an actress, author, chef, daughter, filmmaker, friend, gardener, mother, photographer, singer, teacher, wife, and world traveler.

VALERIE ANDREWS is a former journalist, the author of *Passion for this Earth,* and leader of the Sacred Words project in the Bay Area.

REBECCA ARMSTRONG is a third generation singer and storyteller in the Celtic tradition. She holds a masters degree from the University of Chicago Divinty School and serves as a minister in the liberal religious tradition. She is the international membership director for the Joseph Campbell Foundation.

STUART BALCOMB is a composer, choir director, collector and player of world percussion, artist, and writer. He currently lives in Venice, California, and is writing a novel about alchemy. He also conducts percussion workshops with his wife, Joanne Warfield.

CHRISTY BALDWIN taught mythology for many years. She is the director and producer of the award-winning documentary film, *The Presence of the Goddess.*

JO BEATON has worked in the publishing industry for eight years. She lives on Telegraph Hill in San Francisco.

RICHARD BEBAN is a screenwriter and poet in Venice, California.

JOHN BEEBE is a Jungian analyst and author of *Integrity in Depth.*

JENNIFER BRONTSEMA is a book designer and frequent contributor to collections published nationwide. She lives in Berkeley, California.

STUART BROWN is a former physician and the film producer of *The Hero's Journey: The World of Joseph Campbell,* and *Transformations of Myth Through Time,* and author of an upcoming book on the phenomenology of *Play.* He lives in Carmel, California.

DENISE MURPHY BURKE graduated from Northwestern University. Currently she is a teacher, realtor, and jail literacy tutor.

NAOMI W. CALDWELL lives with her husband in a woodsy setting near the Blue Ridge Mountains of Virginia, where she writes and follows her interests in church, family, and spiritual life.

NICK CHARRINGTON is a music disc jockey, musician, and architect, living in London, England.

SHIRLEY CHRISTINE is publisher of Bridgeline Books in Sonoma, California.

JUDY ISSAC CONLEY is a second year student at Pacifica Graduate Institute in Santa Barbara, California, studying in the counseling psychology program, but whose real passion is the land that speaks to her and the spirits that are alive in the Syrian Hills of upstate New York.

BOB COOPER is a retired teacher and author of *Serenade to the Blue Lady: The Story of Bert Stiles.* He is currently completing the sequel. He lives in Davis, California.

RAND DeMATTEI is a third generation San Franciscan. He has published academic papers based on intuition research with Mobius Group, and is currently an independent business consultant and blues harmonica player.

LARRY DOSSEY is a physician and the internationally acclaimed author of such works as *Prayer is Good Medicine, Healing Words,* and *Recovering the Soul.* He lives in Sante Fe, New Mexico.

PAMELA DuMOND, D.C. is a chiropractor, cranio-sacral therapist, writer, and artist. She is currently completing a book entitled, *A Prayer for Racial Healing: 50 Ways to Promote Unity, Harmony, and Acceptance in America.*

ALEXANDER ELIOT, art journalist, art historian, novelist, and mythologist, was for fifteen years *Time* magazine's art editor. He is author of the world-wide bestseller, *300 Years of American Painting, The Timeless Myths, The Global Myths,* and *The Universal Myths,* and has been the recipient of numerous fellowships.

JANE WINSLOW ELIOT, writer, traveler, journalist, and educator, is board president of Santa Monica's Westside Waldorf School, and author of several books, including *Some Incarnating Games* and *A History of the Western Railroads.*

LESHA FINIW was born in Germany of Ukrainian parents, and maintains an international perspective working as director of development for the Global Environmental Institute. Recent freelance publications include reviews and commentary in the *Design Management Journal, Boston Business Journal,* and *Boston Tab.*

SUSAN FOSTER is working on a doctorate at Pacifica Graduate Institute in Santa Barbara, California. She is a practicing therapist specializing in healing with sound and movement and dream.

ART FRANCE lives and works in Columbus, Georgia, where he is a psychotherapist.

TESS GALLAGHER is the author of several poetry collections, including *Portable Kisses Expanded, Moon Crossing Bridge, My Black Horse:*

New and Selected Poems, and the forthcoming story collection, *At the Owl Woman Saloon.* She is currently the Edward F. Arnold visiting professor of English chair at Whitman College, Washington.

STEVE GEORGE: seven years a monk, twenty years in marketing, always a poet.

ROLF GORDHAMER is a psychologist and the director of the Counseling Center at Texas Tech University.

TREVOR GREEN grew up in Sheffield in a family of nine children, studied at Birmingham Polytechnic, lived on Ashdot Ya'akov kibbutz in Israel for two years, and specialized in design work for ethnic minority groups. Currently he teaches design illustration and three-dimensional graphics at St. Helens College, and maintains a design practice with Gwilt Green Associates in Manchester, England.

ANNE DENTON HAYES is a freelance writer and editor from Oakland, California.

JEANNETTE HERMANN is a professional travel agent and the author of several books on astrology. She lives on a houseboat in Paris and in a house called "Wild Olives" in Provence.

JAMAKE HIGHWATER is director of the Native Land Foundation. He is the author of thirty-four books, including the bestseller *The Primal Mind, Myth and Sexuality, The Language of Vision,* and *Dance: Rituals of Experience.*

JUDITH HIME-EVERSCHOR is married with a bachelor of arts in German and an master of arts in psychology. She is currently working toward licensure as a marriage, family, and child counselor in northern California. She also specializes in working with cancer patients and their families.

ANN B. IGOE is an artist from Santa Barbara, California.

KAAREN KITCHELL has had every job under the sun—tutoring, modeling, waitressing, cook on a schooner, and bookstore clerk. She now lives in Venice, California, and writes fiction.

SOPHIA KOBACKER is an Australian-born writer and traveler. Her passion for indigenous cultures has drawn her into worlds as diverse as Peruvian shamanism, African-American voodoo, and Native American and Australian aboriginal traditions.

STEPHEN LARSEN is the author of *The Shaman's Doorway, The Mythic Imagination,* and co-author with Robin Larsen of *Fire in the Mind: The Life of Joseph Campbell.*

ERIC LAWTON is an internationally renowned photographer and lawyer living in Los Angeles, California. He is the photographer for *The Soul of the World: A Modern Book of Hours.*

JUDITH LUTZ is a playwright, screenwriter, and freelance writer living in Los Angeles, California.

ROBERT MARTIN is the program advising coordinator for San Francisco State University's Multimedia Studies Program and is an independent filmmaker, who is currently completing work on a narrative film entitled *The Music Lesson.*

SHARON MATOLA has a degree in biology from New College, and has worked in a Mexican circus as a dancer and lion tamer. She traveled to Belize as a documentary film assistant and stayed on to develop a zoo with conservation programs. She has written two children's books and co-authored *A Field Guide to the Snakes of Belize.*

BEVERLY McDEVITT is a psychologist and antique collector living in Seattle, Washington, and Penedo, Portugal.

ERICA HELM MEADE is a practicing psychotherapist and the author of *Tell It By Heart* and is currently working on a second book, *Tales of the Uncanny: Intuition, Premonition, and Dreams in Therapy and Beyond.* She lives on Vashon Island, Washington.

LINDA RANIERI MELODIA lives in Queens, New York, where she is an aspiring writer who hasn't quit her day job yet. She loves art, artists, antiques, crying at old movies, and photography.

RICHARD (R.B.) MORRIS is a musician, composer, playwright, poet, and mountain man, whose albums include *Local Man* (with the Irregulars), and *Take That Ride.* He has also written and performed a one-man play based on the life of James Agee, *The Man Who Lives Here is Loony.* He lives with his daughter Frances in Knoxville, Tennessee.

PATRICIA MURPHY, in private practice in the San Francisco Bay Area for fifteen years and a founding board member of The Milton H. Erickson Institute, has relocated to the U.S. Virgin Islands and teaches self-hypnosis.

GERRY NICOSIA is the author of *Memory Babe: The Life of Jack Kerouac* as well as a book of poetry, and the upcoming *History of the Vietnam War Veterans Movement.*

LOIS V. NIGHTINGALE, Ph.D., is a clinical psychologist and is director of the Nightingale Counseling Center in Yorba Linda, California, as well as author of *My Parents Still Love Me Even Though They're Getting Divorced.* She lives with her two children in Yorba Linda, California.

MADELINE NOLD is a psychotherapist practicing in Brookline, Massachusetts, and workshop leader, specializing in comparative mythology and relationships issues. She is currently working on a book, *Magic, Meaning, and Mystery: A Woman's Transformative Journey.*

JOHN AND MARTHA O'BRIEN spend most of their time working

and playing in the hills of Woodacre, California. They're always looking for a reason to go back to Paris.

ELISABETTA ORLANDI studies literature at "La Sorbonne Nouvelle," writes fairy tales, and works at George Whitman's Shakespeare & Company Bookstore in Paris. She hopes someday to open a Shakespeare & Co. in her hometown of Venice, Italy.

PAULA JEAN PFITZER is a photographer and recent graduate of Antioch University, Santa Barbara. She currently resides in Ojai, California, with her sweetheart Yacov, a professional comedian with whom she often cruises the seven seas, and her dog, Spaz.

JEANIE QUINN is a journalist for a small weekly in East Stroudsburg, Pennsylvania and a photographer. She likes sitting down and reading good books.

LISA RAFEL is a writer, chantress, healer, actress, reformed liar, poet, teacher, mother, human, creator, and celebrator of life. Her book, *It Began in Katmandu,* was published in 1990. Her one-woman play, *It's All Right to be Naked,* was presented in Los Angeles in 1992 and in New York in 1994. Lisa teaches about sound and healing techniques all over the world.

LEILA M. REESE lives in San Rafael, California.

MARY REZMERSKI is an aspiring playwright and published poet who lives in Novi, Michigan.

HAYDN REISS is a documentary and commercial filmmaker living in San Anselmo, California. He is a principal of Moondog Pictures. He has produced a documentary on the poets William Stafford and Robert Bly, *A Literary Friendship.* His next project is on the mystic poet, Jalluludin Rumi.

GARY RHINE is an award-winning filmmaker whose work specializes in Native American contemporary issues, including *Wiping Away the Tears of Seven Generations, The Peyote Road, The Red Road to Sobriety,* and *Your Humble Serpent: The Life of Reuben Snake.*

BETTY ROSEN works in the music publishing business in Nashville, Tennessee. She has completed a children's picture book, *The Two of Me,* and is still slugging away at *9 Innings,* a baseball novella.

TRISH SAUNDERS is an astrologer, massage therapist, performer, and dancer, who has lived as an artist in the San Francisco Bay Area since 1987.

DENNIS SLATTERY is interdisciplinary coordinator for the MA in Counseling Psychology Program and Core faculty member of the Mythological Studies Program at Pacifica Graduate Institute. He is the author of *The Idiot: Dostoevsky's Fantastic Prince,* and editor of a collection of essays on William Faulkner and modern critical theory.

HUSTON SMITH is widely regarded as the contemporary authority on the history of religions. He is the author of the worldwide bestseller, *The World's Religions,* and *Forgotten Truths.* He is currently a visiting professor at the University of California at Berkeley.

D. ATESH SONNEBORN, Ph.D., is an ethnomusicologist, composer, and scholar of music in Sufism, who lives in the hills of Northern California.

ROSALIND SORKIN is an energetic widow living in Los Angeles who enjoys riding her bike, acting, and taking risks such as climbing trees, skiing, and sail boarding.

CARROLL STRAUSS is a recovering lawyer who feels she managed to overlook the fact that she was a writer all along, due to a particular gift for overlooking the obvious! She is a member of the C. G. Jung Club of Orange County and the Friends of Jung in San Diego, and she plans to begin formal studies toward becoming a Jungian therapist.

ROBERTO TAKAOKA is a dermatologist in private practice in Sao Paolo, Brazil, where he also lectures on mythological studies.

TERRENCE A. TAYLOR lives in Birmingham, Alabama, where he is a book artist and does limited edition fine press books and one-of-a-kind artist's books for Duende Press, Dolomite, Alabama.

KEITH THOMPSON is a cultural historian and the author of *Angels and Aliens* and *To Be a Man,* and of a forthcoming book about spiritual diversity in America—part cultural study, part personal memoir. He and his wife, anthropologist Marilyn Schlitz, live near Mount Tamalpais in the San Francisco Bay Area.

JAMES VAN HARPER is an actor, comedian, and stuntman, who has always wanted to direct. He also runs a small restaurant china business and is in training for an English Channel swim to raise money for a youth home and AIDS hospice. With pride, he lives in L.A. (Lower Alabama).

KATHERINE VAN HORNE is a portrait, landscape, and performance painter. She grew up on a cattle and lemon ranch and was seen from an early age as both a silent observer and drawer of life on the ranch, for which she has unspeakable gratitude. She is the mother of Samantha and Maria Morgan and Zach Rissel.

VLADAS VITKAUSKAS was the first Lithuanian to scale Mount Everest and has since placed his country's flag on the peaks of the world's seven tallest mountains. He lives in Vilnius where he is a consultant for Lithuania in *The World* magazine.

JOANNE WARFIELD has been a gallery owner and fine art dealer for twenty-five years and is a lifelong student of metaphysics and a certified clinical transpersonal hypnotherapist. She is currently practicing the art of healing with sound and color. She lives in Venice, California, with composer husband, Stuart Balcomb, where they give percussion workshops called "Living in Rhythm."

MARK WATTS is the son of the late author-entertainer Alan Watts and is president of the Electronic University in San Anselmo, California. He produces the weekly public radio series, "The Love of Wisdom" (with Alan Watts), and he is currently editing the spoken-word works of Joseph Campbell.

MEGAN WELLS is a professional storyteller, writer, and performance artist from LaGrange Park, Illinois. Her repertoire of stories and performances includes traditional folklore, mythology, short stories, adapted novels, and original works.

FRED ALAN WOLF is the author of several books, including *The Spiritual Universe, The Dreaming Universes, Parallel Universes,* and *Taking the Quantum Leap,* which won the National Book Award.

POHSUAN ZAIDE is a Vancouver, British Columbia-based psychologist, aspiring writer, and traveler on the road of life. Tantalized by the unknown, she often wanders about in labyrinths and other strange places looking for kindred spirits.

CHRISTOPHER ZELOV is the executive producer of the award-winning documentary film, *Ecological Design: Inventing the Future* and is director of the Knossus Project in Cape May, New Jersey.

BIBLIOGRAPHY

Aziz, Robert. *C. G. Jung's Psychology of Religion and Synchronicity.* Albany: State University of New York Press, 1990.

Becker, Ernest. *The Denial of Death.* New York: The Free Press, 1973.

Bolen, Jean Shinoda. *The Tao of Psychology: Synchronicity and the Self.* New York: Harper & Row, 1979.

Carse, James P. *Breakfast at the Victory.* San Francisco: HarperSanFrancisco, 1994.

Cavendish, Richard. *The World of Ghosts and the Supernatural.* New York: Facts on File, Inc., 1994.

Combs, Allan, and Holland, Mark. *Synchronicity: Science, Myth, and the Trickster.* New York: Paragon House, 1990.

Cousineau, Phil. *The Hero's Journey: Joseph Campbell on His Life and Work.* San Francisco: HarperSanFrancisco, 1990.

Dillard, Annie. *Mornings Like This.* New York: Harper Perennial, 1995.

Flammarion, Camille. Cited by Michell, John F. and Robert Rickard J. M. in *Phenomenon.* London: Thames & Hudson Ltd., 1977.

Freeman, Mara. *Parabola*, Fall, 1995.

Gleick, James. "Unexpected Order in Chaos," San Francisco Chronicle, December 29, 1985.

Greenblatt, Stephen. *Marvelous Possessions: The Wonder of the New World.* Chicago: University of Chicago Press, 1991.

Grudin, Robert. *Time and the Art of Living.* Cambridge: Ticknor & Fields, 1988.

Hesse, Hermann. *Journey to the East.* Translated by Hilda Rosner. New York: Farrar, Straus & Giroux, 1961.

Highwater, Jamake. *Dance: Rituals of Experience*. Third Edition. New York: Dance Horizons/Princeton Book Company, Publishers, 1996.

Hillman, James. Cited in *Puer Papers*. Dallas: Spring Publications, Inc., 1979.

_____. Cited in *Parabola* magazine, "Dream," Vol. VII:2 1982.

James, Henry. *The Lesson of the Master*. London: Penquin Classics, 1986.

Jaworski, Joseph. *Synchronicity: The Inner Path of Leadership*. San Francisco: Berrett-Koehler Publishers, 1996.

Jung, Carl G. *Man and His Symbols*. Conceived and edited by Aniele Jaffe. New York: Doubleday & Company, Inc., 1964.

_____. *Memories, Dreams and Reflections*. New York: Pantheon Books, 1961.

_____. Foreword and Commentary to *The Secret of the Golden Flower: A Chinese Book of Life,* translated by Richard Wilhelm. New York: Harcourt Brace Jovanovich, 1931.

_____. *Synchronicity: An Acausal Connecting Principal*. New York: Princeton University Press, 1973.

Kipling, Rudyard. "The Brushwood Boy" in *The Day's Work*. New York: MacMillian, 1889. Cited in *Parabola* VII:2.

Koestler, Arthur. *The Roots of Coincidence*. New York: Random House, 1973.

Koesler, Arthur, with A. Hardy and R. Harvie. *The Challenge of Coincidence*. New York: Random House, 1973.

Larson, Stephen. *The Mythic Imagination:Your Quest for Meaning Through Personal Mythology*. New York: Bantam Books, 1990.

_____. *The Shaman's Doorway:Opening the Imagination to Power and Myth*. Barrytown: Station Hill Press, 1988.

Lightman, Alan. *Einstein's Dreams*. New York: Pantheon, 1993.

Mansfield, Victor. *Synchronicity, Science, and Soul-Making.* Peru, Illinois: Open Court Publishing Company, 1995.

Michel, John and Robert Rickard. *Phenomenon: A Book of Wonders.* London: Dover, 1968.

Moorhead, Hugh. *The Meaning of Life.* Chicago: Chicago Review Press, 1988.

North, Carolyn. *Synchronicity: The Anatomy of Coincidence.* Berkeley: Regent Press, 1994.

Pauli, Wolfgang. "The Influence of Archetypal Ideas on the Scientific Theories of Kepler." Translated by Priscilla Silz in *The Interpretation of Nature and the Psyche.* New York: Bollingen Series, 1955.

Penzer, N. M., editor. "Kathasaritsagara of Somadeva" and "The Ocean of Story." Cited in *Parabola* VII:2 1982.

Peat, F. David. *Synchronicity: The Bridge Between Matter and Mind.* New York: Bantam, 1987.

Roberts, Royston M. *Serendipity: Accidental Discoveries in Science.* New York: John Wiley & Sons, Inc., 1989.

Progoff, Ira. *Jung, Synchronicity and Human Destiny.* New York: Dell, 1973.

Schopenhauer, Arthur. *On the Apparent Design in the Fate of the Individual.* New York and London: Penguin Classics, 1970.

Shah, Idries. *The Perfumed Scorpion.* San Francisco: HarperSanFrancisco, 1978.

Smith, Huston. *Forgotten Truth.* San Francisco: HarperSanFrancisco, 1976.

_____. "The Way Things Are," An interview by Timothy Beneke, *East Bay Weekly,* March 8, 1996.

Stein, Murray. *In Midlife.* Dallas: Spring Publications, 1985.

Steindl-Rast, David. *A Listening Heart: The Art of Contemplative Living.* New York: The Crossroad Publishing Company, 1992.

Thompson, Keith. "The Astonishment of Being: An Interview with Frederic Spiegelberg." The Esalen Catalog, Fall, 1994.

Vaughn, Alan. *Incredible Coincidences: The Baffling World of Synchronicity.* New York: Ballantine, 1979.

Von Franz, Marie-Louise. *On Divination and Synchronicity: The Psychology of Meaningful Chance.* Toronto: Inner City Books, 1980.

Weber, Renée. *Dialogues with Scientists and Sages: The Search for Unity.* London: Routledge & Kegan Paul Ltd., 1986.

Weschler, Lawrence. *Mr. Wilson's Cabinet of Wonder.* New York: Vintage, 1995.

Wolf, Fred Alan. *The Spiritual Universe: Quantum Physics Proves the Existence of the Soul.* New York: Simon & Schuster, 1996.

ABOUT THE AUTHOR

Phil Cousineau is an author, editor, teacher, adventure travel leader, photographer, and documentary filmmaker. His lifelong fascination with the art, literature, and history of culture has taken him on journeys across the globe. He lectures around the world on a wide range of topics from creativity, mythology, mentorship, and soul to travel and community work.

Born at an army hospital in Columbia, South Carolina, in 1952, Cousineau grew up in Wayne, Michigan, just outside of Detroit. While moonlighting in an automotive parts factory he studied journalism at the University of Detroit. Before turning to writing full-time in 1984, his peripatetic career included stints as a sportswriter and photographer, playing basketball in Europe, harvesting date trees on an Israeli kibbutz, and painting forty-four Victorian houses in San Francisco.

His numerous books include the bestselling *Once and Future Myths; The Art of Pilgrimage; A World Treasury of Riddles; Soul: An Archaeology: Readings from Socrates to Ray Charles; The Soul Aflame; The Hero's Journey: Joseph Campbell on His Life and Work;* and *Deadlines: A Rhapsody on a Theme of Famous Last Words,* which won the 1991 Fallot Literary Award. His books have been translated into seven languages, and he is a contributor to twelve other books, including a collaboration with John Densmore on his bestselling autobiography, *Riders on the Storm: My Life with Jim Morrison and the Doors*.

His screenwriting credits in documentary films, which have won more than twenty-five international awards, include *Ecological Design: Inventing the Future; Wayfinders: A Pacific Odyssey; The Peyote Road; The Red Road to Sobriety; Your Humble Serpent: The Life of Reuben Snake; Wiping the Tears of Seven Generations; Eritrea: March to Freedom; The Presence of the Goddess; The Hero's Journey: The World of Joseph Campbell;* and the *1991 Academy Award-nominated Forever Activists: Stories from the Abraham Lincoln Brigade*.

Currently, Cousineau lives in San Francisco, California, with his companion, Jo Beaton, and their son, Jack

For more information on Phil Cousineau's work, please contact:

Sisyphus Press
P.O. Box 868
San Francisco, CA 94133
www.philcousineau.com

To Our readers

CONARI PRESS publishes books on topics ranging from spirituality, personal growth, and relationships to women's issues, parenting, and social issues. Our mission is to publish quality books that will make a difference in people's lives—how we feel about ourselves and how we relate to one another. We value integrity, compassion, and receptivity, both in the books we publish and in the way we do business.

As a member of the community, we donate our damaged books to nonprofit organizations, dedicate a portion of our proceeds from certain books to charitable causes, and continually look for new ways to use natural resources as wisely as possible.

Our readers are our most important resource, and we value your input, suggestions, and ideas about what you would like to see published. Please feel free to contact us, to request our latest book catalog, or to be added to our mailing list.

Conari Press
An imprint of Red Wheel/Weiser, LLC
P.O. Box 612
York Beach, ME 03910-0612
800-423-7087
www.conari.com